The Art & Pr

of 16th-Century

German Fencing

A guide to the use of Joachim Meyer's rapier

Freelance Academy Press, Inc., Wheaton, IL 60189
www.freelanceacademypress.com

Second Printing

Printed in the UK

ISBN: 978-1-937439-38-5

Library of Congress Control Number: 2018964386

Cover art: Digital illustration by Robert Rutherfoord, based on the drawing from folio 2v of MS Var.82 (the 'Rostock Manuscript')

Interior images reproduced with permission by Roberto Gotti and the M.A.M (Martial Arts Museum) in Brescia, Italy. Photographed by Moreno Dei Ricci, and with public domain licensing provided by the MET

Contents

Acknowledgments

Thank you to:

Heather Whitlock for introducing me to HEMA, it's all your fault!

Joe Lesny and Justin Bozarth for appearing in my early Youtube videos and being my original sounding board

Chris VanSlambrouck and Heidi Zimmerman for giving me a platform and an audience in my pursuit of Meyer's art

Roger Norling for publishing my videos to his blog, HROARR.com, which put me in front of an international audience, and for writing the forward to this book

Ted Elsner and James Reilly who inspire hope in me that this art will be spread far and wide, and for editing the content of this book

Jonathan Tavares, 'Associate Curator of Arm, Armor and European Decorative Arts before 1700,' for allowing me to handle pieces from the Art Institute of Chicago's collection

my fencing instructors at the Chicago Swordplay Guild, John O'Meara and Greg Mele, for taking me under their wing, honing my craft, and giving me the opportunity to teach what I love

to my extended fencing family who have all shaped the way I see, interpret and teach historical, European martial arts: Devon Boorman, Bill Grandy, Puck Curtis, Paul Wagner, and Roland Warzecha

and to my wife and son who give me daily energy and motivation

Forward

My first encounter with Mr. Rutherfoord was seeing some high quality videos posted online, showing an exceedingly elegant and precise fencer displaying Joachim Meyer's rapier techniques, as presented in his fencing treatise of 1570. His body and weapon control was striking and I was very happy to see the rapier artwork of Meyer, for the first time in about 450 years, truly come alive again.

A year or so later, I finally got a chance to meet Mr. Rutherfoord in person in Lincoln, Illinois, even given the opportunity to cross blades with him. This was a very interesting and enlightening experience. While I myself have a fair bit of experience with several other weapons, ranging from dagger to pike, I had none whatsoever of rapier or sidesword. But, while my performance should probably embarrass me, I actually thoroughly enjoyed it, since Mr. Rutherfoord on the other hand, had extensive experience in the teachings of Renaissance fencing masters like Salvator Fabris, Giovanni Dall'Agocchie, Angelo Viggiani, and Joachim Meyer. His stepping, his posture, his stances and his weapon handling may look slow to the eye, but in reality, the experience is quite different and brings to mind the famous quote by Wyatt Earp, where he stated that "Fast is fine, But accuracy is final. You must learn to be slow in a hurry." The experience was very much like I imagine it would be like meeting a true master of the Renaissance, feeling quite exposed as you step up in front of him. It was obvious that Mr. Rutherfoord has a truly uncanny ability to transfer teachings from book to reality, moving fast in a slow way, graceful and precise. This is an experience I wish all fencers would be blessed to have at least once in their lives.

***

Joachim Meyer is without doubt one of the most influential fencing masters, both in modern Historical Fencing and in history, remaining influential for quite some time after his death, with Jakob Sutor von Baden and Theodori Verolini both reproducing large parts of the contents of his treatise in 1612 and 1679 respectively, as well as several 17th-century Italian and Spanish fencing masters, like e.g. Don Luis Pacheco de Narváez, Giuseppe Morsicato Pallavicini and Francesco Antonio Marcelli, naming him alone as the sole German fencing master in their lists on famous fencing masters.

As far as we can tell from church records, Joachim Meyer was born in 1537, in Basel, Switzerland, listed in the records of St. Albanskirche on August 16. His father,

Jakob was probably a cutler, but most likely lived and worked as a papermaker in St. Albans, together with his wife, Joachim's mother, Anna Freund. Meyer moved to Straßburg some time before June 4, 1560, when he married Apolonia Ruhlmann, a widow of baker Jakob Wittgaw, in the St. Wilhelmskirche of Krutenau. The records for the marriage describe him as a cutler from Basel. This may have been a marriage of convenience, where Meyer took on the responsibility of caring for the widow in return for becoming a citizen. It is uncertain where his own mother and father resided, but a Jacob Meyer is listed in the Ammestre, the burgher council of Straßburg in 1549, and then again in 1555, 1561, and in 1567, so it is quite possible that Joachim moved to Straßburg as a child. During the years between 1561-68 he five times applied to the city council to arrange fencing tournaments, and in the last application of 1568 he is listed as a *Fechtmeister*, a fencing master.

It is uncertain if Meyer himself had direct experience of war, but it seems likely, as every household in his time was obligated to provide a man who could serve as town guard, in the town militia and as fire and honourary guard. His time was also filled with armed conflict between Catholics and various Protestant factions, not least with the Calvinist nobility whom Meyer associated with. In his printed treatise of 1570, he directs himself to young boys and experienced soldiers, giving both target groups advice, both on how to train and how to fight. He also sometimes mentions sharp weapons of war, even describing techniques suitable precisely for war, for example a certain looping movement taught with the dusack, but described as good for a strong man to use with a large, two-hand war sword.

Now, it is sometimes argued that the dusack and longsword in Meyer's time were only sport weapons, but that is quite clearly not the case. While true that the wood & leather dusack is a training weapon, it was used to teach the use of the military dusack, an early Germanic sabre which takes its name from a Czech farmer's knife. This was a very common weapon all over Europe well into the late 1600s, and having different names, e.g. backsword, and later "Sinclair Hilt". Likewise, the two-hand swords actually became more important, not less so, on the battlefields, but in increasingly specialized functions, most useful in outnumbered scenarios, e.g. when the lines have broken, and dignitaries, high-ranking officers, banners and cannons, or bridges and other narrow passages need to be protected, or as in examples from the late 1600s, ship captains fighting enemy soldiers that have taken over the ship. There are also a good number of complex-hilt longswords, often carried by older bodyguards depicted well into the first few decades of the 1600s. Clearly though, the rapier, was gaining ground especially among the young and fashionable, as the Italian and Iberian fencing tradition gained influence over Europe. In his time, the fencing treatises available in German on this topic were nearly non-existent, with e.g. Paul Hektor Mair being one of the few examples, and then only in three, single-copy manuscripts of near identical content. Meyer considers the study of this weapon as very important, bringing it up in all his three preserved fencing treatises. It comes into conflict with existing social customs of his time, where in a violent conflict, you are only expected to use the cut against your fellow countrymen, with the thrust generally disregarded as unmanly and dishounourable. But here, contrary to common misconceptions of Meyer, he is actually a proponent of the thrust, telling us that "we" need to learn to use it again, since people from other nations do.

His first fencing treatise, a manuscript kept at the University Library of Lund Sweden (Msc. A40), is dedicated to the young Count Otto von Solms-Sonnewalde and was likely handed over to the count as a personal gift in 1568 when he studied at the formerly Lutheran gymnasium, which in Meyer's time was the academy, and later university, of Straßburg. In the foreword of the treatise Meyer states that the count has asked Meyer both to instruct him in the art of combat, and that he humbly undertook to do so.

The longsword section of this treatise has much of the same content as his printed book of 1570, the *Gründliche Beschreibung der Freyen, Ritterligen und Adeligen Kunst des Fechtens*, but for the dusack and the rapier, the content diverges, and the treatise lacks the grappling, dagger and the polearms, i.e. staff, halberd and pike. This treatise has beautiful, watercolour illustrations by a currently unidentified artist.

In 1570 Meyer's second fencing treatise. dedicated to Johann Casimir, Count Palatine of Simmern, is published. Again, in the foreword he describes how he has both studied under famous and skilled fencing masters, but has also taught many young princes, counts, lords and nobles in the art of combat, and how the Count Palatine has asked him to get his teachings into print. Later, Meyer's former student Count Otto von Solms-Sonnewalde would enter into the military service of Casimir. Both von Solms-Sonnewalde and von Simmern are depicted leading troops on the battlefield in contemporary artwork by Flemish artist Frans Hogenberg, von Simmern leading 4000 soldiers outside of Straßburg in 1576, coming to the aid of the Protestants, and von Solms-Sonnewalde at the Battle of Turnhout in 1597.

This treatise is more extensive, and also adds dagger, staff, halberd and pike. It has some fantastically detailed woodcut artwork, with scenes inspired by Ancient Rome, showing fencers displaying techniques with all the regular weapons of war of his time. This artwork was created by some of the finest woodcut artists of his time: Tobias and Christopher Stimmer and Christoph Maurer, all renowned artists to this day. Also seen in the artwork is the coat-of-arms of the cutler guild, displayed six times in the background and in the frontispice.

A third treatise is preserved, the so called *Fechtbuch zu Ross und zu Fuss* (MS Var.82), today kept at the University Library of Rostock, was still a work in progress at the time of his death. This treatise contains copies of several older treatises which we can be fairly certain Meyer had studied, like a unique copy of Sigmund Ringeck, and copies of "Pseudo"-Peter von Danzig, Martin Syber, Jud Lew, Martin Huntfeltz, Andre Lignitzer, and an anonymous dagger treatise. It also has a rapier section for foot and mounted combat, authored by Meyer himself, and signed as a *Freifechter* of Straßburg in 1570. He describes it as teachings brought together from the Italians, the Spanish, the Neapolitans, the French and the Germans, and the draft for the frontispice dedicates this treatise to Count Heinrich von Eberstein.

Outside of this, a fourth treatise, dedicated to Count Palatine Georg Johann I von Veldenz, is believed to have been displayed as late as in 1882, at the Nationalmuseum in Munich, but this is currently lost in the fog of time. It may also simply just be misattributed to Joachim Meyer, possibly referring to the Cod. icon. 393 treatise in the Bayerische Staatsbibliothek, written by Augsburg City Treasurer Paul Hektor Mair in the 1540s.

Furthermore, he himself, in his treatise of 1570, mentions having completed another book, a fifth book, teaching among other things, dusack, and god willing, he will get it into print. He also mentions how he will present more teachings on both pike, "unmatched weapons" and dagger, at "another place," seemingly referring to another book.

Finally, there must also have existed a manuscript that presented the material for the printed treatise of 1570 to the printer. This too is lost.

Outside of the associations with nobility already mentioned, Meyer also received a position as fencing master at the court of the Duke Johann Albrecht I of Mecklenburg in Schwerin in 1571. This is particularly interesting, as this duke was the first to give the fencing guild the *Freifechter von der Feder* official recognition, with charters and a coat-of arms in 1570, although it would take until 1607 for them to finally receive proper imperial status by Emperor Rudolph II in Prague. It is unclear if Meyer himself was instrumental in the founding of this fencing guild.

Meyer left Straßburg on January 4th, 1571, travelling the 500 miles to Schwerin in the middle of a harsh winter. He arrived at the court on February 10th, 1571, but unfortunately passed away two weeks later, on the 24th of February, possibly from pneumonia, leaving a remarkable, literary martial legacy, behind him.

***

Looking closer at this legacy, Meyer was quite clearly at the forefront of a change from old oral traditions, to new, literary ones, seeking to devise a new way of teaching through a book. As mentioned before, his printed book is aimed both at young, inexperienced boys, as well as experienced soldiers, meant to be read and used without the assistance of a teacher. This was quite a challenge. He strives to systemize and even to redefine terminology to a certain degree, while focusing more on actual mechanics rather than just terms, as this is necessary for the particular context in which the books would be used. Sometimes we see how he redefines or borrows names, like the dagger guard *Schlüssel* taught by e.g. Andre Paurñfeyndt, lending a name to a similar longsword guard with crossed arms, or a *Schwertnehmen*, a disarming technique taught for example by Sigmund Ringeck, but executed with a staff instead of a longsword.

He also teaches the reader how to learn and practice the art of combat, not just how to suppress, capture, maim, and kill an opponent. Unlike most older sources, he also speaks of tactics and psychology, about the characters of men, how it influences their fencing, and how it can be exploited and emulated for deception.

The system he teaches is holistic, working on principles that lie underneath it all, and embodied as techniques with a variety of weapons, ranging from grappling and dagger, to single hand swords, two-hand swords and polearms, perfectly matching the weapons taught in the fencing guilds. The setup in the treatise is systematic, where one part lays the foundation for later ones, so the longsword is the foundation for the dusack, which in turn lays the foundation for the rapier. And all of it serves to prepare you for the polearms, where the staff lays the foundation for the later halberd and pike.

A few concepts are important to know and understand. First of all, like the old masters, he describes *Zufechten* and *Krieg*, the Onset and War, meaning the first approach to the contact, and then the actual in-range fighting. To this he adds the crucial *Abzug*, the Withdrawal, assuming that you can't trust the opponent to instantly die or surrender after you successfully land an attack, which means you have to retreat from the *Krieg* safely with the use of a threat. This particular aspect of the fight is rarely discussed in sources before him.

Other important concepts are *Reitzen*, *Nehmen*, and *Treffen*, i.e. Provoking, Taking and Hitting, which should be read as any attack being capable of either deceiving the opponent to move his defense in a certain direction and thereby giving you an opening to exploit, or an attack being capable of setting aside the opponent's weapon, or to simply hit. Sometimes an attack can do two of these functions at the same time, and they may come in any order. Commonly, Meyer advises to strike from the body to the sword, and the sword to the body, making sure to cover yourself and controlling the opponent's arms or weapon after a successful hit, before retreating. This topic Mr. Rutherfoord expands on quite a bit in the second half of the book.

Noteworthy too, is a particular variant of body mechanics which we seem to see in some of the older sources, like in the treatises of Johannes Lecküchner and Hans Talhoffer: the stances are generally quite low and broad. This particular way of moving includes shifting of weight, from rear foot, to centred, to the front foot, while often "counter-twisting", winding up the torso with the shoulder towards the opposite foot. This can be quite clearly seen throughout his system in the artwork, and it has some quite particular effects on the whole movement of body and weapon.

***

I am quite confident that this work of Mr. Rutherfoord will be highly appreciated and of great service to today's students of Renaissance fencing, and particularly to the students of Joachim Meyer. It is fantastic to see Meyer's great legacy preserved and transmitted to new generations, preserved for eternity, and helped come alive again.

~Roger Norling
Gothenburg, October 25, 2018

part 1 introduction

Since I have undertaken to describe most diligently and truly the art of fighting with those knightly and manly weapons that nowadays are most used by us Germans, according to my best understanding and ability; and since experience shows and it is obvious that combat with the sword is not only an origin and source of all other combat, but it is also the most artful and manliest above all other weapons; therefore I have thought it necessary and good to begin with this weapon, and to discuss it very briefly but clearly in such a manner as is done with all other arts and practices.

Preface

I knew fairly early in my study of Joachim Meyer's rapier that I wanted to start documenting the system as it unfolded in front of me. At first it was a mental process, then expressed itself in the form of videos, both of which are relatively low commitment, but there came a point where I decided it was time I sit and write down what was missing from the visual media of Youtube and the internal ramblings of my mind, and convey it in the written word to a broader audience.

Both writing and fencing share the same shelf of things I find frustrating but rewarding when done well. I started fencing competitively at the age of 15 with a reenactment group, and at times when I was not fencing at the level I expected of myself, I would throw my sword out of anger, sometimes getting it stuck in trees at the park at which we practiced. Twenty years later, I have learned to control my frustrations, but they still linger, and I fear they will always be there until the day I have mastered this art... so maybe forever. Deciding to write this book, or rather the year it took me to organize my thoughts and dig up the motivation to do so, brings back some of the same frustration, but hopefully when it is all said and done, will bring some of the same satisfaction as well.

I have a fairly narrow scope for this book, which is to describe the nuances I find between the lines of Meyer's text, and explain to the reader how I have come to my conclusions. It would be a waste of both my, and my readers', time restating Meyer's own words, but where it is necessary in elucidating a point, I will share important quotes he makes on the subject. With this in mind, it would be useful to have a copy of Meyer's *Kunts des Fechtens* open while reading through.[†] Meyer is at times very explicit in his instructions, and at others, expects his readers to understand that he is not going to restate some important detail for the nth time for completeness' sake or to waste ink. And I fear this often gets translated to the modern audience as an omission of action rather than an omission for expedience. In fact, Meyer has written his rapier work for an audience whose grasp of the art is somewhat limited, due to the fencing conventions of his time and place, so the details I have to add are either from earlier in his writings, or only told to us once as a general guideline, or pulled from other systems of the time, which Meyer admits he is glossing from.

I think, most practitioners of physical arts are visual and kinesthetic learners. Unable to be with my reader, I have attempted to make the images very clear, choosing to illustrate the footwork diagrams and sword engagements and limit the photography

† This book is an interpretation of Joachim Meyer's art presented and translated by Dr. Forgeng in "The Art of Combat," published by Greenhill Books in 2006.

to only the times where my illustrative skills fall short (though my profession is in the latter). For those that prefer learning through the written word, I hope I will not fail you, but as I have already admitted, putting 10,000 words on paper is as frustrating for me as committing 10,000 perfect lunges, or even sometimes one word and one lunge.

Introduction

Joachim Meyer states the art of the thrust has been lost to the modern German,[1] and needs to be rediscovered through the use of the rapier as taught to him by the French, Spanish, Italian and Neapolitans.[2] He also readily admits that the forefathers of his tradition knew the proper use of the thrust "permitting [it] in earnest cases against the common enemy".[3] It is apparent that the 'true principles' of the art, as expounded upon by Henrick von Gunterrodt writing in 1579 (soldier and owner of the MS. I.33 'Tower Manuscript,' Europe's oldest-known fencing text) were embedded in the German art since the very beginnings of its practice.[4] This fact should be no surprise to anyone who has held a sword of *any* century. The sword coming to a point is no accident, it is intentional, and its use was well understood. Only when certain conventions of a culture prohibit the use of the thrust (like for the German people in the 15th and 16th centuries) against "sworn-in soldiers or other [Germans] who had come into conflict with each other"[5] does its use fall to the wayside. Though the rapier did not exist in the 13th and 14th centuries, it is my contention that if either the priests of the Tower Manuscript or Johannes Liechtenauer (considered to be the father of German swordsmanship in the 14th c.) were handed one, its use would not be lost on them.

Note the entire heart of the art of combat lies in this final guard, which is called Longpoint; and all actions of the guards or of the sword finish or have their conclusion in this one, and not in others.[6] *-Tower Manuscript I.33*

Joachim Meyer, almost three centuries later echoes this statement:

The Longpoint in the rappier is the end of all thrusts that take place long from you, for all thrusts that in hitting do not end in the Longpoint are too short.[7]

then later states:

> *Now since the [fight from Longpoint] is so diverse that it is impossible to present in a single form, I will offer some examples from which you can sufficiently deduce and learn how you shall act in any given situation*[8]

and then finally admonishes his reader:

> *When you find yourself in rappier combat or any other weapon, then approach him with extended, straight, and firm parrying, and take heed what he will execute against you...*[9]

The advice Meyer gives us is nothing new and is actually summed up nicely in a few short lines from Sigmund Ringeck (believed to be one of the earliest practitioners in the Liechtenauer lineage in the early 15th century):

> *...direct your point with outstretched arms against his breast or face. If he then strikes from above to your head, wind your sword against his blow and thrust to the face. Or, if he strikes from above or below against your sword and wants to strike your blade to the side, change-through and thrust to his opening on the other side. If, however, he hits your sword with strength, let it snap around and hit him with it on the head.*[10]

What Meyer states as an art with preference given to the point and an extended sword-arm (Longpoint), having been learned from "foreigners," actually has a very strong foundation within his own lands. Luckily, modern readers and practitioners have access to many transcribed and translated works, which can help them not only get an understanding of what was being taught abroad, but also how Meyer wished to convey this art to his fellow Germans.

German, One-Handed Swords of the Late 16th Century

The form of single-handed swords that existed in Germany in the late 16th century informs their intended use, which ranged from a battlefield weapon, to personal sidearm, to practice implement for use in the fencing halls. The blade needs to be broad enough to deliver a debilitating cut while nimble enough to control the point for the thrust. Swords of this period usually have more complex hilts than their counterparts in the first half of the century and the centuries before. As worn armor falls to the wayside, protection for the hand becomes more of a necessity.

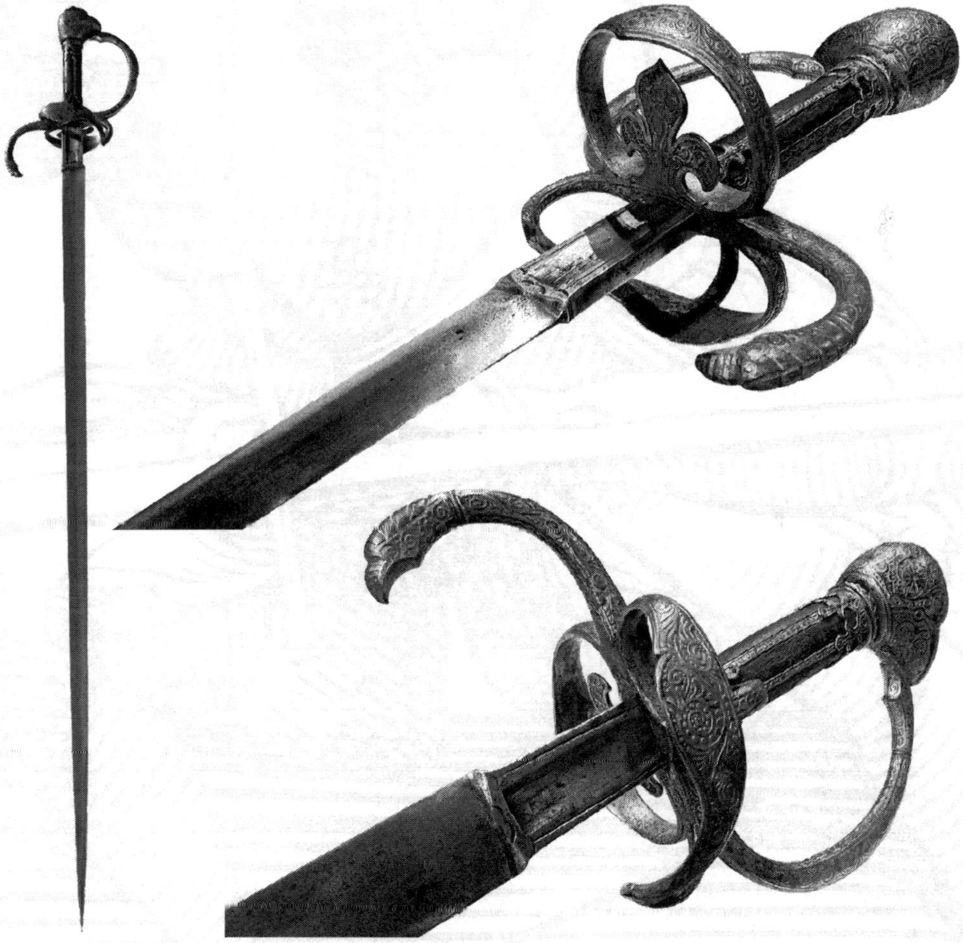

The above weapon is an example of a sword used on horseback, featuring a turned-up rear cross, knuckle bow and side rings on either side. The outside ring contains a fleur-de-lis, protecting the top most fingers from wayward thrusts, but also prevents the index finger from gripping the ricasso. The opposite side features a thumb-ring for better control of the blade. The entire hilt is engraved and has decorative bird heads on the pommel and rear cross. The overall length is 114 cm (42 inches) with a blade length of 93 cm (36.75 inches). It dates to approximately 1570.

The 16th century is also when we see a divergence of swords: those specialized for the battlefield, and those used exclusively for the duel and self-defense, commonly known as the rapier. With only one opponent to consider (in contrast to the chaotic nature of the battlefield), the thrust becomes the preferred attack and a weapon that maximizes that need is developed. The blade becomes narrower and longer to extend the steel out towards the opponent.

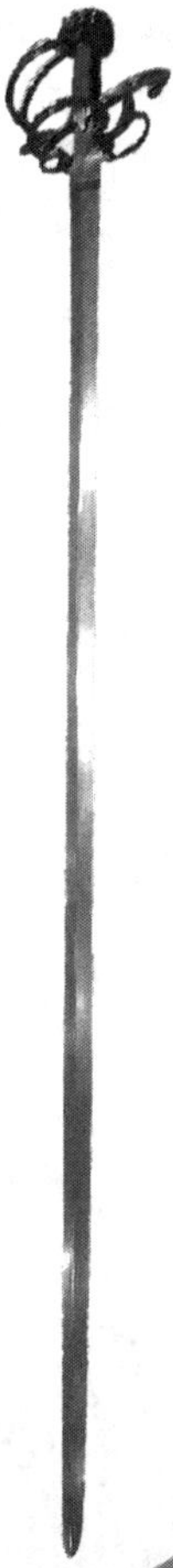

Though the thrust becomes the preferred method of attack, the cut is still a viable means of debilitating the opponent when delivered to the face, neck, hands and other soft tissue targets.

The above weapon is an example of the sword's evolution into what is known as the rapier. A thrust oriented weapon with a long, narrow blade, and complex hilt. This piece was probably used by the Duke of Saxony's body guard as a side arm. It features a fluted, mushroom shaped pommel, with accompanying fluted side rings. The handle is wrapped in copper wire providing the hand with friction to grip it. The guard rings come up under the beginning of the blade, resting on an Ionic-styled ricasso. The overall length is 120 cm (47.5 inches), and dates to the 1590s.

To further protect the hand, solid plates are added between the posts of the guard to protect from thrusts directed there. Elaborate ornamentation is added to the hilts during this century as the sword becomes just as much a fashion statement as it is a means to protect one's life. Those that can afford expensive weapons can also hire personal fencing masters in the training of its use.

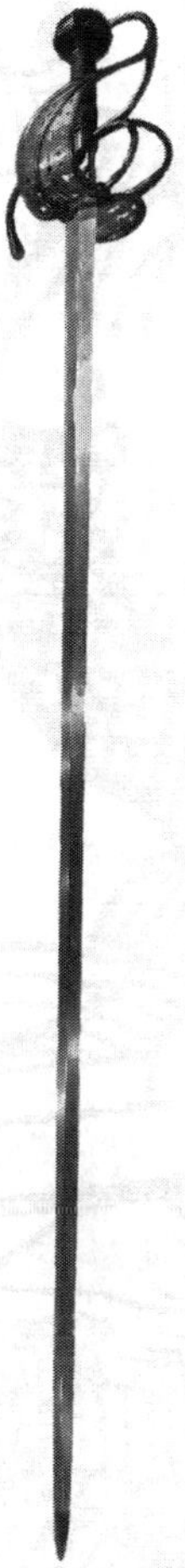

As the 16th century gives way to the 17th, the blade becomes even longer and hilt more elaborate. The thrust becomes the primary way to dispatch the opponent; the longer the blade, the less useful and cumbersome the cut becomes.

Another example of a rapier, this piece features an etched and pierced guard with smooth, rounded posts. The pommel is octagonal with a matching etched motif. This piece also has a wire wrapped handle for grip and dates to the end of the 16th century. The overall length is shorter than other contemporary examples at 109 cm (43 inches).

Meyer's Rapier & How to Hold It

Meyer never gives us any specifics on the sword he details the use of, except to say it is a rapier. From the illustrations in the manual it looks fairly simple compared to the more complex hilts found in the later 16th century, composed of a front and rear cross, a knuckle bow, and an outside ring. This is possibly because what Meyer shows is a training sword, one solely to be used in the fencing halls.[11]

As common with many single handed swords of the time, the blade has a front edge, aligned with the knuckles, referred to as the 'long-edge', and the opposite edge which is referred to as the 'short-edge.' When the sword is held in the right hand with the long-edge downward, the flat of the blade facing the right is the outside-flat, which is also where the outside-ring resides. The opposite side of the blade is called the inside-flat. It should be noted that as the sword turns through space, the outside ring always denotes the outside-flat, which is important for understanding the diagrams throughout this book.

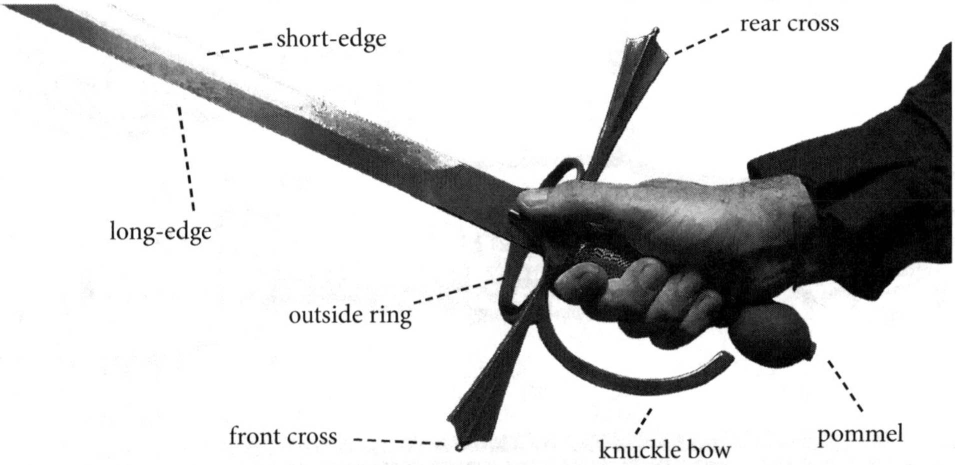

The length of the blade is divided into two parts. The half of the sword closest to the hilt is called the Strong, while the half closest to the point is the Weak. These divisions are important in elucidating a very important concept — the sword is a lever, with the hand acting as a fulcrum. Pressure applied to the Weak (*schweche*) is difficult to resist, while the same pressure applied at the Strong (Stercke) can be withstood more easily.

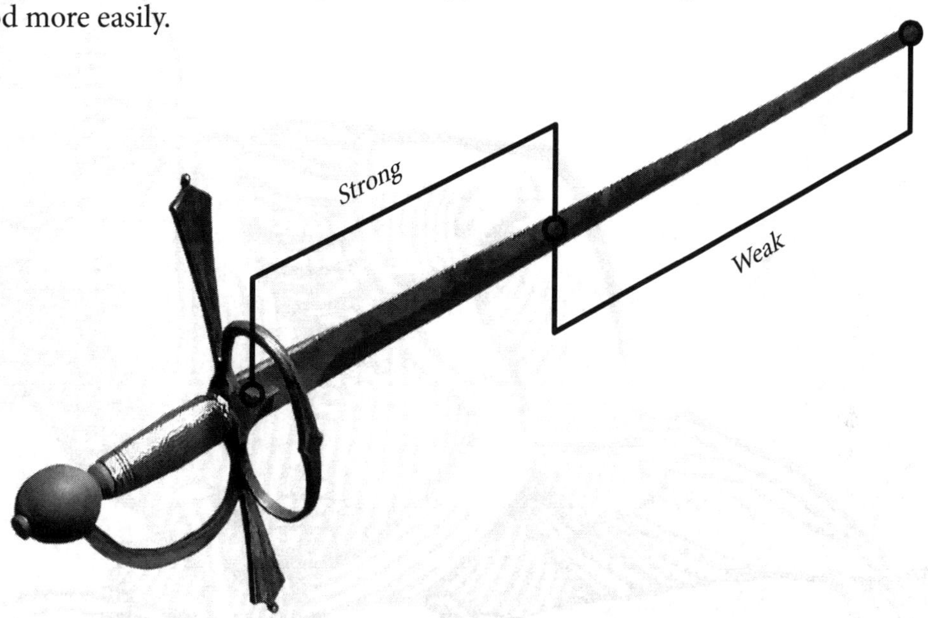

The divisions have important tactical considerations, and can be further broken down into four parts. The Hilt (*Creutz)* is important for protecting the hands while also used during grapples. The Strong, for Winding (*winden)*. The Middle (*Mittel)*, for the Takings (*Nehmen*), which borrows from both the Weak and the Strong. The Weak for cutting, Changing-Through (*durchwechslen)*, and the point at the end for thrusting.

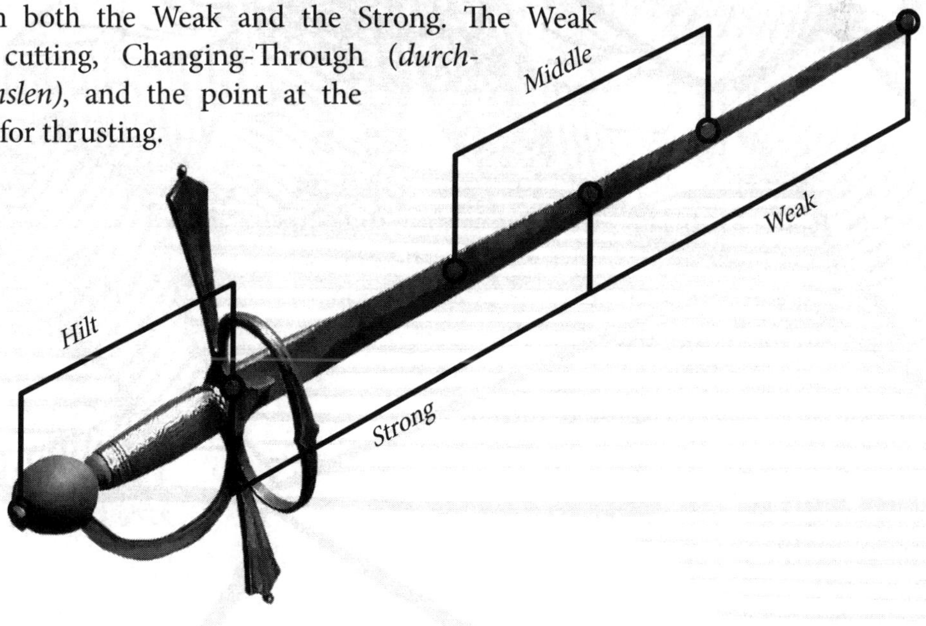

Holding the sword is fairly straight forward, but wielding it requires the arm to turn the sword through some extreme positions. Because of this, the hand should be slightly rotated on top of the handle, allowing the sword to rotate further to a high left position than it could otherwise.

Here we can see the sword held in the "Left Ox," a guard where the long-edge is rotated up and to the left. To support the sword from beneath without having to rotate the hand inside the guard, the hand should initially reside slightly over the handle so that when it turns with the arm, the hand is situated as pictured.

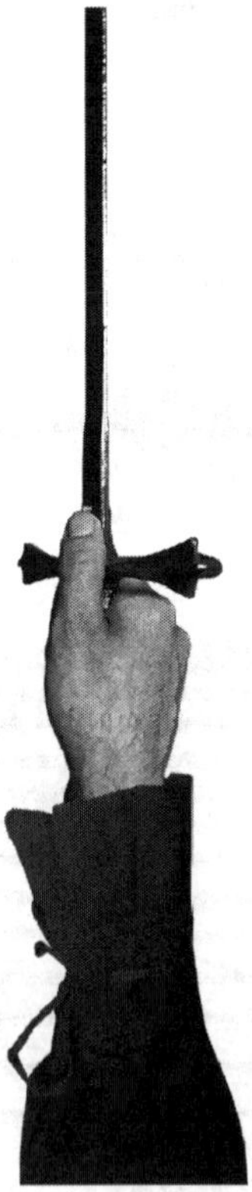

Because the sword does not have any hardware above the cross, it becomes more important to protect the closest appendage to it: the thumb. The thumb should always hide behind the blade and be positioned to the opposite side of the engagement. When we meet our opponent's weapon with the long-edge, the thumb should hide closer to the short-edge, and vice-versa. The position of the thumb also allows us to rotate the sword from guard to guard by pressing against the rear cross as the hand, arm, and body turn.

Proper grip is more than understanding how to hold the weapon, but rather how the sword hand relates to the structure of the swordsman's arm and body. When turning the sword, the motion should not be made from the wrist, but rather should stay in a straight line with the forearm. This allows the entire arm to brace the sword when clashing against the opponent's and when cutting and thrusting to the target. The exception to this rule is if the sword has not yet met the opponent's blade or has been removed from it, then manipulating the sword from the wrist becomes the quickest means to do so (i.e. cutting around and moving under the opponent's weapon).

incorrect

correct

Above: the wrist, forearm and upper arm are not in alignment. Any pressure applied to the blade will necessarily be resisted by the wrist alone

Above: the wrist, and entire arm are in a line behind the long-edge. Pressure applied to the long-edge will transfer along the entire arm and is thus much stronger than in the previous image

Explanation of the Cutting Diagram

The diagram below, a recreation of the one Meyer illustrates in his 'Rostock' manuscript (MS Var.82, Folio 2v), depicts a superimposed space between the two fencers. The outer circle is approximately three hand widths wide at arms length and describes the area in which our hilt/hand exists. The sword hand should never leave the outer limits of this circle. The inner circle approximates the outline of our opponent's torso. Later in this text I will show the swords as they exist in this space from our perspective. The location of the hilt and point of the sword are important in understanding the relationship between the blades and how the blades move through space. The opposite page further explains the lines and targets on the opponent.

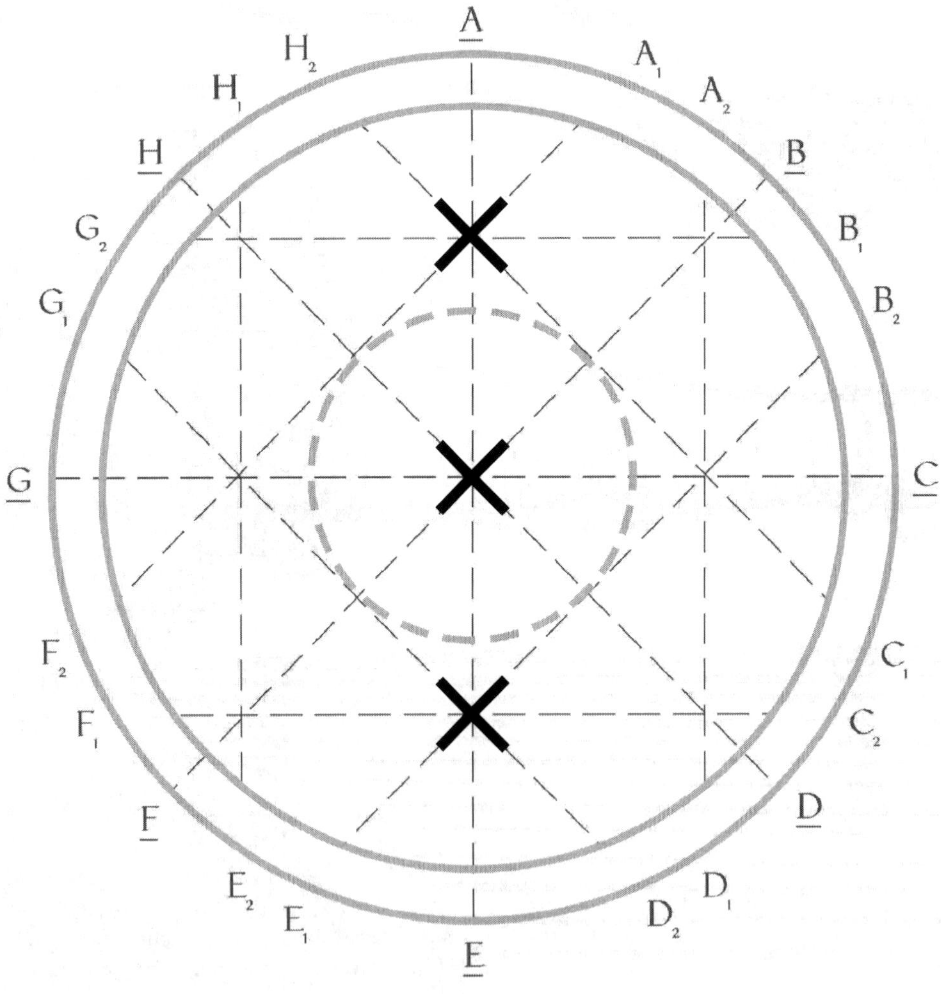

The opponent's primary targets:

Following the vertical line of AE:

- G_2B_1: Their Neck
- GC: Their Belly
- F_1C_2: Their Knee

Following the vertical line of H_1E_2:

- G_2B_1: Their right shoulder
- GC: Their right flank

Following the vertical line of A_2D_1:

- G_2B_1: Their left shoulder
- GC: Their left flank

The Upper Cross - through the neck

The Middle Cross - through the belly

The Lower Cross - through the leg

The primary cuts through the targets:

Vertical (with the long edge)

- AE: Scalp Cut (*Scheidelhauw*) *
- H_1E_2: Supressing Cut (*Dempffhauw*) on the left †
- A_2D_1: Supressing Cut (*Dempffhauw*) on the right †

Vertical (with the short edge)

- H_1E_2: Squinting Cut (*Schielhauw*) on the left
- A_2D_1: Squinting Cut (*Schielhauw*) on the right

Diagonal (with the long edge)

- A_1F_2: Shoulder Cut, Defense Stroke & Wrath Cut from the right through the upper cross
- H_2C_1: Shoulder Cut, Defense Stroke & Wrath Cut from the left through the upper cross
- BF: Hip Cut from the right through the middle cross
- HD: Hip Cut from the left through the middle cross
- B_2E_1: Thigh Cut from the right through the lower cross
- G_1D_2: Thigh Cut from the right through the lower cross

Diagonal (with the short edge)

- HD: Crooked Cut (*Krumphauw*)

Horizontal (with the long edge)

- G_2B_1: Neck Cut from the left through the upper cross
- GC: Belt Cut from the left through the middle cross
- F_1C_2: Leg Cut from the left through the lower cross ‡

* EA: the "other" Scalp Cut

† E_2H_1 & D_1A_2: 'Wing Cut', like clipping the wings or striking the arms from below

‡ Meyer refers to this as the "Foot Cut" but explains he means the entire leg from the knee down

The Rose

Meyer's work mentions a concept called 'the rose,' but he never really defines what it is. He mentions it once in his rapier section, saying: *reverse this high thrust into a low thrust through the rose.*[12]

He mentions the rose more often in his previous two books on the longsword and dusack, each seemingly referring to the rose as a means to change one action into another by going through *it*. It is my belief that the rose Meyer refers to looks like a rose as it is depicted in the 16th century. If we add petals to our cutting diagram we get a means to attach or go from one cut line to another, usually going around the opponent's blade in the process. Below is a possible depiction of what the rose might look like, though it is possible these petals attach at other points in the cutting diagram or even are transmutable depending on where our blade is and where it needs to go.

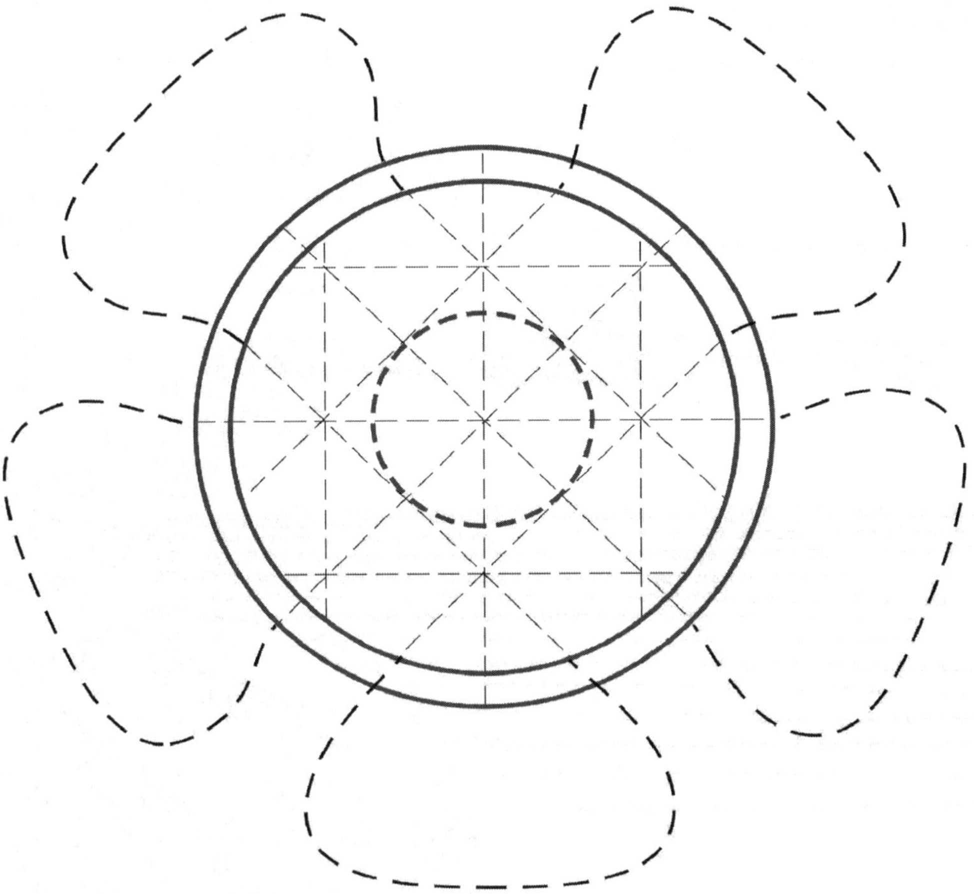

Explanation of the Footwork Diagram

The diagram below shows up on Plate F of *Kunst des Fechtens* under the figure forming the guard of Straight-Parrying, but Meyer never mentions its existence nor refers to it. Its placement under this particular figure might help demonstrate the importance of that particular position. Once I start to discuss footwork as an overall concept and for specific actions I will place feet on the diagram and discuss why the feet are moving the way they are. For now, here is a short break down of how I have interpreted the steps Meyer introduces in his longsword section, and subsequently carries over into his other weapons forms.[13] To start, the left foot begins on C, with the right foot on B.

C to B (gather of the rear foot)
B to A (step forward on the right foot)
C to E (triangle step to the right)
C to G (triangle step to the left)
C to E & B to D (double triangle right)
C to G & B to F (double triangle left)
C to B to E (broken or stolen step right)
C to B to G (broken or stolen step left)

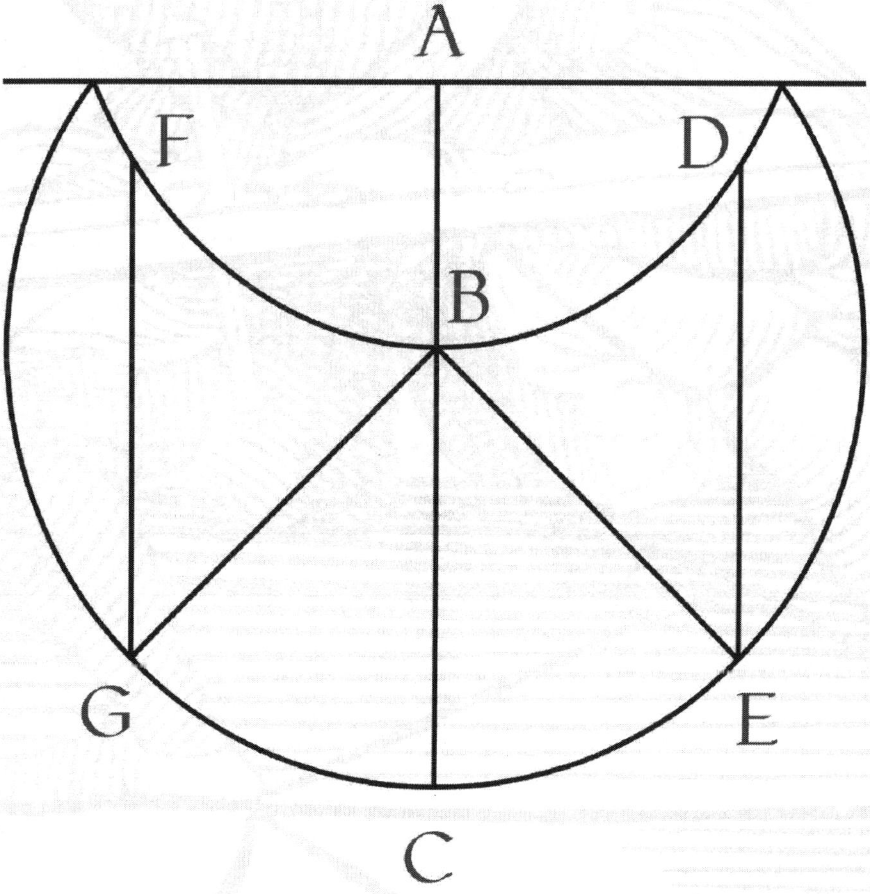

part II the guards

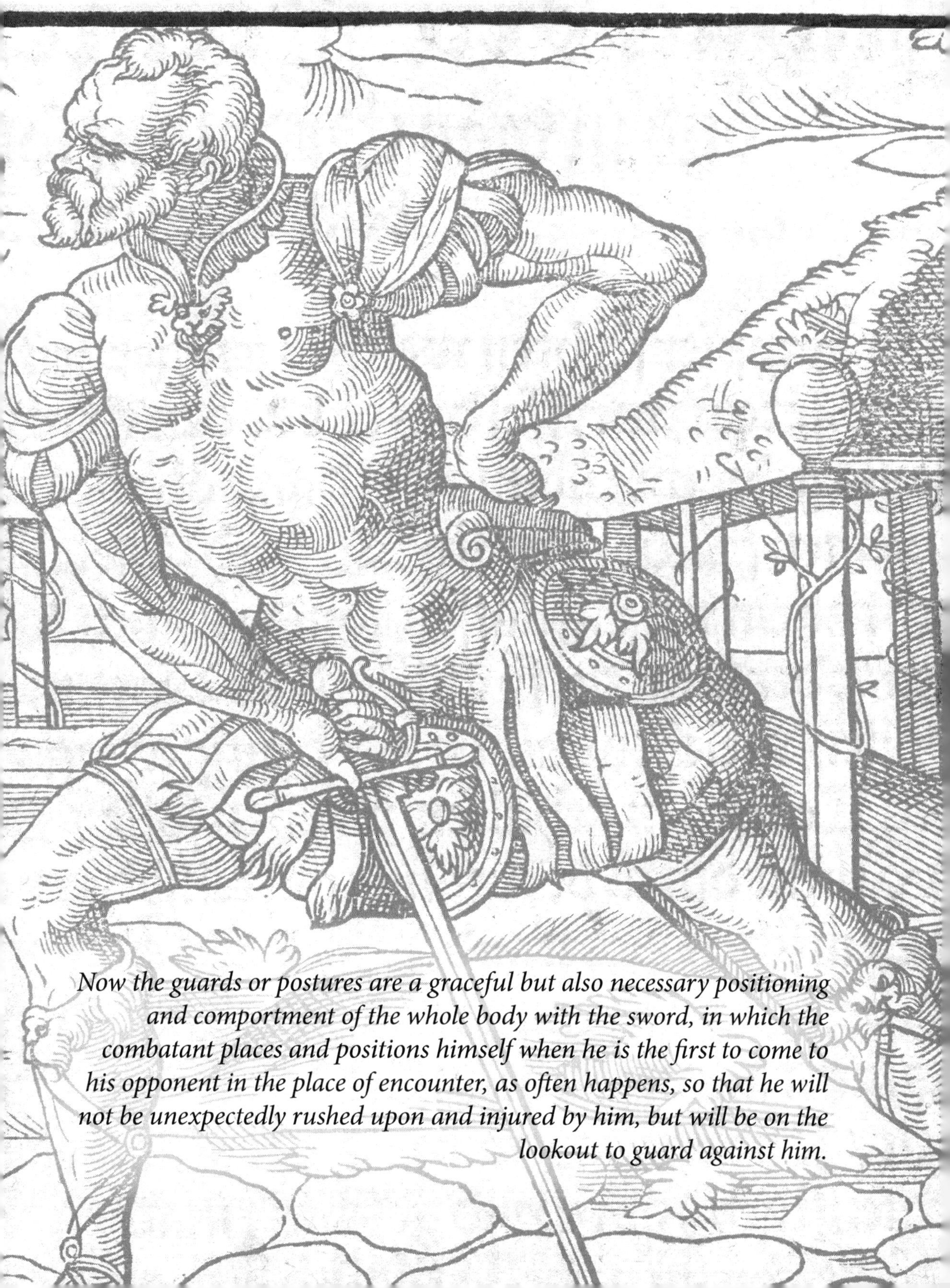

Now the guards or postures are a graceful but also necessary positioning and comportment of the whole body with the sword, in which the combatant places and positions himself when he is the first to come to his opponent in the place of encounter, as often happens, so that he will not be unexpectedly rushed upon and injured by him, but will be on the lookout to guard against him.

Meyer is clear in his description of his guards, and gives us some useful information about how he expects us to use them. As he explains his techniques, he uses the guards as way points, telling us which guard to start in, go through, and end in. Without rehashing Meyer's text here, I want to give you some useful ways to think about the guards. First and foremost, Meyer has a guard for each of the nine quadrants the fencer is divided into, making an octothorp-grid of guards. The top row are the high guards; the middle row, the middle guards; the bottom row, the low guards. Vertically, the right column are the right guards; the middle column, the straight guards, and the left column, the left guards. Some of these positions can be utilized with the point forward and some with the point away. For instance, both high guards on the left and right have variants with the point forward and point away. Meyer refers to the high, point-forward positions as the Ox (*ochs*), while the high, point away positions are simply the high guards (*oberhut*), though he tells us they are really the Ox for the Thrust and the Ox for the Cut, respectively.

This is our first clue that Meyer has a specific intention for each guard, or rather, what each guard is useful for. We could go through each technique and chart out the guard's proceeding action and make assumptions about the tactical implications of each, but at this point I would rather refer to a contemporary of Meyer, Angelo Viggiani. Viggiani explicitly states that each and every guard, or rather any position in which we hold the sword, can be broken down into four categories:

- High & Low
- Offensive & Defensive
- Perfect & Imperfect
- Wide & Narrow

Viggiani goes on to explain each category's usefulness: high guards are useful for offense, low guards for defense; right guards for offense, left guards for defense; point-forward is useful for delivering thrusts, point-away for cuts; wide guards expose a target, while narrow guards protect one. You will notice that both the high/low and right/left categories are assigned offense and defense. This means the a high-right guard would be better suited for an offense and a low-left guard would be best used for a defense.

If we were to count the number of times Meyer uses each of these guards in the *vor* and *nach* (making an offense and receiving an attack) they would line up with these categories. These categories are not just how Viggiani would like us to use each guard, but rather what a sword is best able to do held in an arm attached to the right side of a human body.

Category 1. High guards are offensive because the sword can drop to a target more easily than it can rise to one, allowing gravity to assist in the strike. They also strike the more vital targets, such as the head and neck. They cover the body less than the low guards and are thus less secure in their engagements. The low guards are defensive because they are more able to cover the vital areas of the body and cover the opponent's weapon more securely. They are also defensive because as a parry is made from a low to high, it will rise into a high guard, allowing it to drop to the opponent just after a parry has been made.[14]

Category 2. Guards on the right are offensive because when the arm and sword are aligned with the right shoulder they can strike farther. Meyer supports this point when referring to Longpoint as the farthest extension of the arm and sword.[15] Guards on the left are defensive because parries from the left to right move all attacks outside of our presence sooner than their counterparts, and when the parry terminates on the right, aligned with the dominant shoulder, the weapon is ready to make its maximum extension towards the opponent.

Category 3. Point-forward guards are optimal for the thrust because the point is already forward and does not need to make any further motion for it to arrive on target. The converse is true for guards with the point away; the edge is directed towards the target and thus should be employed.

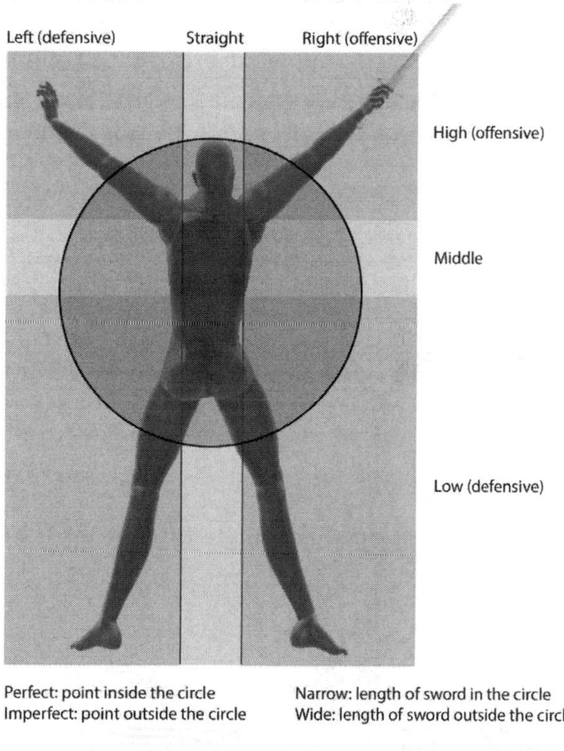

Perfect: point inside the circle
Imperfect: point outside the circle
Narrow: length of sword in the circle
Wide: length of sword outside the circle

Category 4. Wide guards, or guards where the sword's length is not in front of the body, naturally expose it and are thus used to invite the opponent to attack. Narrow guards, or guards where the majority of the sword lies between both fencers, are used to constrain space and/or the opponent's sword.

With these four categories established, we can break down Meyer's guards into their uses.

Note: Viggiani and other Bolognese masters would seem to make narrow guards opposite those of the high guards. For instance, high guards are never categorized as narrow, possibly because high guards cover the body less than the low guards. However, there are degrees of 'narrowness' and 'wideness,' and 'lowness' and 'highness,' and the same is true with the other two categories as well.

Right Ox for the Thrust (*Ochs*)

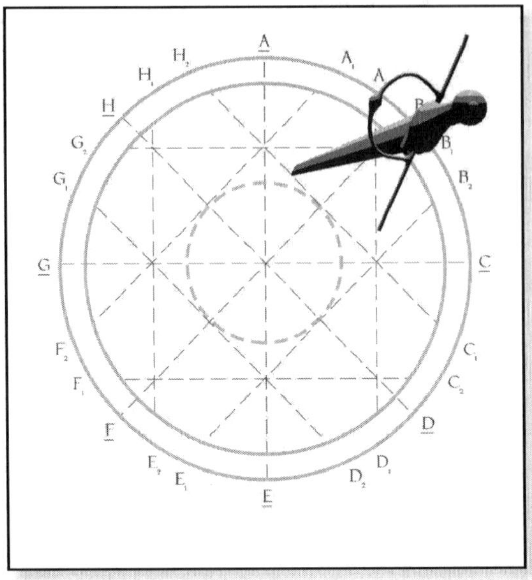

The Right Ox occupies the high-right quadrant while threatening the opponent's face with the point. To support this position of the arm, the left shoulder comes slightly forward along with the left hip. The sword arm is straight and extended forward above the head. Because the hand is held up and to the right with the point angling back to the center, the palm will somewhat face the opponent. The long-edge is in line with the arm, and directed up and to the right. Common with all of Meyer's rapier guards, the right foot is forward with the toe directed at the opponent. The posture is somewhat erect with a slight incline forward. The chin is raised to assist the straightening of the back. The center of mass is between the feet, not to the inside or outside, which would add instability to the posture.

- *hand in upper right*
- *point at the opponent's face*
- *palm right and somewhat forward*
- *left shoulder somewhat forward*
- *body more erect*

- *High*
- *Offensive*
- *Perfect*
- *Narrow*

see Appendix E, Plate B

Left Ox for the Thrust (*Ochs*)

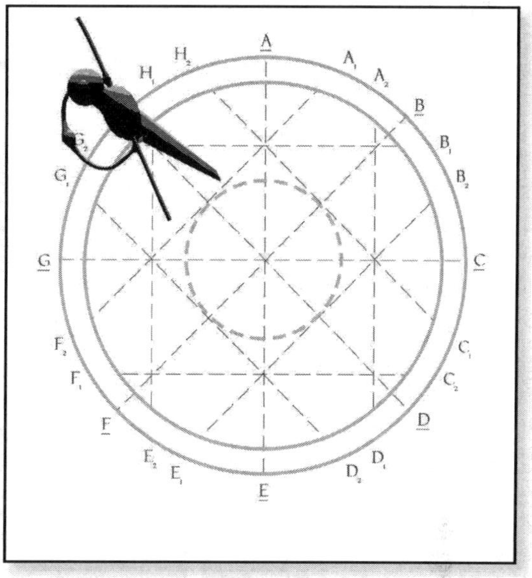

The Left Ox is the contrary posture to the Right Ox. It occupies the high-left quadrant while also threatening the opponent's face with a thrust. Other than being held on the left side, the guard is very much the same: the arm is extended up and forward, and the long-edge follows the alignment of the arm. The body is also somewhat inclined forward with the center of balance between the feet. However, because the arm is extended to the left, the left shoulder and hip are brought back allowing the body to turn to support the position of the arm. Contrary to the Right Ox, where the palm is somewhat facing the opponent, the Left Ox has the palm away from them. Meyer frequently refers to this position as 'palm away.'

- *hand in upper left*
- *point at the opponent's face*
- *palm right and somewhat backward*
- *left shoulder back*
- *body more erect*

- *High*
- *Defensive*
- *Perfect*
- *Narrow*

Right Ox for the Cut (*Oberhut*)

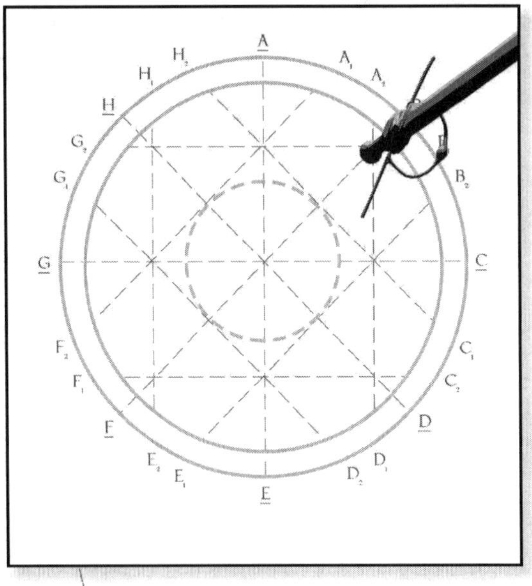

Both Ox guards have a cut variant position. Instead of threatening with a thrust, they threaten with a cut. Though Meyer mentions they are also called the High Guard, he seems to prefer calling them Ox for the Cut. Other than the hand rotating the sword behind us, this guard is identical to the Right Ox for the Thrust.

- *hand in upper right*
- *point high and back*
- *palm to the left*
- *left shoulder somewhat forward*
- *body more erect*

- *High*
- *Offensive*
- *Imperfect*
- *Wide*

Left Ox for the Cut (*Oberhut*)

Just like Right Ox for the Cut, Left Ox has the same cut variation. In it, the arm and body position remaining the same following its counterpart. Again, instead of threatening with a high thrust from the left, this guard threatens with a high cut from the left.

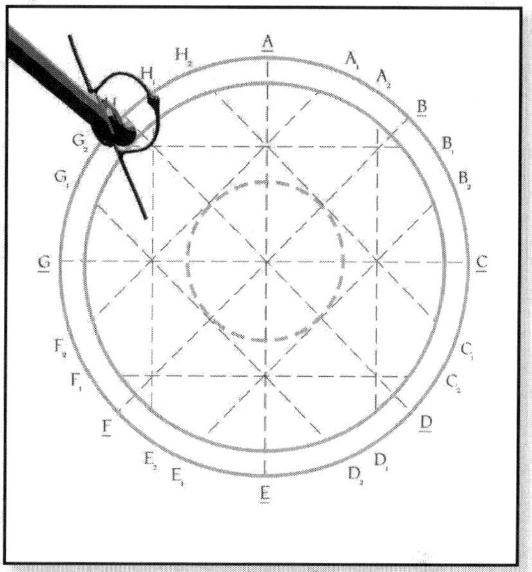

- *hand in upper left*
- *point high and back*
- *palm to the left*
- *left shoulder back*
- *body more erect*

- *High*
- *Defensive*
- *Imperfect*
- *Wide*

Straight High Guard (*Oberhut*)

The Ox for the Cut also has a central or middle variation called the Straight High Guard. Meyer says that even though the point is somewhat forward, this guard is only for delivering a cut.

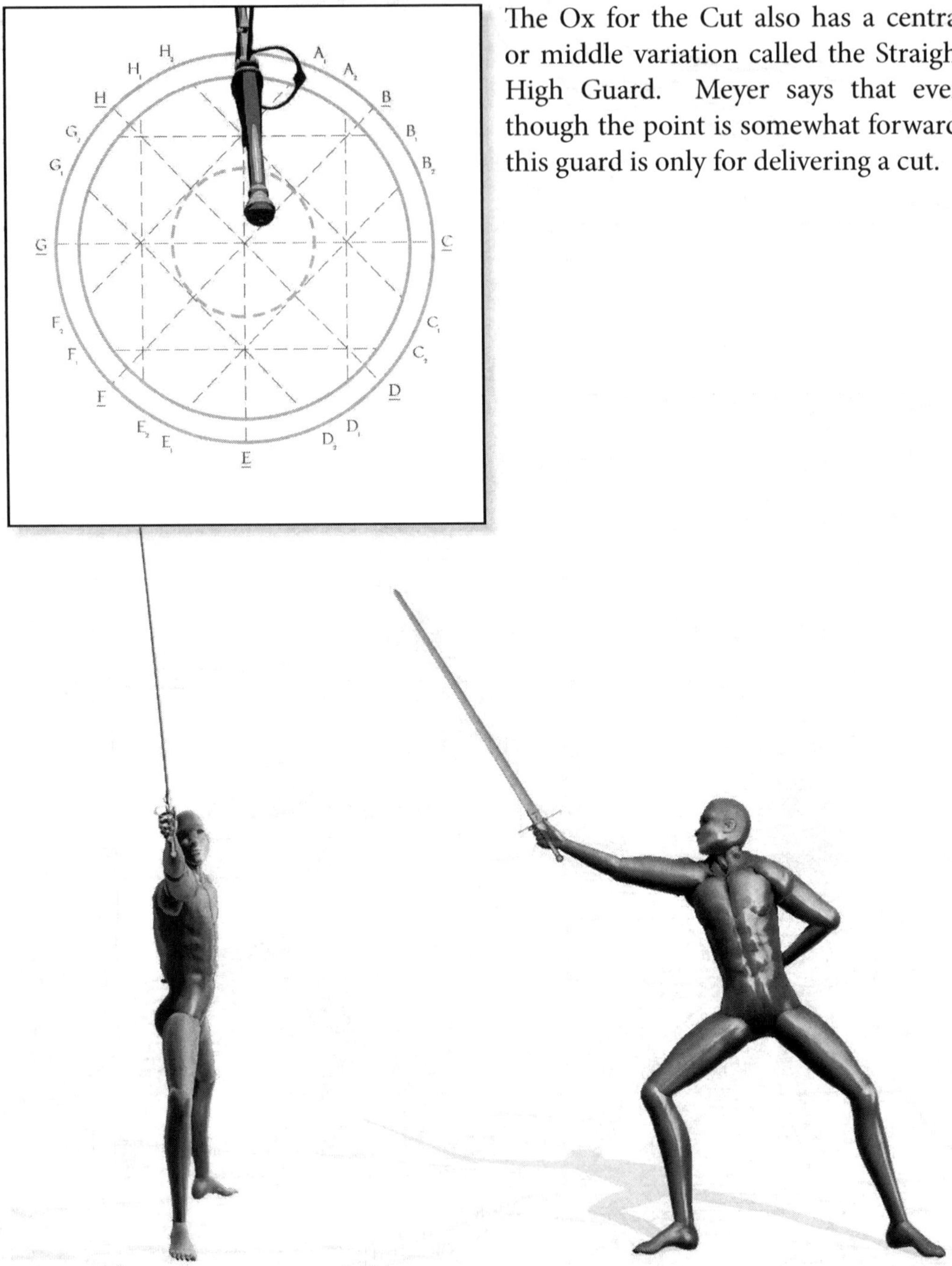

- *hand central*
- *point high and forward*
- *palm to the left*
- *left shoulder back*
- *body more erect*

- *High*
- *Straight*
- *Imperfect*
- *Wide*

Straight Iron Gate (*Eisenport*)

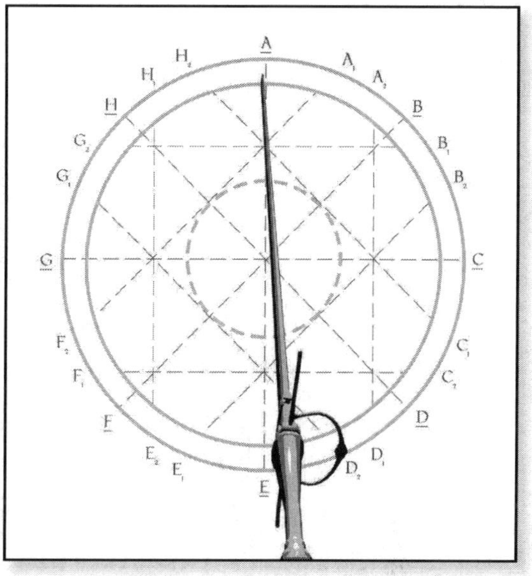

By dropping the entire sword and arm to the bottom of the circle while leaving the point near the center we form Iron Gate. Meyer states this guard is good for crowding in on the opponent (coming to the bind) and also good for intercepting the opponent's cuts and thrusts (parrying), much like an iron door. This guard is a neutral position before committing the weapon to either the left or right Iron Gate. It keeps the sword uncommitted until it needs to serve a specific function. Notice the lower the guard, the lower and more inclined the body. A simple way to think about how the body moves with the sword is that wherever the sword needs to be employed, the body moves behind it, not only hiding behind it, but supporting its position.

- *hand central*
- *point face level and forward*
- *palm to the left*
- *left shoulder back*
- *body lowered*

- *Low*
- *Straight*
- *Perfect*
- *Narrow*

see Appendix E, Plate C

Iron Gate on the Right (*Eisenport)*

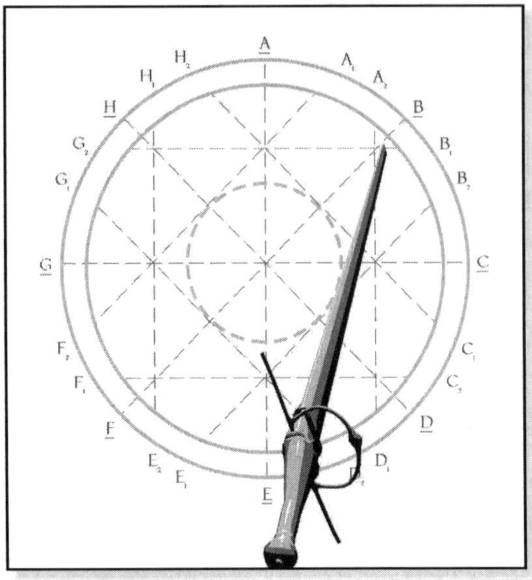

Iron Gate on the Right is formed like the neutral or straight variant, except the hand, point, and long-edge move to create an opposition, or cover, to the outside or right side. To support this position of the sword, the left shoulder and hip are slightly rotated forward. This action keeps the body straight behind the position of the sword while also fortifying it.

- *hand and point to the right*
- *point face height and forward*
- *palm to the left*
- *left shoulder somewhat forward*
- *body lowered*

- *Low*
- *Offensive*
- *Perfect*
- *Narrow*

Iron Gate on the Left (*Eisenport*)

Opposite the Iron Gate on the Right is the Iron Gate on the Left. The hand, point and long-edge are moved to the left to create a barrier to the inside. The left shoulder is turned back to hide the body behind the position of the sword. The inside or left side of the fencer is the most naturally exposed portion (because the sword is held in the right hand, attached to the right side of the body), so this position moves to protect that opening.

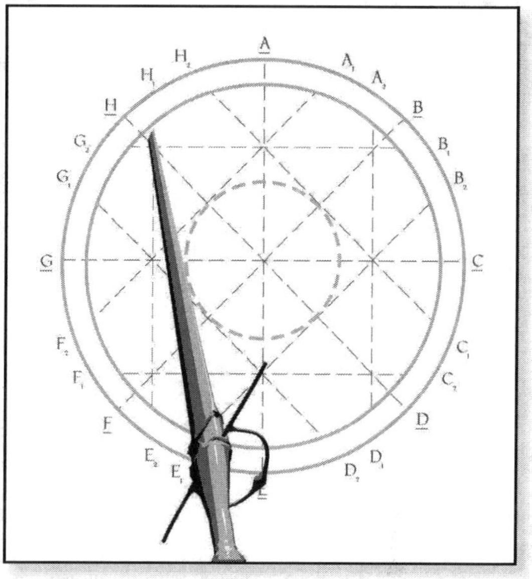

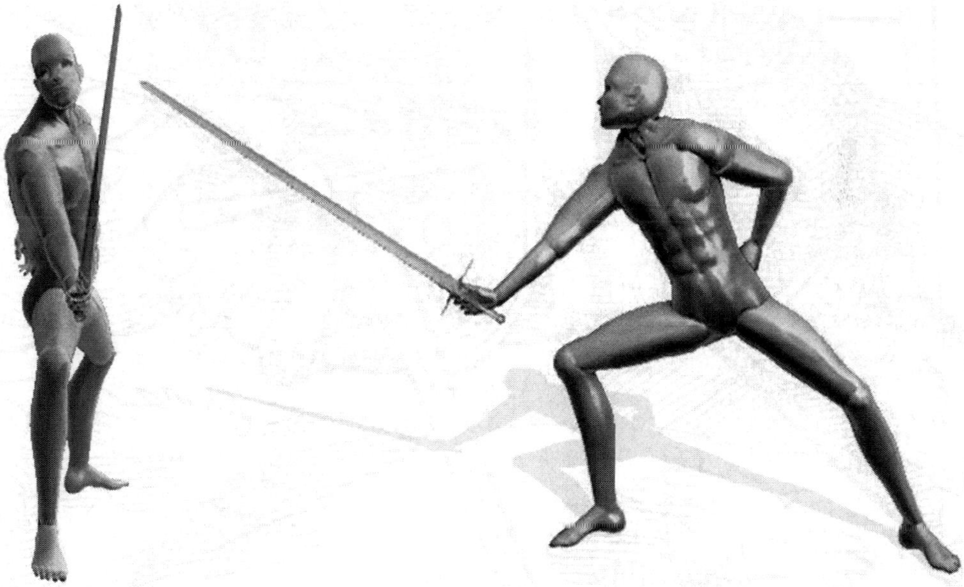

- *hand and point to the left*
- *point face height and forward*
- *palm to the left*
- *left shoulder back*
- *body lowered*

- *Low*
- *Defensive*
- *Perfect*
- *Narrow*

PLOW ON THE RIGHT (*Pflug*)

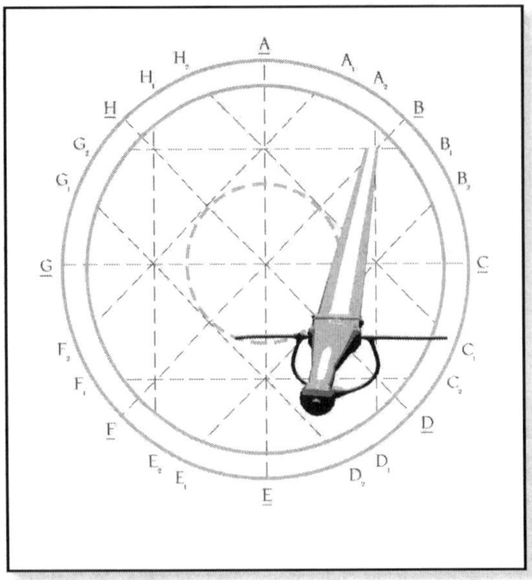

The Plow in Meyer's art is a 'supinated' position (with the palm up) as opposed to inward like Iron Gate, and is described as a position like the low thrust, but 'formed as a guard.' In his description of the Plow, he mentions the point should extend toward the opponent's belly, but when he uses it in his techniques, states the point should be directed at their face. The thumb should extend over the inside flat of the blade to give more control to the use of the point.

Meyer uses the Plow to create strong engagements on the opponent's weapon to the inside and outside while also using it as a position to invite a cut to the head in order to run-in and grapple. The body orientation leans in the direction of the blade, further taking the opponent's blade out to the side it has been opposed.[16]

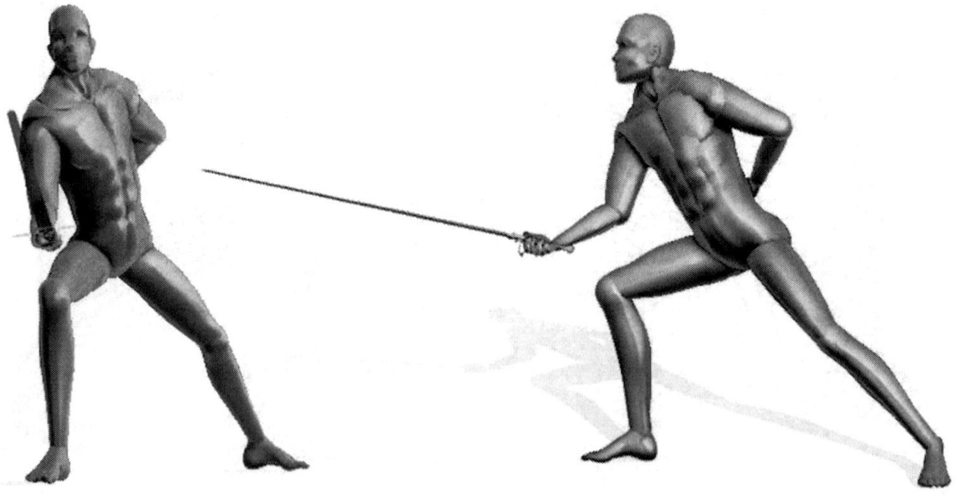

- *hand and point to the right*
- *point forward*
- *palm up*
- *left shoulder somewhat forward*
- *body lowered*

- *Low*
- *Offensive*
- *Perfect*
- *Narrow*

Plow on the Left (*Pflug*)

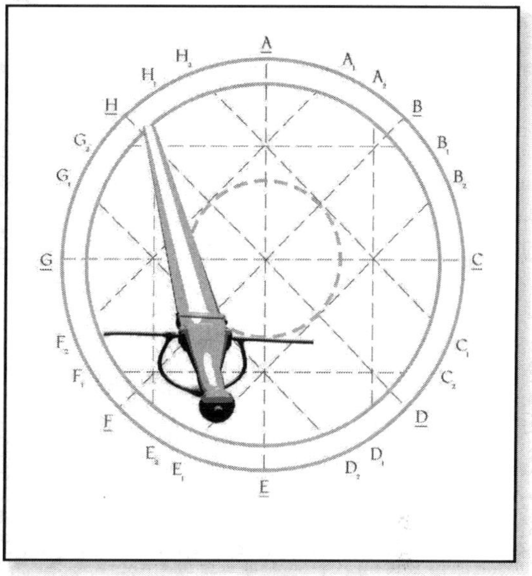

When the same guard is formed on the left, the palm remains up, using the long-edge to create opposition to the inside. The body is low with the feet wide apart, as if just finishing a low thrust to the inside. Like other positions where the sword is held to the left, the left shoulder and hip are rotated back to hide the body behind the sword with the right side extended as far forward as possible.

Plow can also be formed in the middle with the hand directly in front of the forward knee and point straight ahead. Plow, is an oddity in Meyer's rapier, and possibly a holdover from the earlier German sources, as its use seems secondary to the other 'perfect' guards.

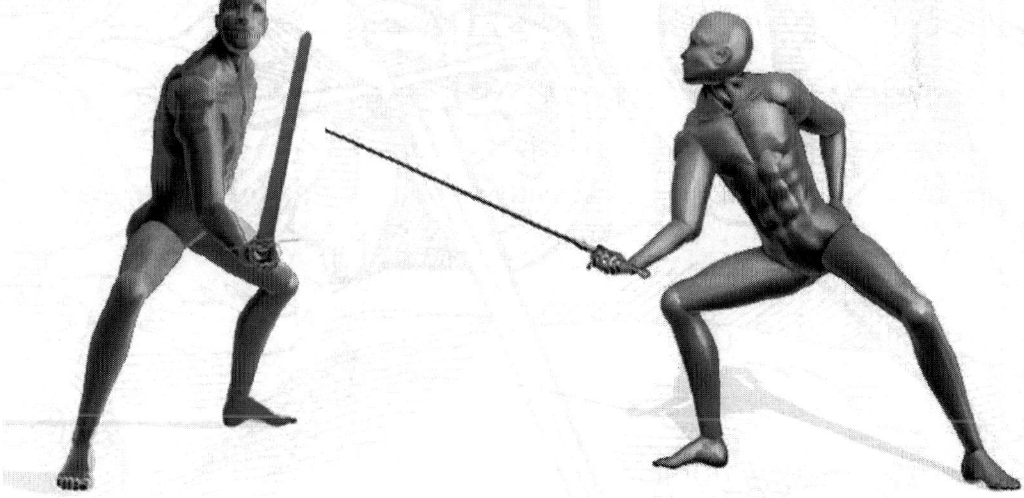

- *hand and point to the left*
- *point forward*
- *palm up*
- *left shoulder back*
- *body lowered*

- *Low*
- *Defensive*
- *Perfect*
- *Narrow*

Low Guard on the Right or Side Guard (*Nebenhut*)

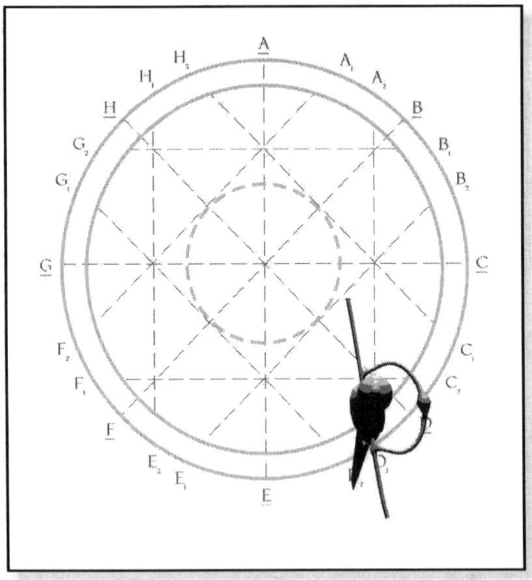

The Low Guard on the Right, or Side Guard, is the end position of a diagonal cut from the left. It is similar to the Right Iron Gate except the point is dropped toward the ground, removing the threat of the point and widening the guard. The main function of this position is to entice the opponent to attack the upper targets, so that we may execute a pre-planned parry and counter (though Meyer expects his fencer to know how to attack from this position as well). The left shoulder and hip are brought forward, almost square with the right, allowing the sword to exist in the lower right quadrant. The feet are wide with the body extended forward, similar to all low guards in this art.

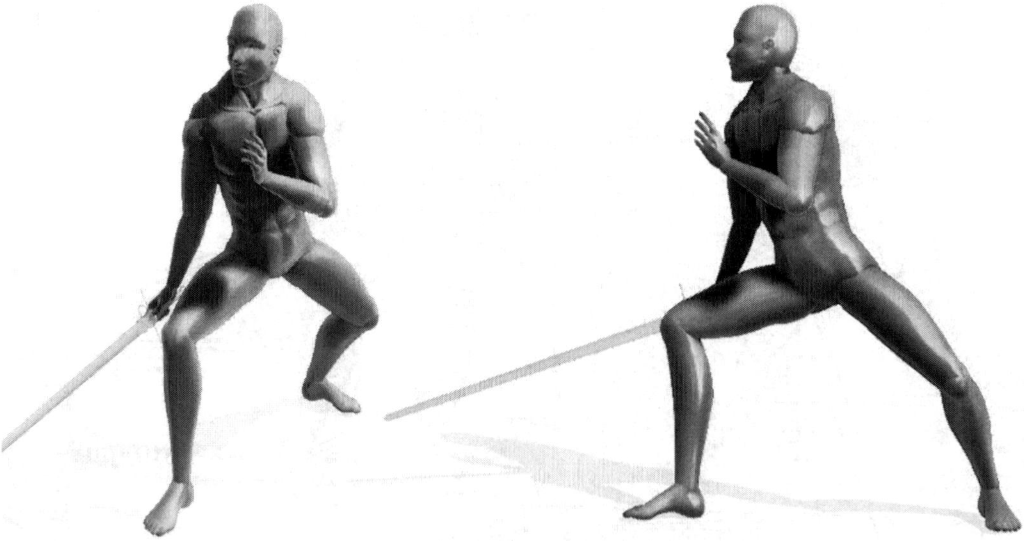

- *hand and point to the right*
- *point low and forward*
- *palm to the left*
- *left shoulder somewhat forward*
- *body lowered*

- *Low*
- *Offensive*
- *Imperfect*
- *Wide*

see Appendix E, Plate D

Low Guard on the Left or The Change (*Wechselhut*)

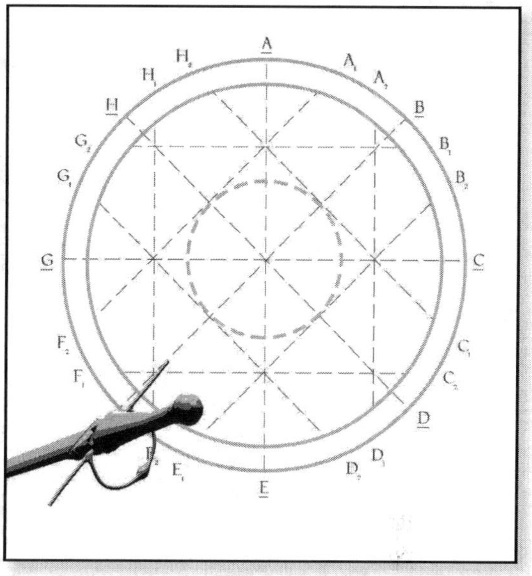

The Low Guard on the Left, or The Change, is the end of a diagonal cut from the right, offering an opening or target for the opponent over the sword arm. This position along with the Left Iron Gate is the most defensive position in Meyer's art. While the Left Iron Gate defends the inside with the long-edge and point, the Low Guard on the Left provides a strong position to make a parry with the short-edge directed towards the center. Meyer seemingly does not intend to use this position to attack as he does not give us a single technique where this guard is used in the *Vor* (to initiate an attack). Rather, similar to the Low Guard on the Right, Meyer wants us to form this guard to invite an attack so that a parry and subsequent counter can be made.

- *hand and point to the left*
- *point low and away*
- *palm up*
- *left shoulder back*
- *body lowered*

- *Low*
- *Defensive*
- *Imperfect*
- *Wide*

see Appendix E, page 222

STRAIGHT LOW GUARD (*Alber*)

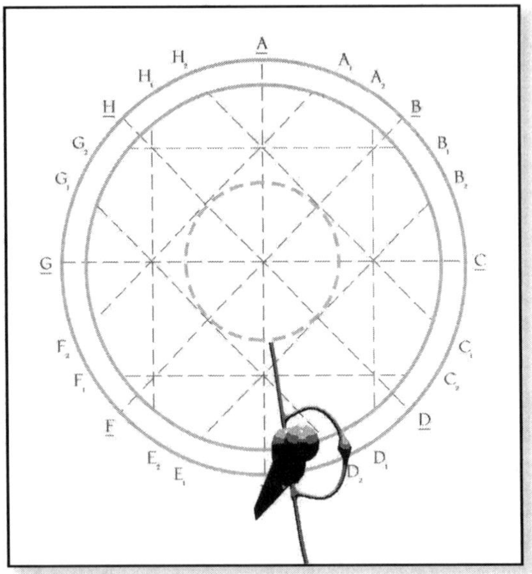

Meyer states that the Straight Low Guard is simply the end of a vertical cut where the arm is outstretched and point lowered towards the ground. He does not intend to use this position to make a defense from, but rather makes note of it simply to reinforce the idea that all guards can be formed on the right, left and middle.

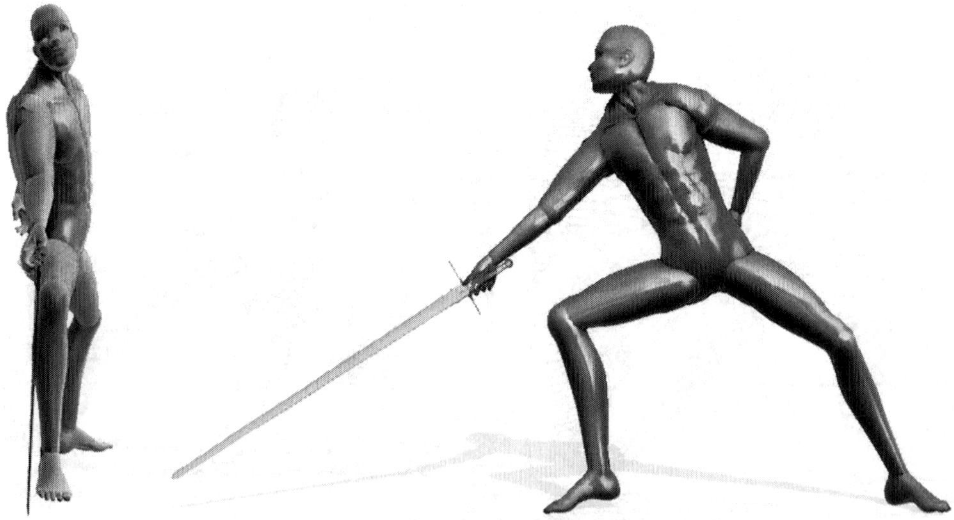

- *hand and point central*
- *point low and forward*
- *palm to the left*
- *left shoulder back*
- *body lowered*

- *Low*
- *Straight*
- *Imperfect*
- *Wide*

Middle Guard on the Left (*Mittelhut*)

The Middle Guard on the Left is not a guard that Meyer makes note of while listing his guards in his rapier book. It is a guard he defines in the previous book on the dusack. However, Meyer does mention it three times within the rapier section, describing it as an end position to a middle cut from the right. For the sake of being thorough, I have decided to include it here.

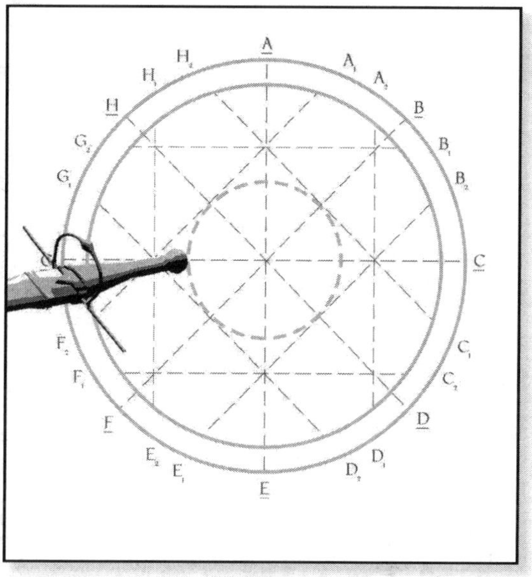

- *hand and point to the left*
- *point back*
- *palm down*
- *left shoulder back*
- *body more erect*

- *Middle*
- *Defensive*
- *Imperfect*
- *Wide*

Middle Guard on the Right (*Mittelhut*)

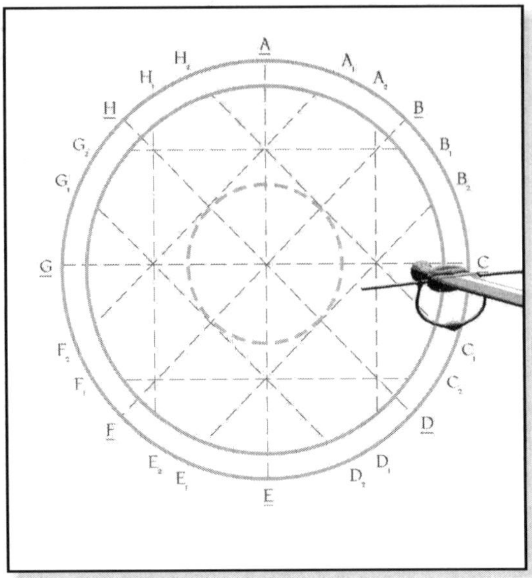

Middle Guard on the Right is not a guard that Meyer describes or ever uses, yet it can be created if one follows Meyer's logic that every position can be formed on the right and left. From the illustration below it should become apparent that a Middle Guard on the Right exposes the body too much in the course of a rapier fight, and is possibly why Meyer opted to not include it.

Similar positions are mentioned within contemporary Italian traditions and earlier German sources.[17]

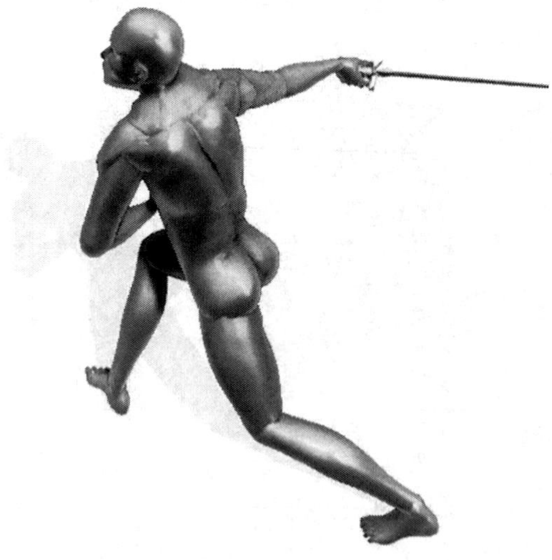

- *hand and point to the right*
- *point back*
- *palm up*
- *left shoulder forward*
- *body more erect*

- *Middle*
- *Offensive*
- *Imperfect*
- *Wide*

Straight-Parrying (*gerade Versatzung*)

The Straight-Parrying is the primary guard in Meyer's rapier art. It can be thought of as the straight variation of the Middle Guard. The sword is held slightly below the right shoulder, point extended towards the opponent's face with the long-edge turned down. The body is profiled with the left shoulder and hip turned to the back in order to hide the body as much as possible behind the sword. The Strong of the sword lies in the middle, protecting the forward-most targets. The arm is in a perfect line behind the sword so as not to present itself to the opponent. The lower body is refused from the opponent in case they wish to strike there, with the weight firmly on the forward, right foot. With the sword in a central and middle position, the sword can easily rotate to the right or left to meet the opponent's weapon with the long-edge. This position can also be considered Longpoint (the end of all thrusts) formed as a guard.

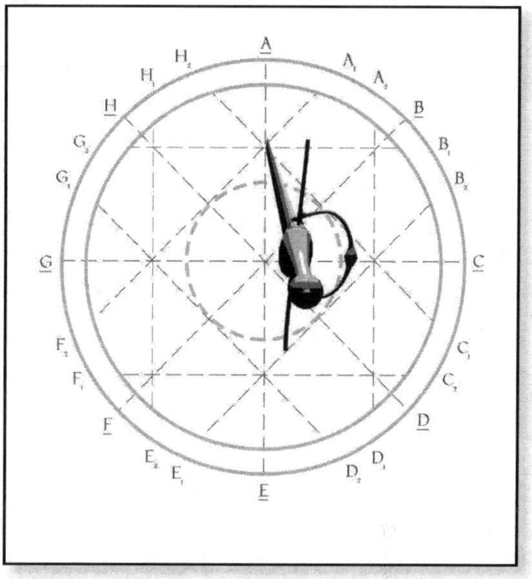

- *hand and point central*
- *point at face height*
- *palm to the left*
- *left shoulder back*
- *body more lowered*

- *Middle*
- *Straight*
- *Perfect*
- *Narrow*

see Appendix E, Plate F

LONGPOINT (*Langort*)

In the practice of rapier, the guard or position of Longpoint is exclusively the end position of the longest possible thrust through the extension of sword, body and foot. To maximize this extension, the height of the hand is always level with the shoulder in order to form a straight line to the target. If the hand is lowered or raised from the height of the shoulder, the point is pulled away from the target and the thrust is shortened. While Longpoint is the ideal, it is also necessary to form attacks that do not end in their longest possible extension depending how the weapons engage. In some instances positions that favor a stronger occupation of the opponent's sword, or a position that works around their weapon are more favorable in a given engagement. It should be understood that anytime the sword strays from the Longpoint, it has been shortened, and space needs to be managed to overcome this.

Cuts likewise make contact with the target in positions similar to Longpoint, but because the edge is employed during the cut, the angle of the wrist causes the hand to be slightly lower than the shoulder when cutting from above, and slightly higher when cutting from below. Cuts that originate from the dominant side end with the hand slightly to the inside, while cuts from the non-dominant side not only end with the hand to the outside, but also with the body turned (as will be discussed later). Cuts also tend to follow through Longpoint into one of the other positions discussed above. The key similarity between thrusts and cuts that move through Longpoint is that they both should be executed with the dominant shoulder at the height of the target being struck, not only to maximize the distance at which the attack can reach, but also to hide the body behind the weapon.

From the preferred guard of Straight-Parrying, Longpoint is simply a further extension of the hand and foot. If we stray from Longpoint during or after the attack (and as we withdraw from the fight), we should quickly come back to Longpoint (or Straight-Parrying) to maintain a certain degree of safety and threat of the point to the opponent.

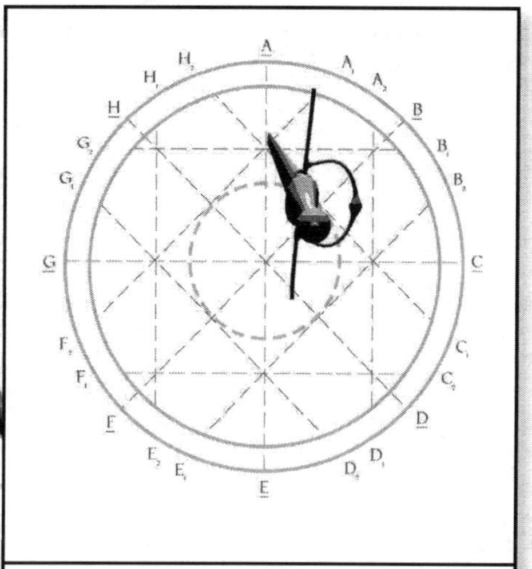

Longpoint to a high target

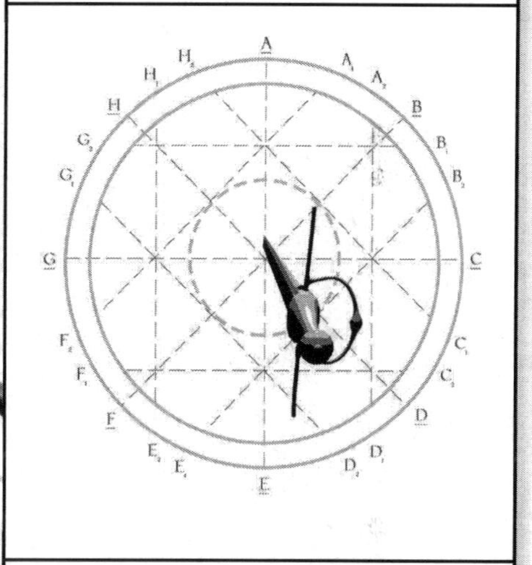

Longpoint to a middle target

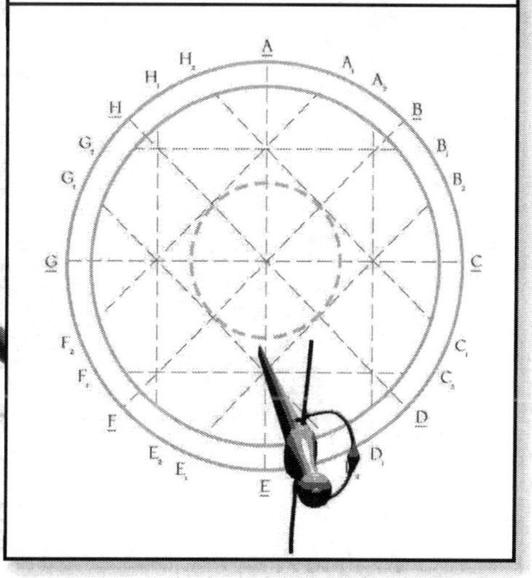

Longpoint to a low target

High Longpoint: see Appendix E, Plate D & G
Middle Longpoint: see Appendix E, Plate B & E

part III the cuts & thrusts

Transforming Between the Guards

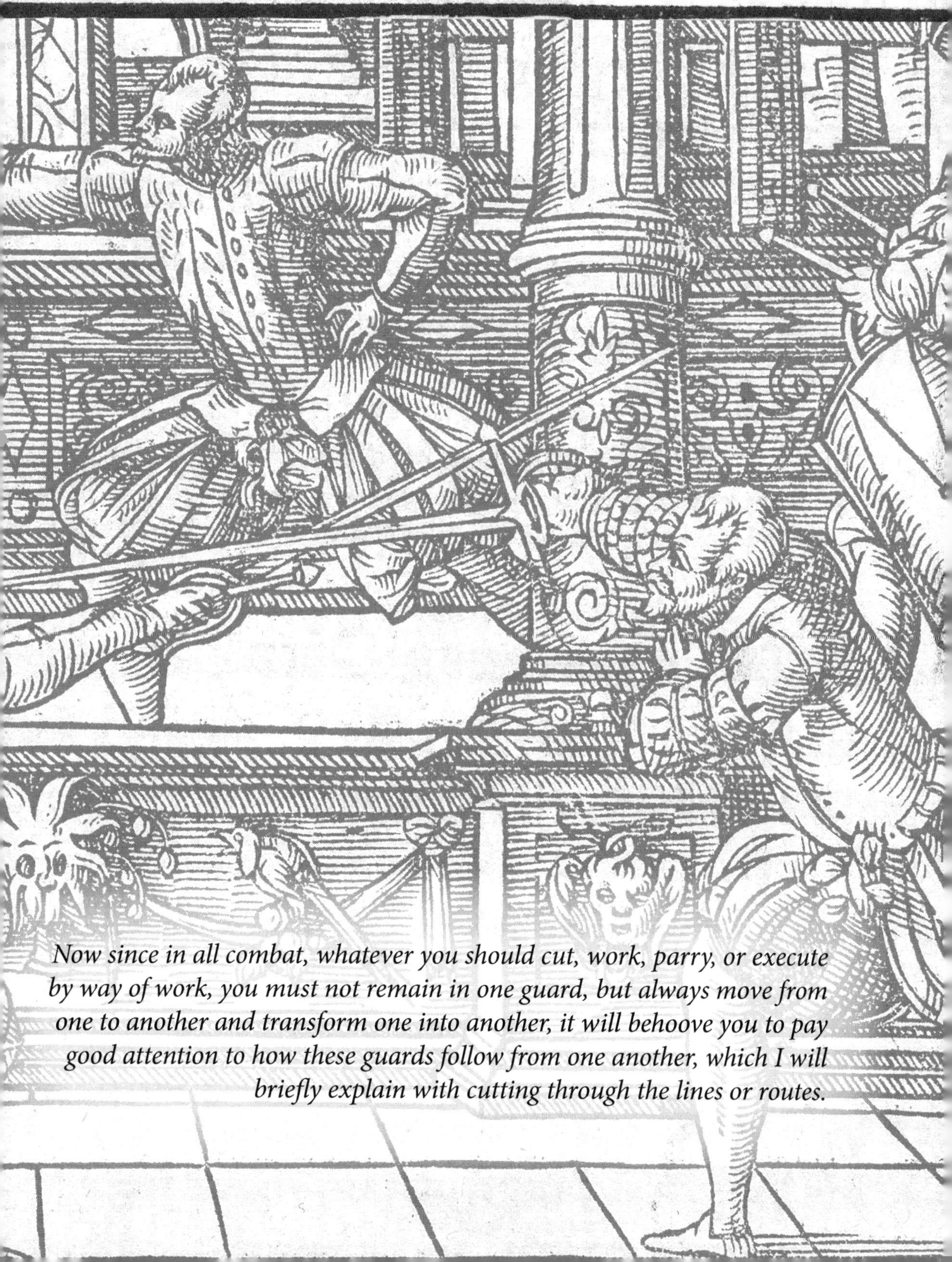

Now since in all combat, whatever you should cut, work, parry, or execute by way of work, you must not remain in one guard, but always move from one to another and transform one into another, it will behoove you to pay good attention to how these guards follow from one another, which I will briefly explain with cutting through the lines or routes.

The Cuts

The cuts and thrusts, independent of their intent, are the forceful transitions between the guards. They are the actions between a preceding and subsequent rest.[18] These actions always start in one guard, transition through Longpoint (or some facsimile thereof) and finish in another guard. For instance, a descending, vertical cut (*Schiedelhauw)* will begin in Straight High Guard, fall into Longpoint, and then have its conclusion in Straight Low Guard. If the descending cut is made along the diagonal (*Oberhauw schlims*), it starts in Ox for the Cut, lowers into Longpoint, then finishes in a low guard on the opposite side. Conversely, an ascending cut (*Unterhauw*), will start in a low guard, flow through Longpoint, and end in a high guard. Middle cuts (*Mittelhauw*) begin on either the left or right, pass through Longpoint, and end on the opposite side. These are the four primary paths that cuts travel, though Meyer further distinguishes these cuts into the following groups:

1. The vertical cuts can be straight down the middle, and thus retain the name Scalp Cut (*Scheidelhauw)*, or can also be made down either the left or the right side, and are given the name Suppressing Cut (*Dempffhauw).*

2. The descending, diagonal cuts are made by starting on either the right or left and are given names based on their function and temperament, or where they strike the opponent or their weapon. For instance, when they strike the opponent, they are called Wrath Cuts (*Zornhauw*). When these Wrath Cuts strike through the upper-cross, they are the Shoulder Cut; through the middle-cross, the Hip Cut; the lower-cross, the Thigh Cut. However, when the descending, diagonal cuts are made against the opponent's weapon, they are designated as Defense Strokes (*Wehrstreich*), again, high, middle and low.

3. The middle cuts also can begin on the left or right, and end on the opposite side, and are also made high, middle and low (through the three crosses) and are called: the Neck Cut, Belt Cut, and Foot Cut, respectively.

4. The low cuts, or ascending cuts, follow the same path as the descending cuts (both vertical and diagonal), but have their origin in the low guards, and borrow the naming convention of their respective high cut.

Since no blow can be reasonably performed without ending in a guard, the virtue of a fencer is to be found in the raising and lowering of the guards.[19]
-Antonio Manciolino, 1531

All of the preceding cuts are made with the long-edge of the weapon, though they can also be made with the short-edge (or the flat as Meyer points out). One short-edge cut is given a unique name in Meyer's rapier system, borrowed from the longsword – the Squinting Cut (*Schielhauw*), a vertical, descending cut through the middle (though the hand is turned either way to turn the short-edge downward, changing its function to either side). In the cases where the short-edge is employed, passing through Longpoint becomes more difficult (especially when making descending, short-edge cuts) and so the cut is thus "shortened." These shortened or reversed cuts are better suited in making defenses (parries) rather that strikes to the target.

All cuts, like the guards they pass through, should be made with a straight and extended arm. This adds structure to the cut while reducing the time the weapon needs to travel into and through Longpoint (the furthest extension of our attack). Because this art is primarily a form using a single weapon (without an accompanied shield or companion weapon in the other hand, though one could be employed), the sword must be both our weapon and shield. This means that as the sword is brought into a particular guard to prepare a cut, the sword should begin to travel first, into the space ahead of us, before the body. The more the sword departs from Longpoint, exposing the body to a greater degree, the more the sword needs to return to this position before the feet carry the body forward into danger.

This means that from the guard in which the cut is prepared, the sword should travel first, ahead of the body and feet. Once a degree of safety has been satisfied, but before the extension of the cut into Longpoint, the foot raises, then as the extension of the cut pulls the body forward into Longpoint, the foot falls (at some distance further than it was before). An anonymous, Italian, author writing sometime in the first half of the 16th century in Bologna, summarizes the transformations of the guards this way: "based upon [the guards] usage, as placements into which a man may put himself, and from which a man may **safely move his sword hand, and then his feet**, as following they must..."[20] [emphasis mine].

Scalp Cut (*Scheidelhauw*)

The Scalp Cut is a vertical cut beginning in Straight High Guard. As the sword is lowered, it passes through Longpoint connecting with the top of the opponent's head, then lowers as much as possible through the target, ending in Straight Low Guard. Because this cut travels 'straight,' beginning and ending in the middle column, it lacks the ability to make a cover to either side and is thus employed more as a deceptive strike, or when the opponent's weapon has moved out of the way to either side (by their choice or our making).

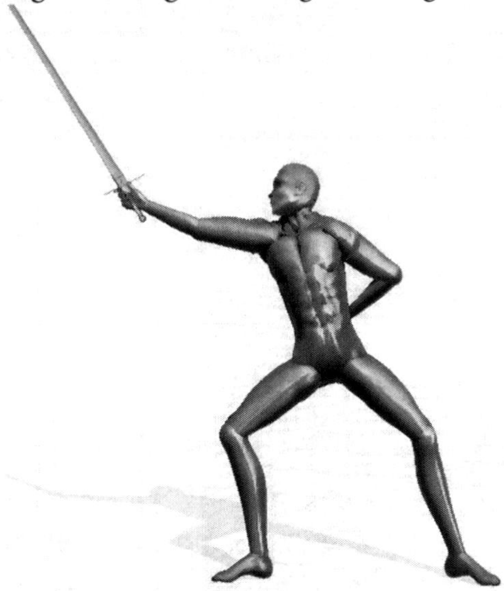

If the sequence is reversed, starting in Straight Low Guard, we can call it a low, reversed, Scalp Cut, meaning that its origin is from below, and reversed because the short-edge is employed.

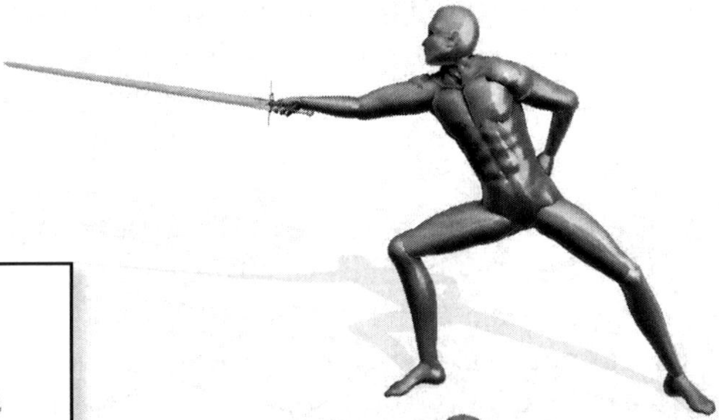

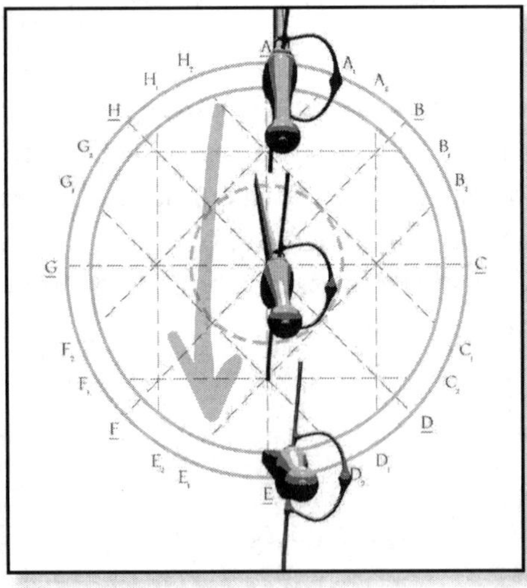

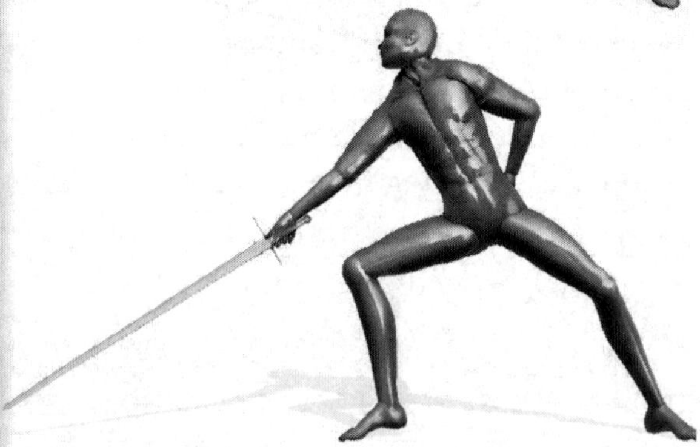

Suppressing Cut (*Dempffhauw*)

The Suppressing Cut is a vertical cut made downward to either side through the shoulders. Its primary function is to displace the opponent's weapon from our presence. From Straight High Guard the sword is dropped straight down through the right or left shoulder, through Longpoint, and then continues downward with the entire body, similar to a low Longpoint, but with the sword held at an upward angle. If the Suppressing Cut is made through the opponent's left shoulder (down our right, vertical) then as the body is lowered past Longpoint, the shoulders and hips should rotate behind the position of the sword (as shown in the last figure below). This rotation supports the outside opposition made between the weapons (discussed in the chapter on parries), but also hides the body behind the sword to the opposite side. If the cut is made through the opposite shoulder, the body should stay profiled, with the left shoulder and hip to the rear.

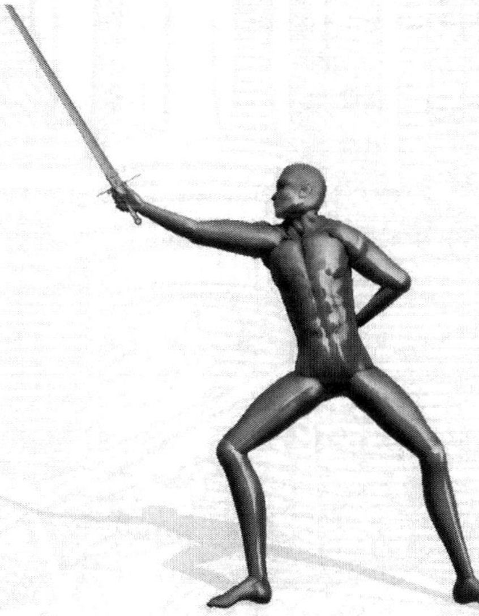

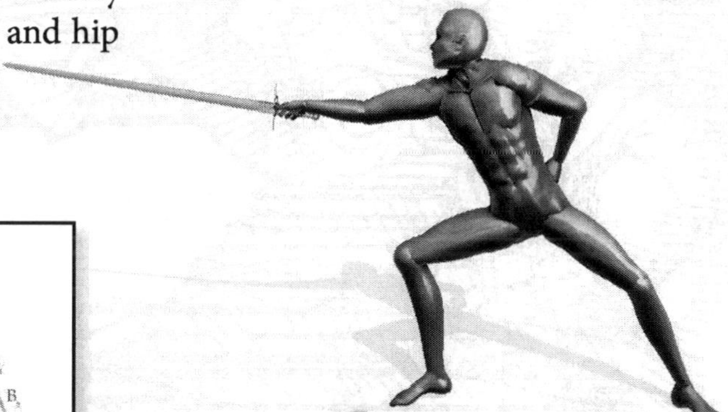

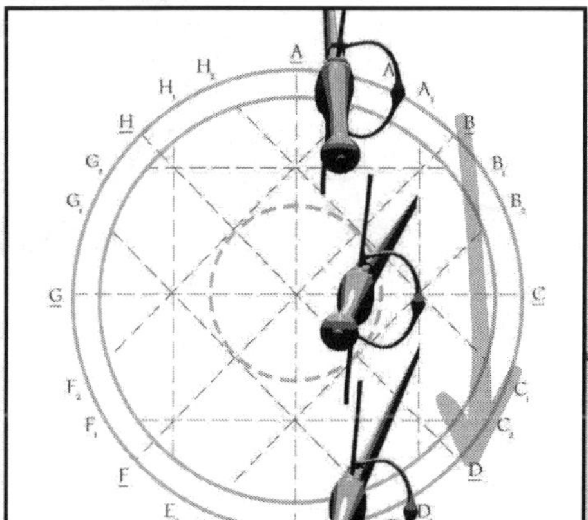

see Appendix E, Plate G

Squinting Cut (*Schielhauw*)

The Squinting Cut is a reversed Suppressing Cut from above. From Straight High Guard, as the long-edge is lowered, the hand turns up through a Left Ox-like position when opposing a cut to our left, and up through a Right Ox-like position when opposing to our right. This descending, short-edge cut does not come through Longpoint and is thus 'shortened.' As the opponent's blade is suppressed with the short-edge (or flat) our point moves over their weapon striking a target on the same side their blade was opposed.

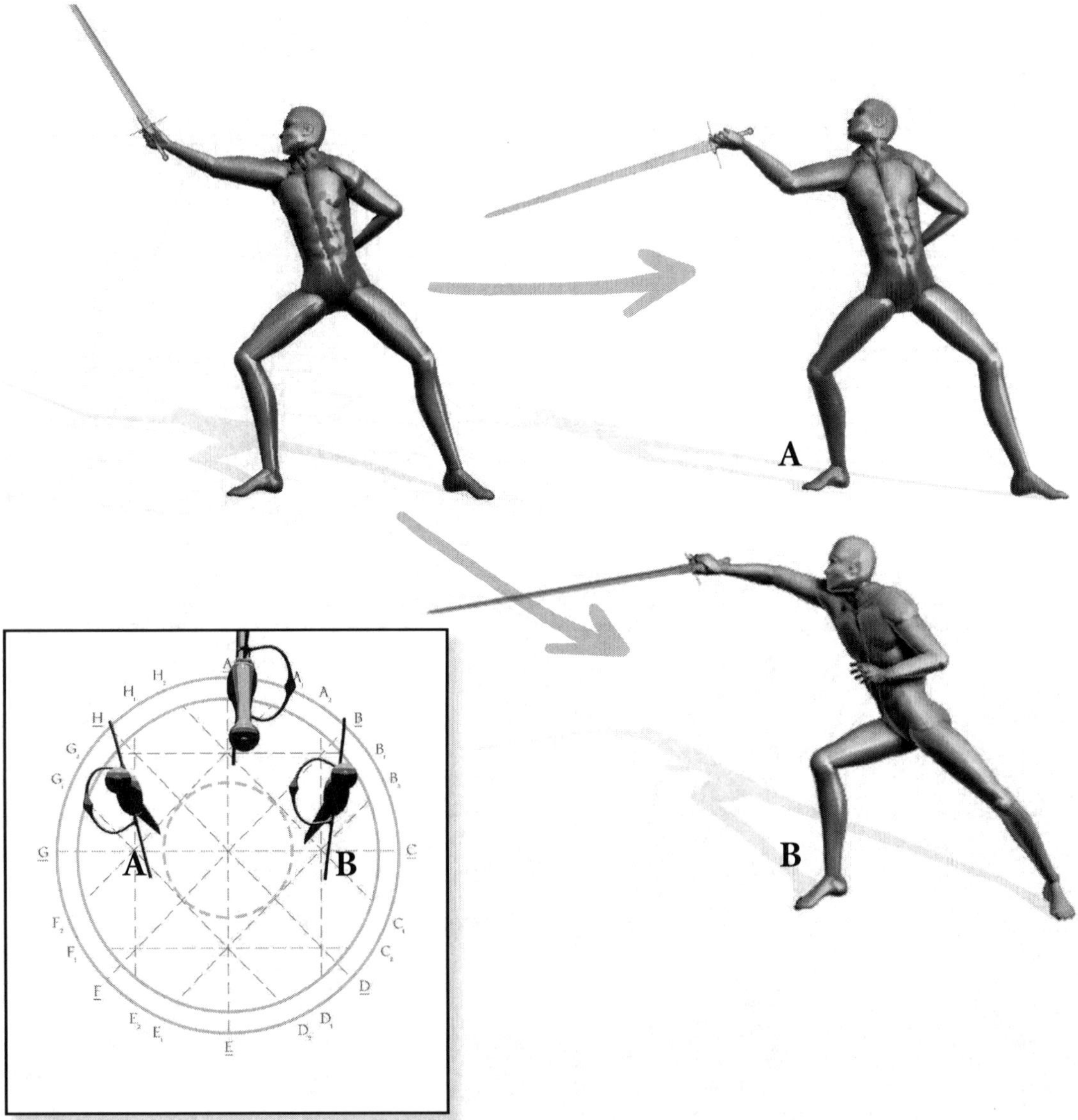

WRATH CUT (*Zornhauw*)
from the right

The Wrath Cut from the right is the most natural cut as it has its origin on the dominant side and works with gravity as it descends through space. From Right Ox for the Cut, with the left shoulder and hip somewhat forward, the hand begins to fall, bringing the point forward. Then the left shoulder and hip are rotated back, pushing the right shoulder and hip forward, maximizing the extension into Longpoint.

This rotation not only adds power and speed to the strike, it positions the body behind the sword as it make contact in Longpoint and continues through the target into Low Guard on the Left.

Depending on the height of the target being struck, the right foot and body extends to form any variation of Longpoint (high through the face, to low through the legs).

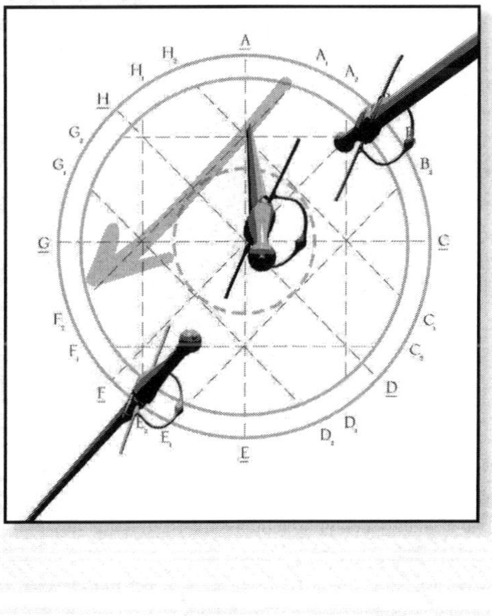

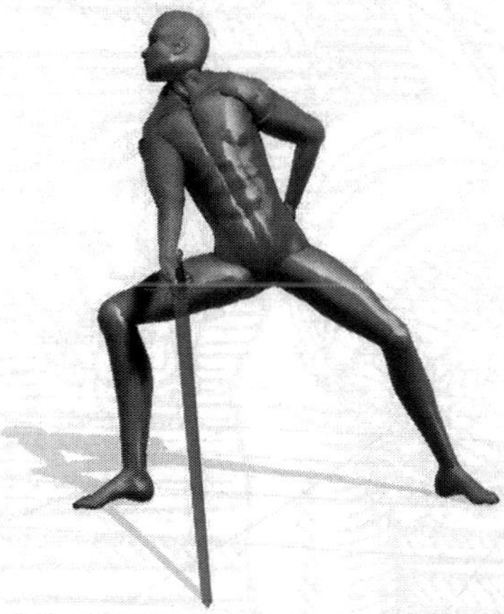

Wrath Cut (*Zornhauw*)

from the left

Converse to the Wrath Cut from the right, the same cut is made from the left, but following the opposite cut line as well as the body turning the opposite direction. Starting in Left-Ox for the Cut, with the left shoulder and hip to the rear, the hand lowers pulling the point forward. In this instance, to add power and speed to the cut, the left shoulder and hip rotate forward through Longpoint and to the cut's conclusion in Low Right Guard.

Because the left shoulder and hip begin a rotation forward, they pull their counterparts back, thus slightly reducing the extension of this cut when made from this side.

Both Wrath Cuts from the left and right can be reversed. Beginning from the Low Guard, the short-edge is raised through Longpoint and finish in their respective High Guard.

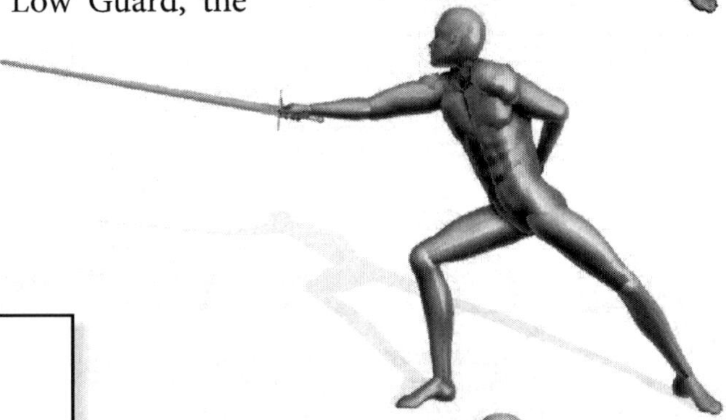

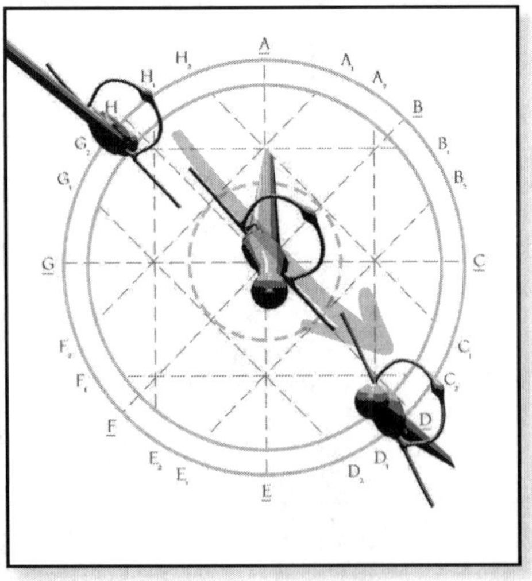

Half Cut
from the right

The same Wrath Cuts can also be 'halved,' meaning they do not fall into the low, imperfect guards, but rather end with the point forward. From the same starting position of Right-Ox for the Cut, and the same rotations of the body, the point is brought forward and left into Longpoint.

When the descending, diagonal cut from the right is instead made to the opponent's weapon (a Defense Stroke), the half cut should be made 'short' into Iron Gate on the left. This position gives us a good purchase on the opponent's weapon and control over it, as will be discussed in the following chapters.

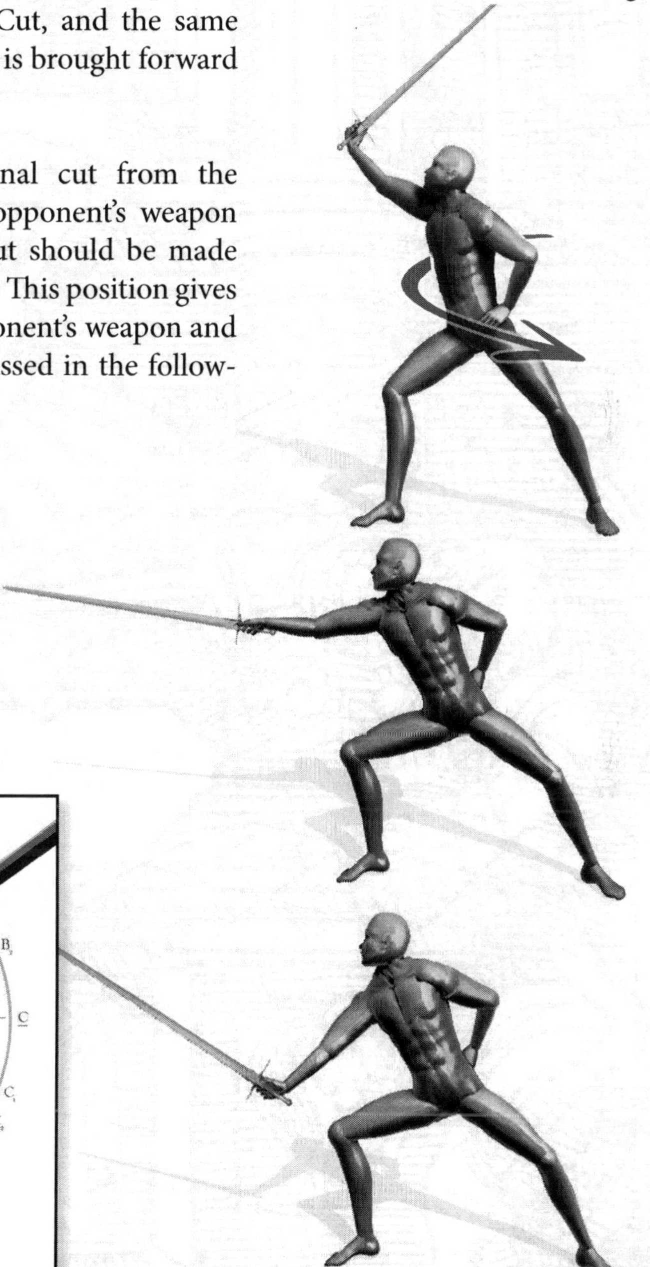

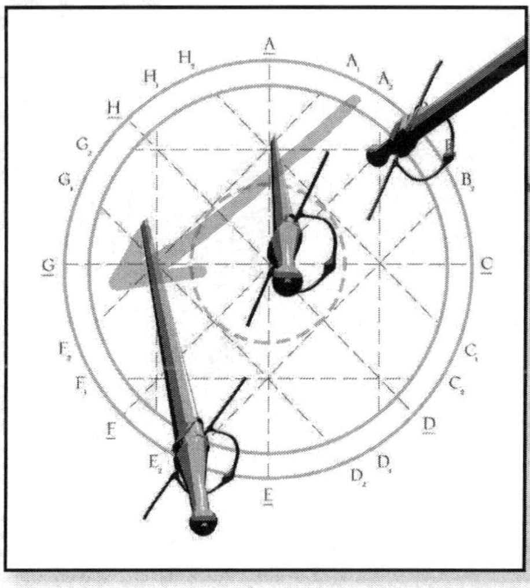

Half Cut
from the left

The same half cut can be made from left to right, with the same rotations of the body as its 'full' counterpart (Wrath Cut from the left). Again, the cut can be made into Longpoint and then fall into Right Iron Gate, or be made into Right Iron Gate if made as a Defense Stroke.

Due to the rotation of the body to the outside, and the somewhat shortened nature of this long-edge cut, a Defense Stroke from left to right makes this action a strong parry to the outside.

Like the 'full' Wrath Cut, half cuts can be reversed. Starting in Iron Gate, the short-edge is raised and extended through Longpoint, and from there can assume another narrow guard. For instance, an ascending, short-edge cut from Left Iron Gate is made into Longpoint, then finishes by lowering into Right Iron Gate, or continues to rise and turn into Right Ox for the Thrust. These actions are suited for controlling the opponent's sword and will be discussed in the chapter on Taking.

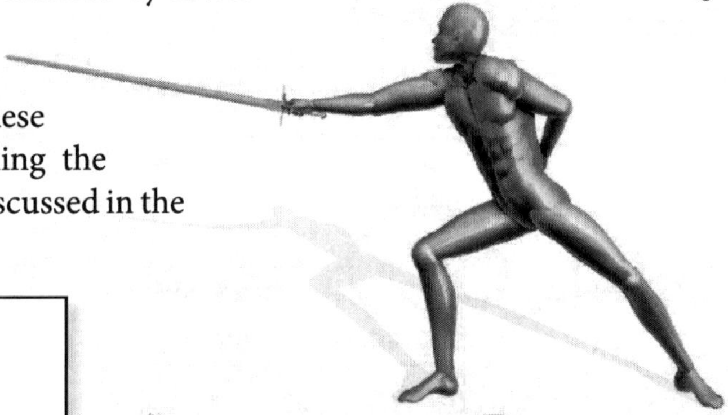

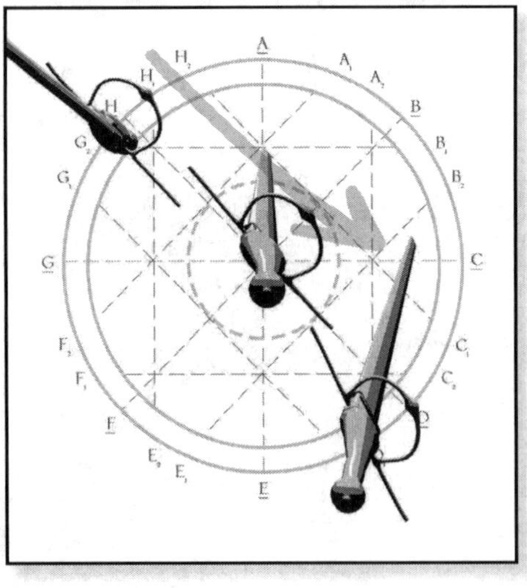

Low Cut (*Unterhauw*)
from the left

The Low Cuts with the long-edge begin in positions similar to their respective low guards but with the long-edge turned to face the target. The Low Cut from the left begins in the Low Left Guard but with the hand turned over as to present the long-edge forward. As the hand raises, the point is extended forward through Longpoint with the long-edge up and hand somewhat higher than the point. As the cut passes through the target (or the opponent's weapon if made as a parry), the sword continues up into Right Ox for the Thrust.

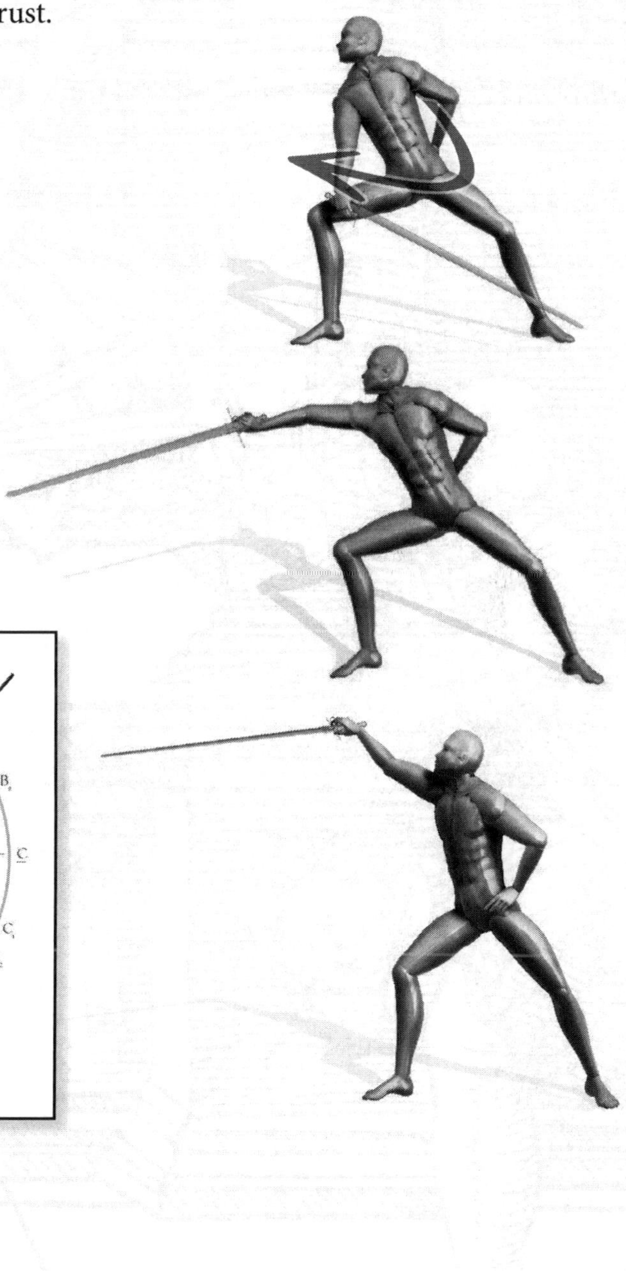

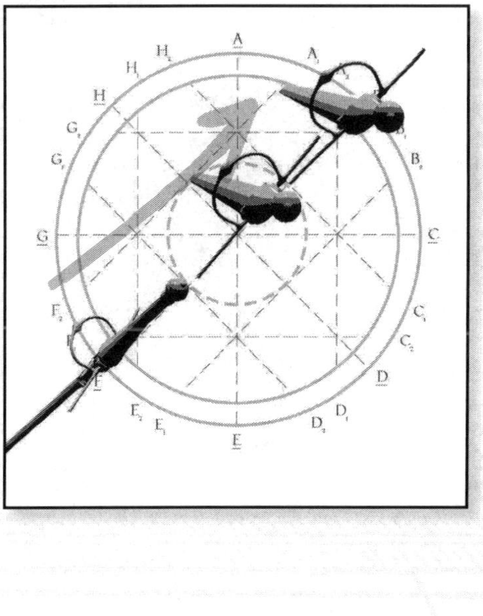

Low Cut (*Unterhauw*)

from the right

The Low Cut from the right starts in the Low Right Guard but with the palm facing upwards as to turn the long-edge forward. As the hand raises and sends the point forward, the body uncoils from its starting position, sending the sword forward through Longpoint with the long-edge up and to the left. As the weapon extends through its target, it finishes in Left Ox for the Thrust.

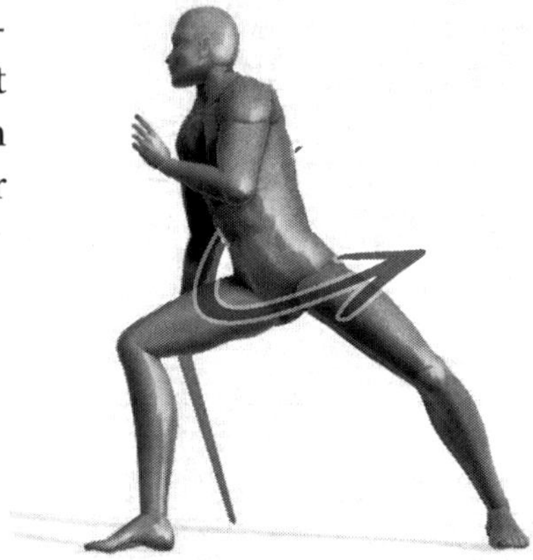

Reversing this action gives us the Crooked Cut.

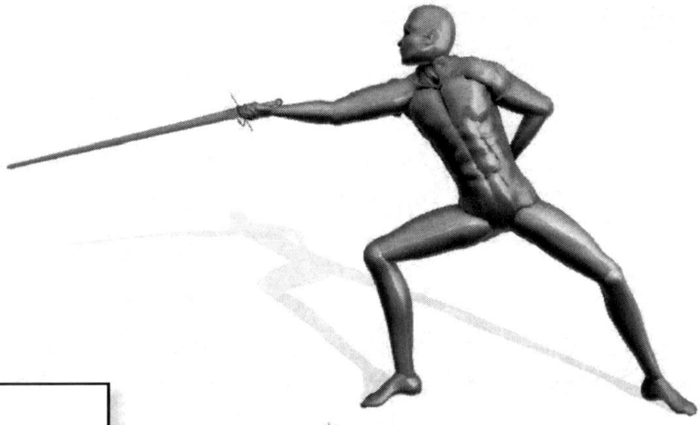

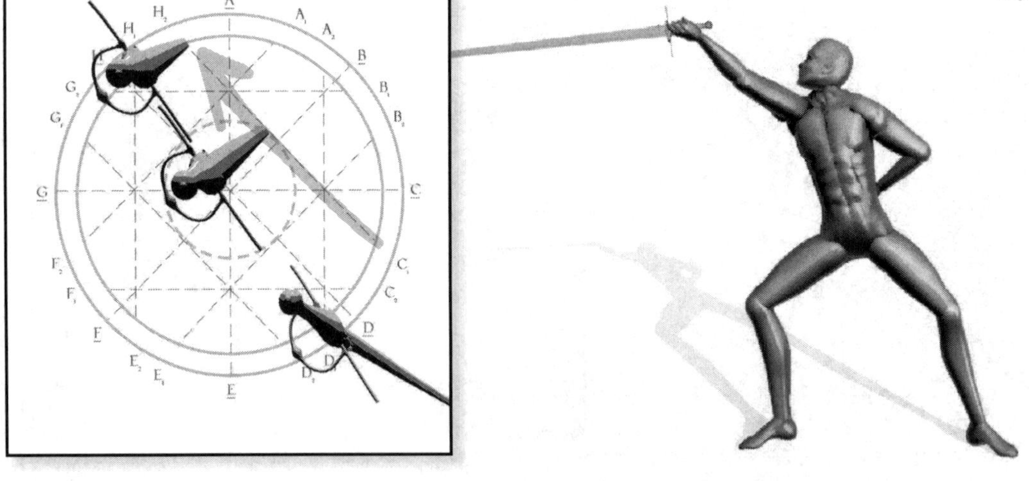

Crooked Cut (*Krumphauw*)

The Crooked Cut is an action Meyer seemingly leaves out of his rapier section, though describes actions that could be categorized as such.[21] The main function of this cut is to remove the opponent's weapon from our presence with a descending, short-edge cut. This descending cut starts from Left Ox for the Thrust, when presented with the rapier (unlike with the longsword, where it is executed from the low guards). The short-edge lowers and finishes in the position shown by the lower figure.

After the Crooked Cut has displaced the opponent's weapon, the long-edge is brought to bear, finishing with a thrust (see the chapter on Taking).

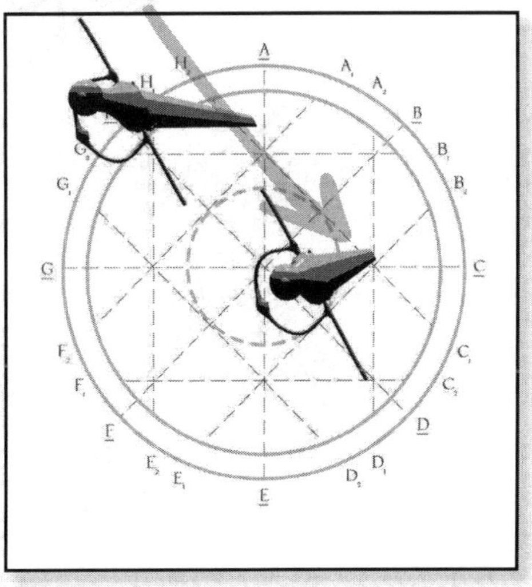

Middle Cut (*Mittelhauw*)

The Middle, or horizontal cuts, are made in the same fashion as the diagonal cuts, except for the angle of their path. Cuts from the right to left are assisted by rotating the body counter-clockwise when viewed from above, while cuts from left to right are powered by rotating the body clockwise, when viewed in the same perspective.

The Middle Cuts pass through high, middle, or low Longpoint striking the target with the palm up when cutting from the right, and palm down when cutting from the left. Though Meyer does not distinguish between the names assigned to these cuts when made to the opponent versus those made to their weapon, they are just as suited for making attacks as well as defenses, displacing the opponent's weapon to the side, as opposed to downward with the Defense Stroke.

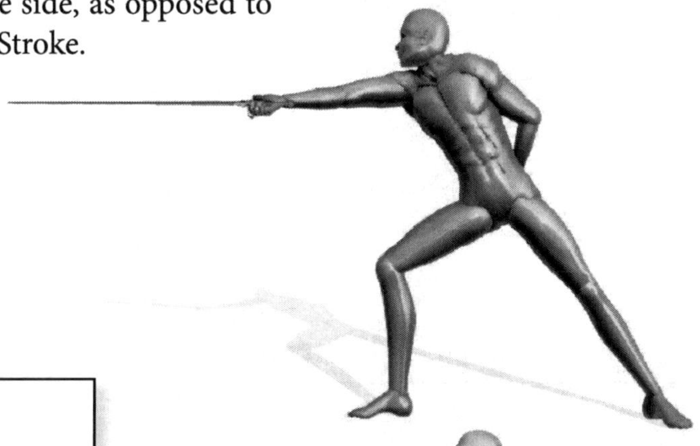

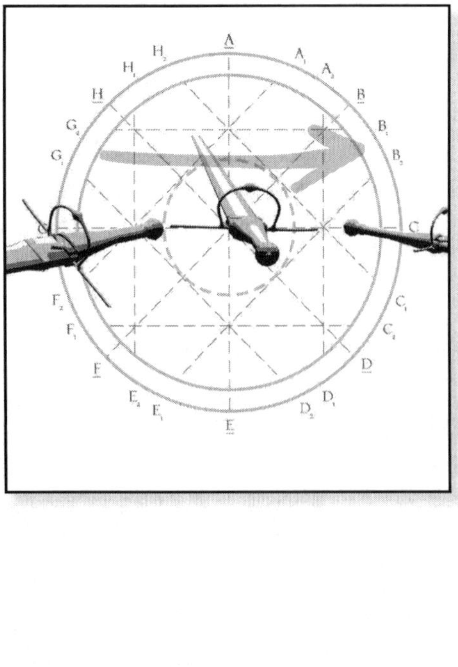

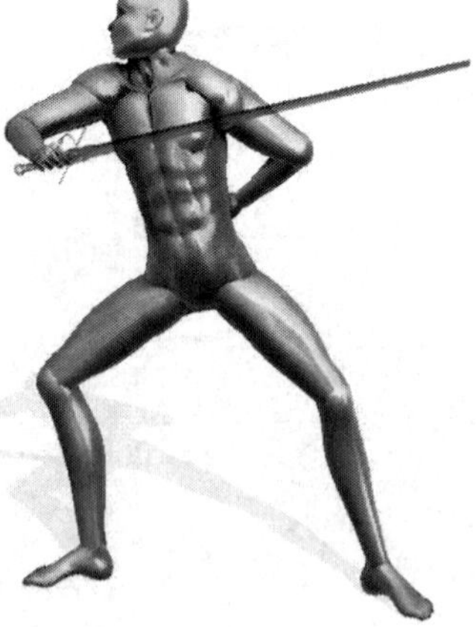

Turning the Body with the Cuts

Cuts, whether delivered to the opponent or their weapon (vertical cuts excluded), require a turn of the body to give them additional force. As the weapon is pulled through space by the arm, the body turns, pulling the dominant shoulder with it. As the arm begins the action, the body finishes it, allowing the arm to relax in its delivery in order for it to stay nimble and prepared to change course (if need befalls it). *All* cuts from right to left are supported by a counter-clockwise turn, and converse for the cuts from left to right, whether they are with the long-edge or the short, descending or ascending, or even with the right or left foot forward, stationary or stepping.

From Right-Ox for the Cut, the right side is forward, but with the chest and left shoulder somewhat square to the opponent

Making a descending, diagonal cut (Wrath Cut - *Zornhauw*) from right to left into The Change, the body rotates counter-clockwise, hiding the left shoulder behind the right

From the Left-Ox for the Cut, the left shoulder starts behind the right

Making a descending, diagonal cut (Wrath Cut) from left to right into Side Guard, the body rotates clockwise, bringing the left shoulder forward and chest more squarely forward

Thrusts

The thrust is nothing more than assuming Longpoint from a point forward (perfect) guard with a quick, and supported extension of the arm and body.

From any perfect guard, the sword-arm begins to extend, pulling the right shoulder forward as the left shoulder rotates back. As this happens, the weight of the body is transferred to the rear foot. This weight transfer can be completed by taking a step on the rear foot (as will be discussed in the next chapter) or by simply bringing the hips over the rear leg. As the arm extends, it pulls the body forward. As the body comes forward (while keeping the weight on the rear foot), the front foot lifts. As the front foot lifts, the weight is propelled forward by pushing off the rear foot, allowing the front foot to catch and support the body as it extends and lands on the ground further forward than it was before.

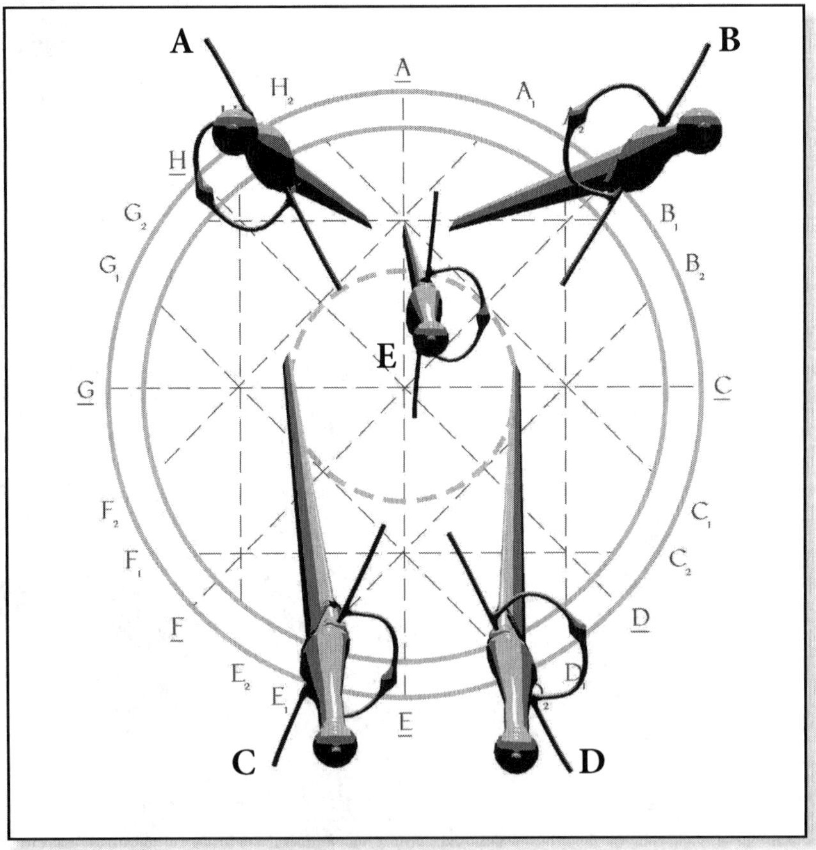

Thrusts can originate from the right or the left, and from below or above, or directly in the middle. Likewise, the end of the thrust terminates in the same four quadrants or directly through the center. **A:** Left Ox or a High Thrust on the left **B:** Right Ox or a High Thrust on the right **C:** Left Iron Gate or a Low thrust on the left **D:** Right Iron Gate or a Low thrust on the right **E:** Straight Parrying or a thrust into Longpoint

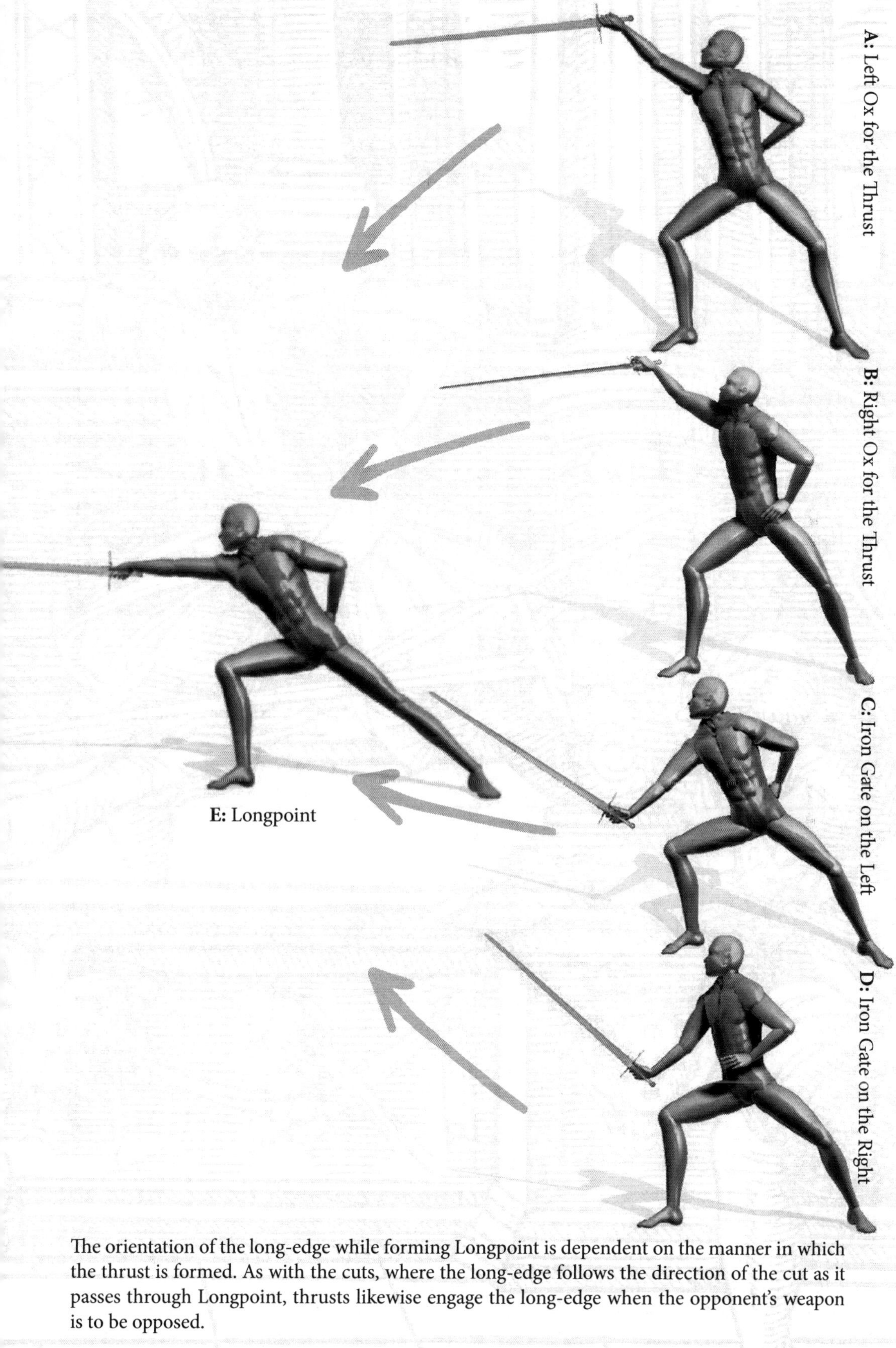

The orientation of the long-edge while forming Longpoint is dependent on the manner in which the thrust is formed. As with the cuts, where the long-edge follows the direction of the cut as it passes through Longpoint, thrusts likewise engage the long-edge when the opponent's weapon is to be opposed.

It is not always necessary for a thrust to end in its longest possible extension, nor is it always prudent. Thrusts may also end 'shortened' with the Strong moving to the opponent's Weak in order provide a greater degree of security. Or, as the thrust is made, the short-edge can turn into their weapon forming an angle behind their blade, allowing the sword to sneak in behind their position. The smart fencer must always determine the balance between the extension of the thrust (offense), and its ability to provide cover (defense).

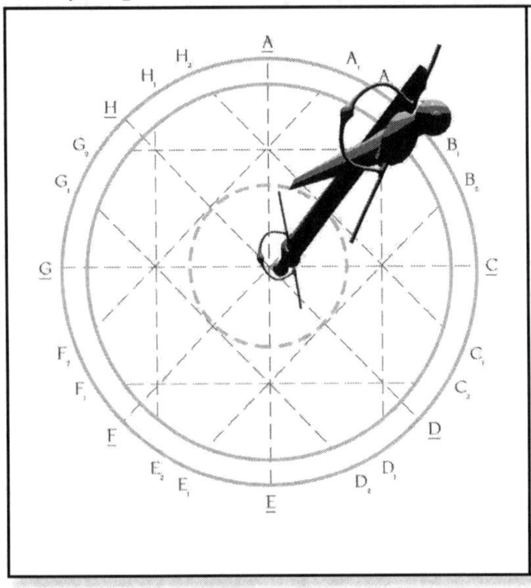

Above: A High Thrust on the right, on the outside, in order to occupy the opponent's weapon with our Strong against their Weak making a barrier as the attack is made

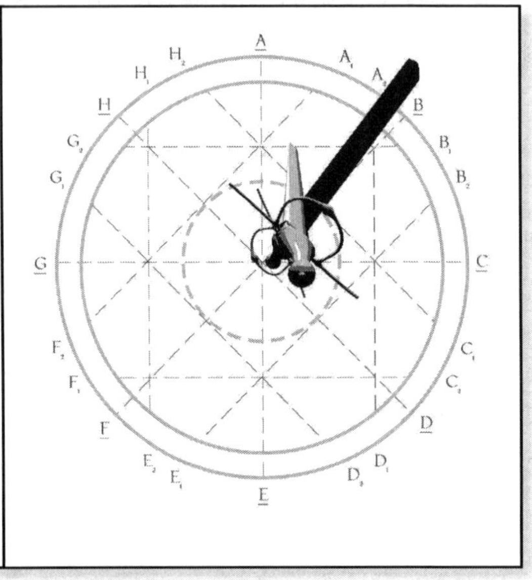

Above: The sword thrusts into Longpoint, sacrificing a strong engagement for more reach (but still with the edge turned against their weapon)

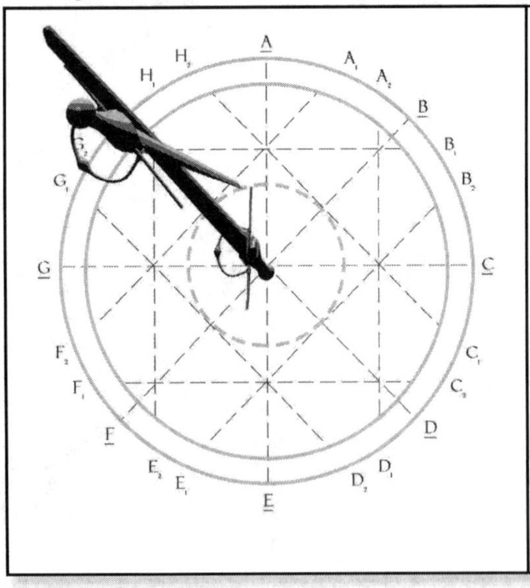

Above: A High Thrust on the left, on the inside, in order to occupy the opponents weapon with our Strong against their Weak making a barrier as the attack is made

Above: The sword thrusts into Longpoint, sacrificing a strong engagement for more reach, coming off their blade in the process

Transforming the Cuts & Thrusts

In fencing, there are times when it is useful to immediately turn one action into another, whether it is redoubling an attack, parrying an attack and returning one of our own, or to feint an attack and deliver another somewhere else. All actions of the sword can be broken down to either cuts or thrusts, and to turn one into the other without pause will give us an advantage in the fight.

To transform a cut into a thrust is a matter of ending the initial cut with the point forward (a half cut) and then without halting the forward motion of the weapon, extending the point to the target from the place the cut ended. The initial cut can be a parry, beat, or feint, meant to draw the opponent's weapon away from the intended target, while the thrust moves in for the strike immediately after. The tactical uses of these will be discussed in the chapter on Provocations.

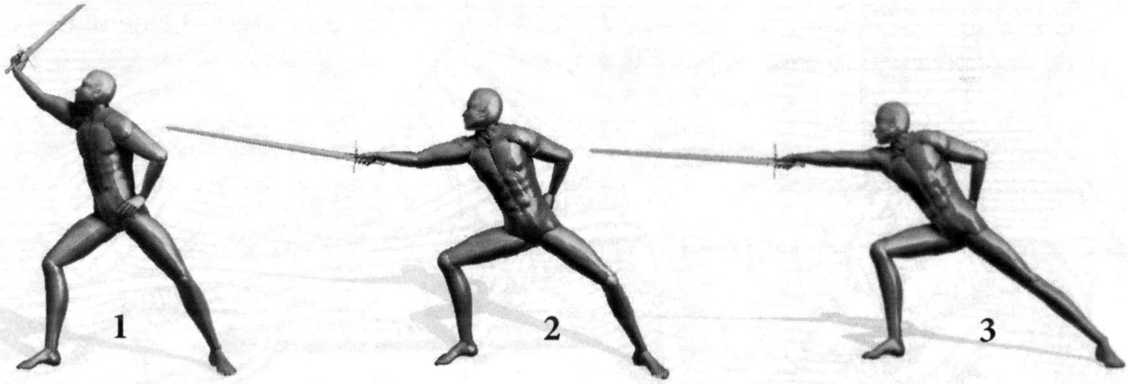

Above: The cut is prepared in Right Ox for the Cut. As the cut descends, the point comes into presence of the opponent and is then pushed forward as a thrust.

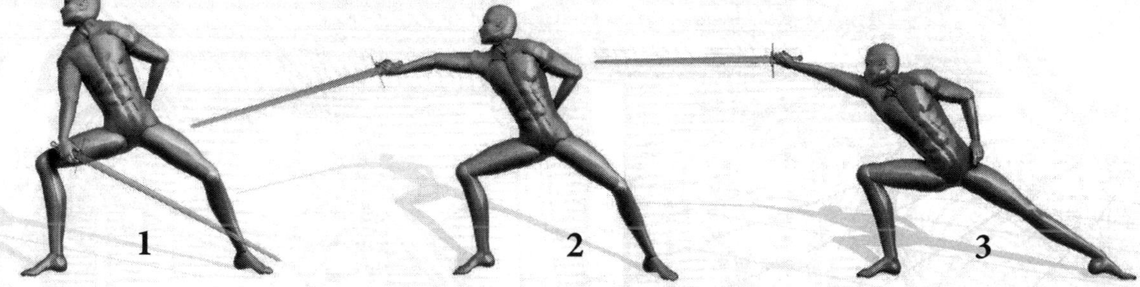

Above: The cut is prepared in Low Left Guard. As the cut ascends, the point comes into presence of the opponent and is then pushed forward as a thrust.

Transforming thrusts into cuts takes a nimble wrist and a keen sense of timing. As the arm extends for the thrust, the wrist should relax, allowing the short-edge of the sword to come closer to the body. With the arm fully-extended, the point should be allowed to loop around, finishing in a cut with the long-edge. If the thrust begins high, in Right or Left Ox for the Thrust, then the point will drop low as the hand remains stationary in space, only allowing the wrist to bend, finishing as a descending cut.

If the thrust begins low, in Left or Right Iron Gate, or either Plow, then as the short-edge is brought in, the point will raise, loop around and finish in either an ascending or descending cut.

Like the transformations of cuts into thrusts, the thrusts into cuts are varied in their application. The initial thrust can be a feint, a parry (Setting-Off), or meant to physically move the opponent's weapon out of the way. Once the thrust has accomplished its goal, and is subsequently diverted from its original target, it should be abandoned and transformed into the cut.

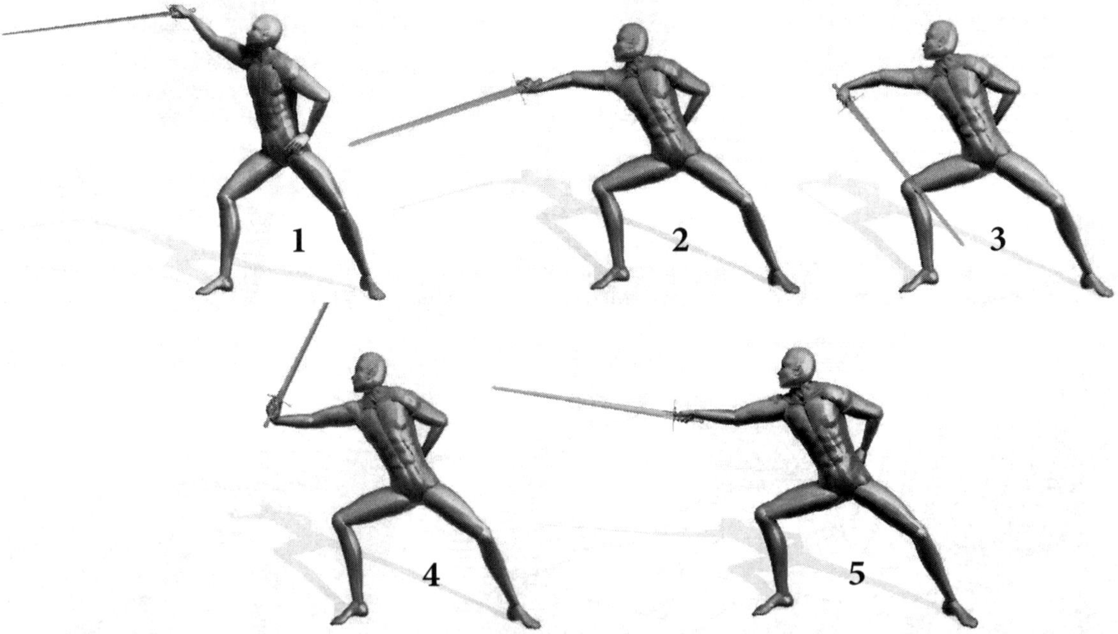

Above: From Right Ox for the Thrust, the arm extends with the long-edge up. As the point is pushed forward, it drops down and to the left, turning behind the body, then raises up through Right Ox for the Cut, and finishes as a Wrath Cut from the right (or the action could finish as a descending short-edge cut – Squinting Cut).

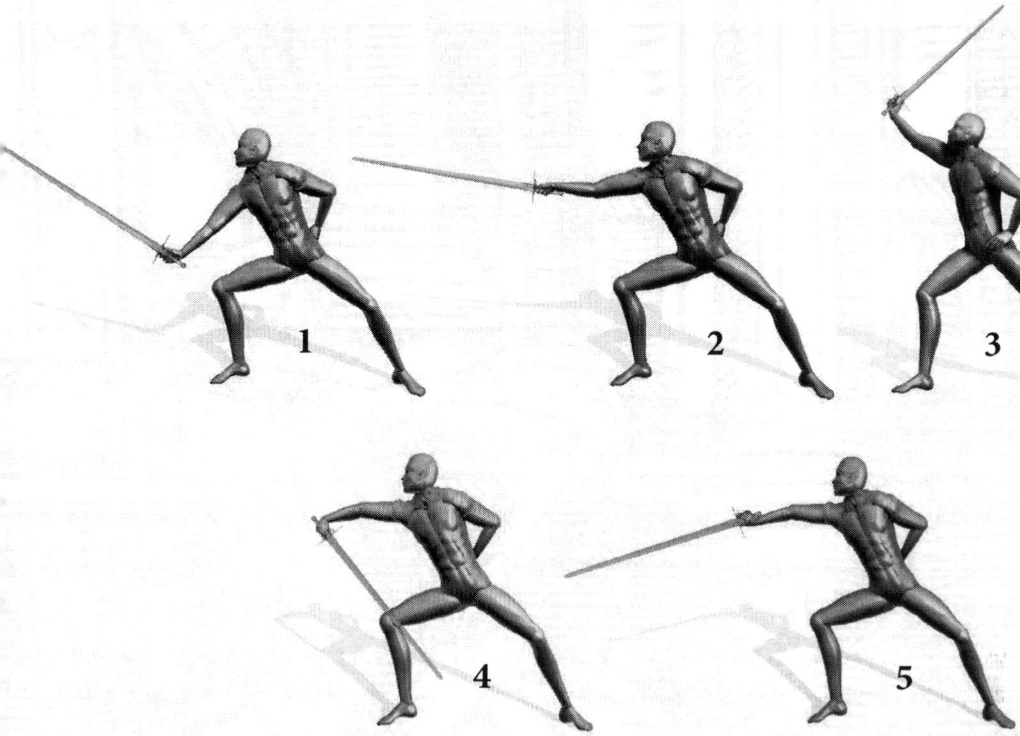

Above: From Iron Gate on the Left, the arm extends with the long-edge down. As the point is pushed forward, the point is raised up through Right Ox for the Cut. The point continues its motion to the rear, falling down and to the left, and finishes as a Low Cut from the left.

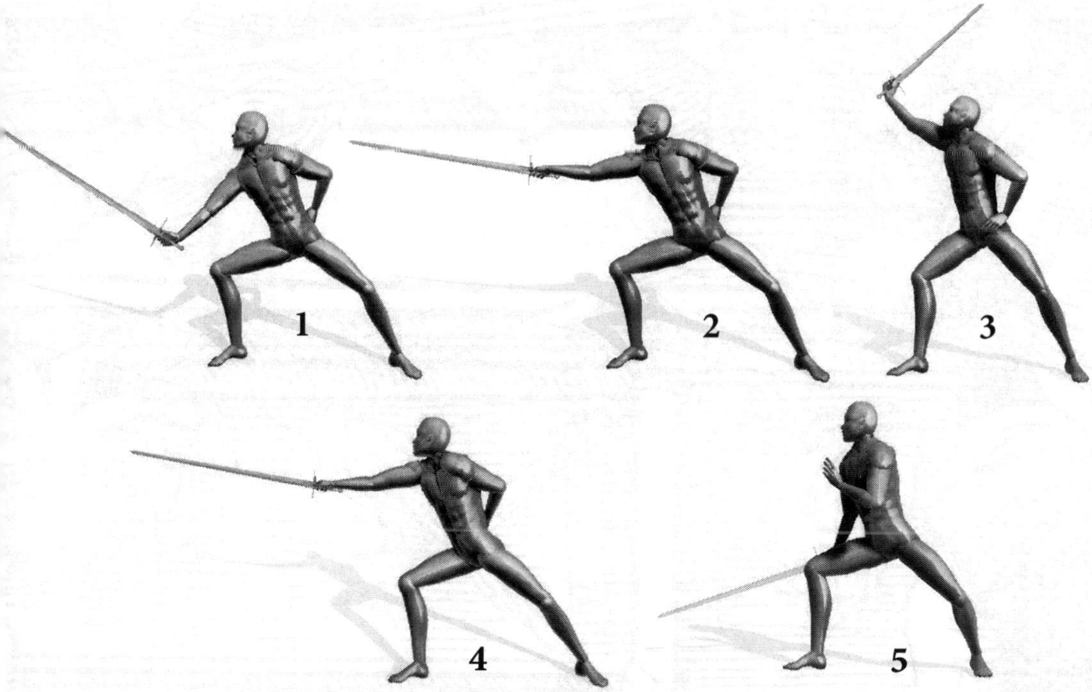

Above: From Iron Gate on the Left, the arm extends with the long-edge down. As the point is pushed forward, the point is raised up through Right Ox for the Cut. The point continues its motion over the head to the left through Left Ox for the Cut, and makes a descending long-edge cut through Longpoint, finishing in Low Right Guard.

part iv staging the fight

Now combat with the sword is in essence a practice in which two opponents strive against each other with the sword with the intent that one will outmaneuver and overcome the other with intelligence and nimbleness, artfully, finely, and manfully, with cuts and other handwork; so that if it were necessary in earnest cases, through such practice one may be more quick and skillful, and more judicious for the protection of his body.

Space

When two fencers face one another they will have both adopted a guard, ready to execute actions. The distance at which these fencers face each other will ultimately dictate the types of actions they should perform and the respective time they can be completed in. Meyer tells us when the swords have bound at certain points along the length of the weapon, we are now at a particular stage of the fight and should consider the space for completing our actions. This first distance or stage of combat is the **Onset** (*Zufechten*).

Thus when you are so near him that you can just reach the weak of his blade with your weak in the bind, then you may well execute sweeping cuts and thrusts against him, either with deceiving or else with other pulled cuts. For although he should crowd in at your opening when you come around with your weapon, yet he still cannot rush upon you, since you can be ready to crowd in with your incoming strike as quickly as he can with his.[22] *-Meyer*

The Onset is the point at which we can start to describe the fight and how it will unfold. We can start to create opportunities through deceptive actions and are yet far enough away the opponent can not immediately strike us with their own devices.

Onset: a distance or stage of the fight where the points can just meet at their Weaks (or roughly a "fathom" as he describes in the Longsword section, though this might be slightly further due to the extended nature of the rapier fight). From here, point forward guards can be formed but it is also safe to pull the sword into open (wider) positions.

As the fight progresses, the fencers will find themselves closer to each other, arriving there either through simply stepping forward or a combination of stepping and actions of the sword. When they are now bound with their swords at their middles, they are at the **Middle** (*Mittel*), or **Handwork** (*Handarbeit*), quite literally, the middle of the fight.

> *When you have come so near one another that both blades bind in the middle, then you must not cut around, nor go away from his blade without particular opportunity, for as soon as you go away from his blade, he can rush upon you with chasing. But be mindful of the techniques that can be executed on his blade, and if he over commits to a cut or else makes himself open, be sure to crowd after him.*[23] *-Meyer*

When in the Middle, it is crucial that the sword be used to control the space between us and the opponent. If our sword leaves the Bind (literally meaning the swords have been bound to one another) then the opponent can immediately strike to the opening, possibly before we are able to credibly deal with the threat.

Middle/Handwork: a distance or stage of the fight where the blades can bind in their middles. The sword should be used as a barrier and not leave the bind unless there is an appropriate opportunity to do so. If the sword is pulled away at this stage, then the opponent can more easily strike with little motion.

As soon as an action has been made in the Middle, then either fencer can opt to Withdraw from the engagement. This is the final stage of the fight, not when a fencer has struck the other, but rather when one fencer withdraws from the fight and creates space between themselves and their opponent. From here, the engagement is either over or can begin once again.

Moving from the Onset to the Middle
basic stepping

Much depends on stepping, therefore see that you give every stroke its step. For when you cut at his opening and do not step with the foot from the side from which you have cut, then the cut is useless.[24] *-Meyer*

The process of moving from the Onset to the Middle is a necessary skill that needs to be understood in order to enter a distance at which we can strike the opponent without having them be able to do the same. From the Onset, cuts and thrusts do not have the potential to Hit until the feet are in such a position to allow the body to be carried forward to apply the weapon to the target. This is not to say that the fight begins or only has true consequences in the Middle, because that which dictates the advantages we might gain as we arrive in the Middle are first secured (or lost) in the step before (literally).

The primary intent on making any action from the Onset is to prepare a cut or thrust that will lead us to and through the Middle. This process involves: first, the position we find ourselves in, then transitioning to a new position to prepare our action, and finally, using that action to bring us into the Middle. This means of entry is most easily seen with a cut from above with a gather step.

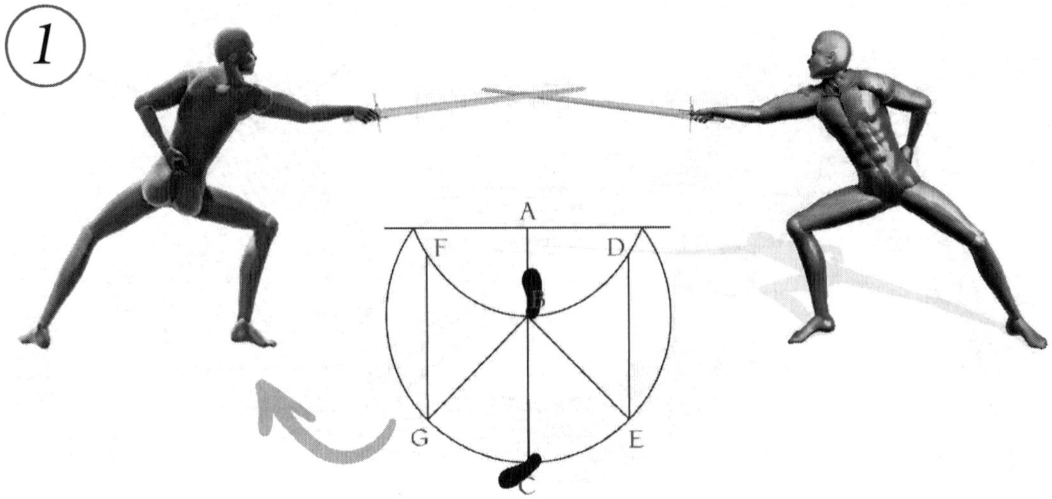

Fig1: Each fencer starts in Straight Parrying in the Onset.

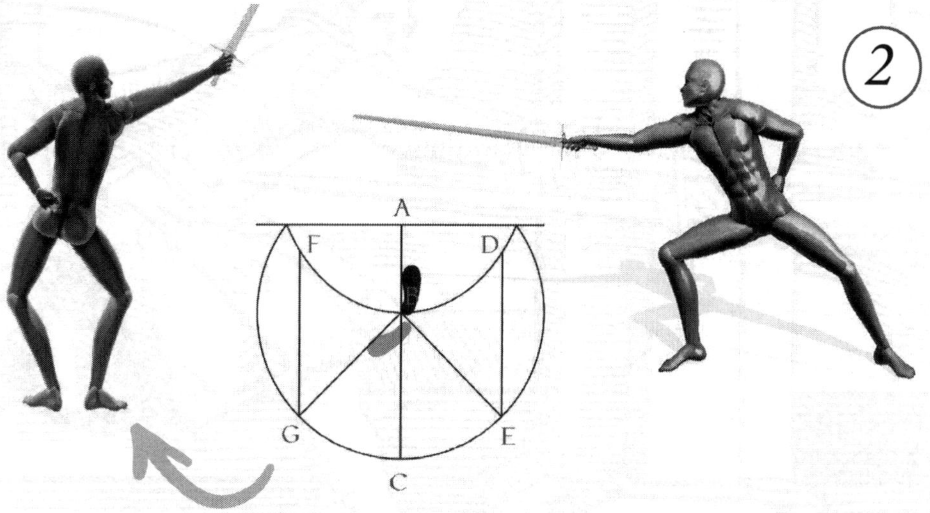

Fig2: The fencer on the left brings the sword up in front of their face to Straight High Guard in order to prepare a vertical cut, while also gathering their rear foot close to the forward foot, settling the weight on the rear foot.

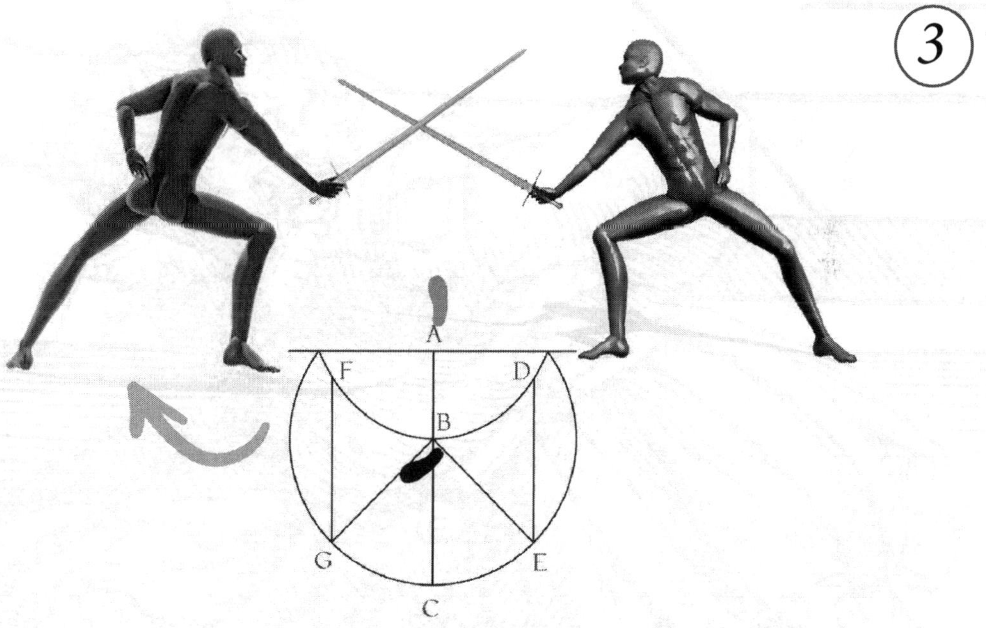

Fig3: The fencer on the left allows the sword to fall, delivering a vertical cut through the space between themselves and their opponent into the guard of the Iron Gate. They have bound their blade to the opponent's, coming to a temporary position of rest in the Middle.

4

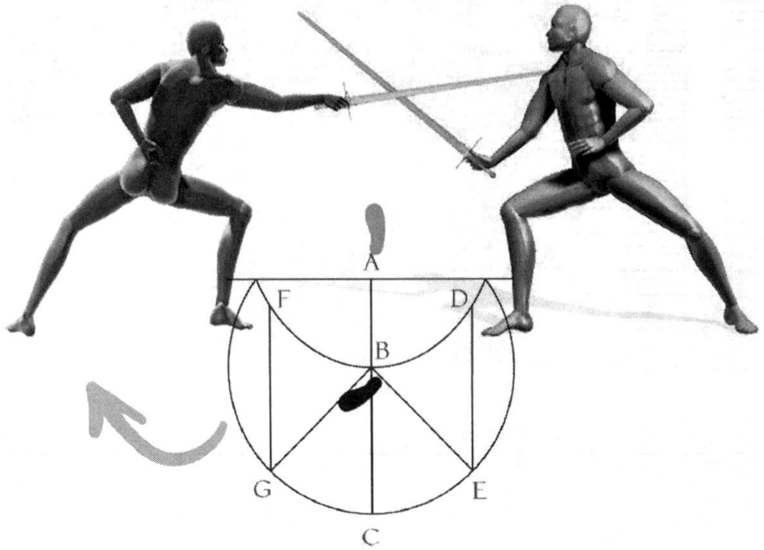

Fig4: From the Middle, the fencer strikes the opponent while using their own sword to defend themselves. Additional footwork can be made to maneuver from the previous stage to the Hit, and will be discussed more fully in the next chapter.

5

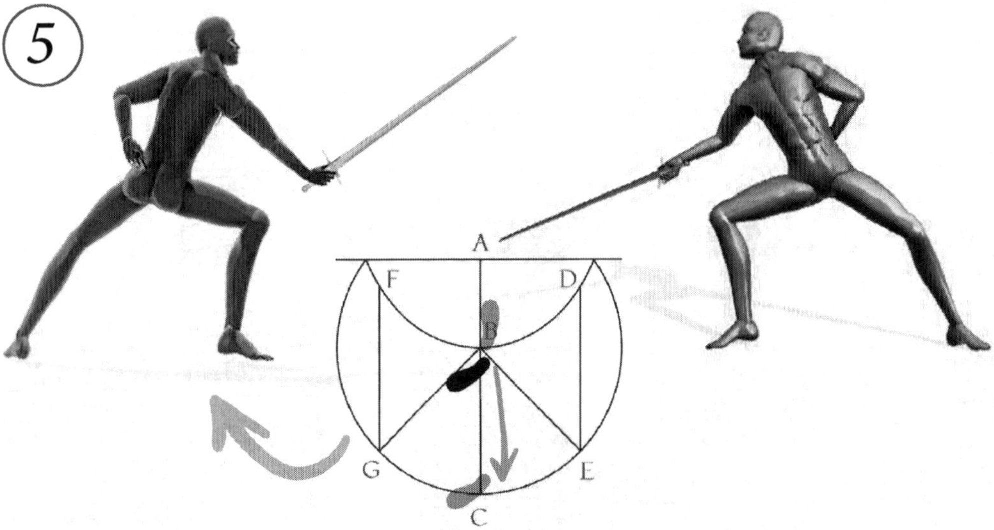

Fig5: After the attack has succeeded (or failed), the fencer withdraws from the fight by reassuming Straight-Parrying, or by making diagonal cuts to the Strong of the opponent's sword (Defense Strokes - *Wehrstreich*), driving it away, by first recovering the forward foot and then stepping back with the rear foot.

Your work firstly drives to the [weak], then to the strong, then to the body[25] *-Meyer*

With this establishment of closing distance, we can say the left foot determines the distance at which the right foot can extend, bringing the body and sword to a position in the Middle where we will ultimately strike the opponent.

The left foot, which generally starts on C, can move directly forward to B, or along the perimeter of the outside arch to either F, to the left, or D, to the right. In fact, the left foot is capable of moving anywhere on the diagram that is required to allow the right foot to extend more easily and readily to the opponent.

The freedom it has to move either left or right gives further allowance to the sword to ultimately be delivered to that corresponding side. For instance, if the intent is to deliver a cut from the right, then the sword can be prepared while the left foot moves to D. Conversely, if a cut is to begin from the left, then as the cut is prepared the left foot can move to F.

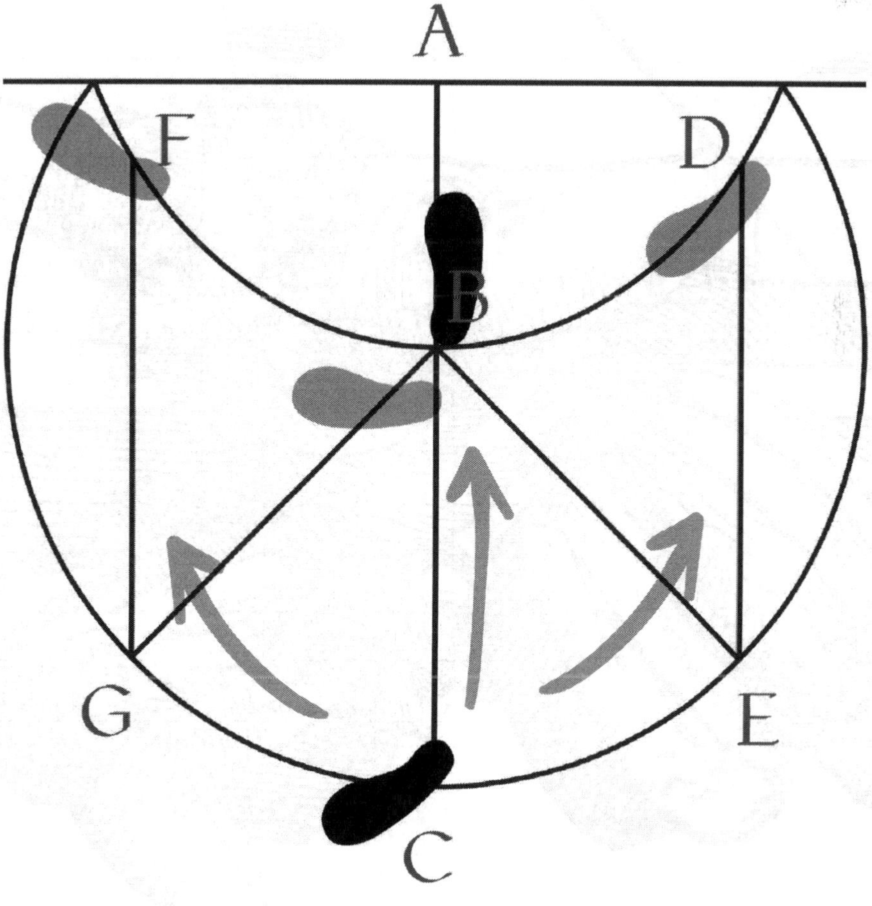

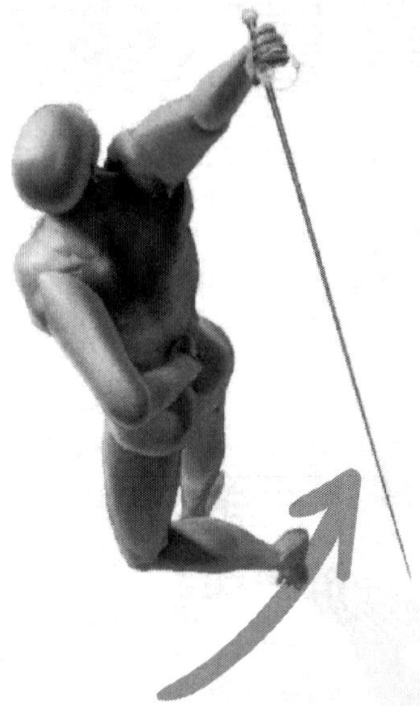

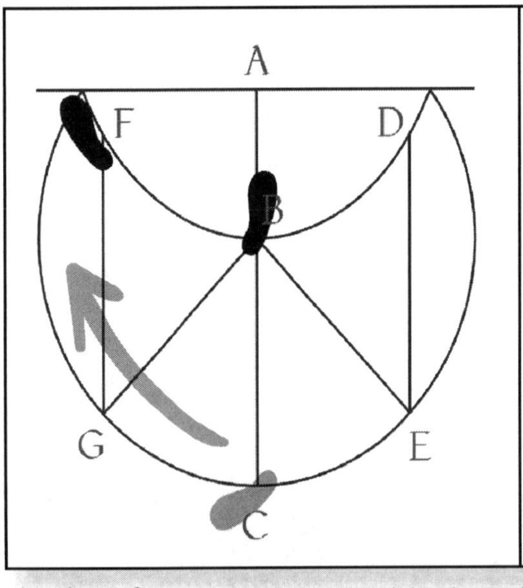

The above figure prepares a cut originating from the left through Left-Ox for the Cut while bringing the left foot forward and to the left. This both allows the right foot to extend for the cut while also moving the position of the body to the side it will be cutting.

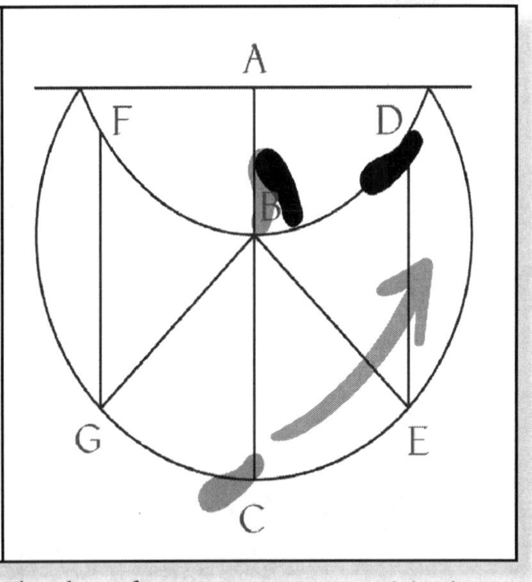

The above figure prepares a cut originating from the right through Right-Ox for the Cut while bringing the left foot forward and to the right. This both allows the right foot to extend for the cut while also moving the position of the body to the side it will be cutting.

Time

Since your opponent may possess the same information as you, and can counter all this, you need to know beforehand upon what opportunity you may come to him. For daily experience attests how much depends on the opportunity, no matter how good it is, may be usefully carried out, if it is not used at its proper time.[26] *-Meyer*

When two fencers face each other, they are drawing upon a library of techniques, and if both are competent in the art then the fight becomes less about who can execute their actions better, but rather who can use them in their proper time and place within the fight.

Throughout German fencing, there has existed the concepts of the *Vor*, *Nach* and *Indes*, translating to: Before, After and Instantly, respectively. The Before refers to the fencer who is first to:

...attack your opponent [...] in the first Onset, and further drive on, so that he cannot come to his undertaking or device, but must restrict himself to parrying so that he [must] defend himself from you.[27] *-Meyer*

The fencer acting in the Before is the first to press the opponent with a credible threat. Conversely, the fencer acting in the After is:

...when you are rushed on by your opponent [...] so that you cannot carry out your intention.[28] *-Meyer*

The fencer in the After is thus in obedience to the fencer in the Before and must quickly act to gain the Before from their opponent through techniques that are specifically designed to defend while creating a threat. Acting this way is called *Indes*.

There is thus a constant changing and transformation between the Before and After, for now your opponent gets it, now you in return. But he who has the After, that is, is so crowded upon that he must always parry, shall be well mindful of the word Instantly, and not forget it, for through it he must rush back to the Before, if he wishes to withdraw without harm. But whoever does not pay attention to it, even though he conducts himself fiercely, he will nonetheless never learn to execute anything good.[29] *-Meyer*

This concept of *Indes* or Instantly is a bit tricky to illustrate, but Meyer mentions that his peers view *Indes,* a German word, closely tied to the word *Intus*, a Latin word meaning 'inside.' Meyer would seem to prefer the German usage meaning Instantly, but it is important to apply both usages. *Indes* must both be thought of as an action that happens *instantly* and *inside* or *within* the opponent's action.[30] If the fencer in the After is to take the initiative away from the one in the Before, then they must act instantly, *within* the opponent's action.

Thus, the word Indes admonishes you to have a sharp lookout, which involves seeing and heeding many things at once. Also you may learn sufficiently from your opponent's body language, what kind of techniques he intends to use, and what they will entail by way of opening, and where they will offer you opportunities. For the whole art of combat lies in all these things that the word Indes admonishes you. [31] *-Meyer*

The Three Actions

All actions of the sword can be broken down into three main categories, they are: Provoking, Taking and Hitting.

Provoking is:

...to deceive the opponent, provoke him, make him angry, and to drive him out of his advantage[32] *-Meyer*

Taking is:

...you put [his blade] off with a countercut, or catch it with parrying[33] *-Meyer*

Hitting is thus:

...if he reveals himself somewhat with an opening on one side or another, you can also correctly place your stroke upon him with advantage.[34] *-Meyer*

We must understand that *all* actions of the sword must fall into one of these three areas so that no motion is wasted and all opportunities can be taken advantage of.

...one shall use some cuts for provoking, to bring him out of his advantage; some for taking, that is when through this provoking you have goaded him to cut, you put it off with a countercut, or catch it with parrying; and thirdly some for hitting, as you will see...[35] *-Meyer*

Provoke

From a high guard, a Wrath Cut can be made to Provoke, drawing a reaction from the opponent that can be exploited.

Take

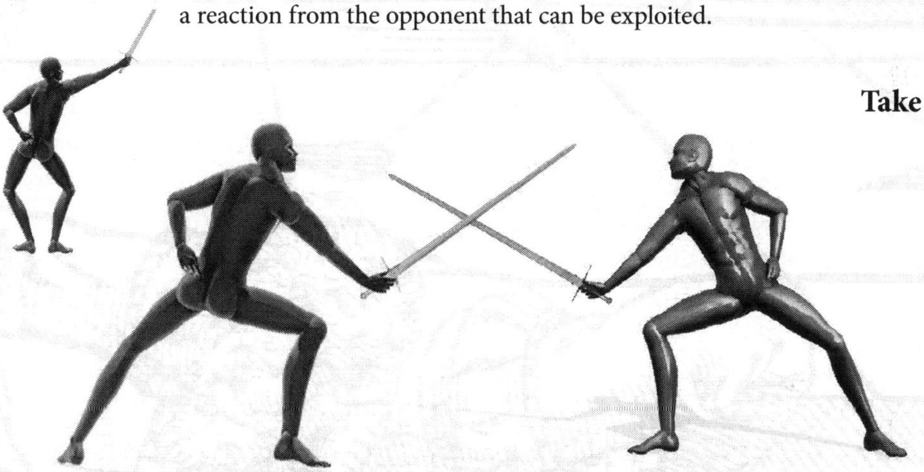

The same cut can be used to Take, to beat the weapon out of the way, making room for us to operate more freely (Defense Stroke).

Hit

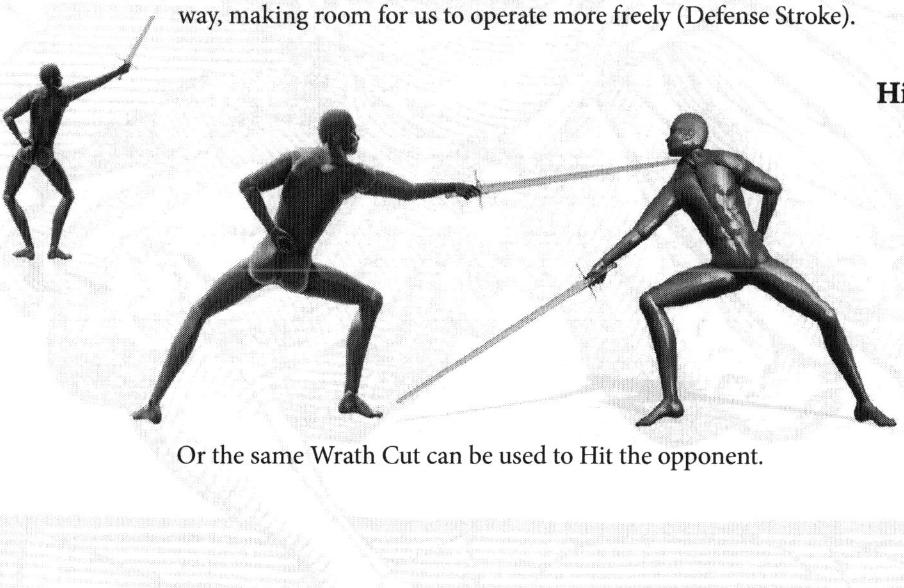

Or the same Wrath Cut can be used to Hit the opponent.

Position, Space, Time & Action

all four together make the fight

With these four concepts of position (guards), space (the Onset, Middle, and Withdrawal), time (Before, Inside, and After) and action (Provoker, Taker, and Hitter), we can build a fight.

From the Onset, both fencers in a particular guard, should seek to Provoke the other to gain some advantage of position and time while they move through the Middle. From the Middle, the blades can bind and thus Take and Parry. The one who uses position and time best will inevitably make themselves safe while Hitting the other, and then safely withdraw from the fight.

Both the fencer in the Before and the one in the After can draw upon actions of the Provoker, Taker and Hitter. The fencer in the Before, Provoking their opponent, can either simulate an attack (a feint/deception) or can invite the opponent to attack, assuming the After. This can be done through making themselves open in one place or another by Changing-Off from guard to guard. The fencer in the After can also Provoke the fencer in the Before by acting Instantly or within the opponent's Provocation. This can be done by also feinting an attack or acting as if they are going to Take their blade, but then remove their weapon before the bind occurs so that the other's falls away without harm.

Both fencers, the one in the Before and the one in the After, can also Take as they approach the Middle. The fencer in the Before can choose to Provoke the opponent to draw their sword into a predictable position, and then once in that position make a cut or other action to further drive it away. The fencer in the After can Take by means of parrying the opponent's attack.

When in the Middle or passing through the Middle, the fencer in the Before, by first either Provoking or Taking, or a combination of both, can seek to Hit the opponent by virtue of forcing them to move their blade into such a position that they can Hit and not be Hit in return. The fencer in the After can and should only Hit once they have gained the Before, either by Provoking or Taking, Instantly, within the opponent's actions, so that they can safely Hit without being Hit themselves.

To understand all of these subtleties, it is important to understand how the blades interact with each other. Before we can understand how to Provoke from the Onset, we need to understand what we are provoking and what advantages and opportunities exist within the fight. To do this we must start in the bind, in the Middle of the fight. By understanding the Middle and the binding of the blades, we can then understand how to act in the Onset. In the following chapters we will look at the functions of the three actions and then return full circle to discuss their relationship to space and time.

thus you have provoking, taking and hitting, which is to provoke the stroke, to parry or set off the stroke you have provoked, and at once to countercut back to the opening. And I do not mean that you should not hit with the Provoking Cut or also with the Taker if you can; it is so named only because the chief intention is either to provoke him out of his advantage or to take out and bear off his cut - whether you can also hit his with this doesn't matter.[36] *-Meyer*

part v taking

Handworks in the Middle Binding

For it is by no means enough to have begun well and rightly, if you do not also press after judiciously, for the greatest art depends on this, and it all falls under this chapter concerning handwork.

Establishment of the bind, and when to avoid it, is a required skill within Meyer's rapier system. During the course of an engagement between two individuals armed with a sword, both seek to strike while not being struck while moving their weapons through the space between them. When the swords come to cross at their Middles a bind is a safest way to control the outcome of the fight.

When in the bind the sword is your shield, and it should be used as a barrier to first protect yourself before it is used to offend your enemy.

You should not cut to the body until you have made yourself secure with [the takings], not only to cut or thrust to his body, but so that after delivering the cut you can recover your weapon and body without harm.[37] *-Meyer*

Whether the opponent is seeking to strike with a thrust or a cut, they can not bring their attack to its conclusion if their point is kept out of the center circle (as illustrated by the dashed circle in the middle of the diagram). To achieve this, we should work to keep their blade as close to the outer circle as possible through various actions on their sword, known as the Takings.

In all bindings you should keep his blade in the outer circle, so that you have his body fully with your point, then he can not harm you.[38] *-Meyer*

A fencer can use eight chief sword positions as a barrier to keep the opponent's sword in the outer circle. Four are with the sword falling over the opponent's, binding above (an Overbind): two in Iron Gate, both to the inside and outside; and two in Left and Right Ox, with the point directed to their respective sides.

The four others are from beneath the opponent's blade (an Underbind); two, in similar positions to the Left and Right Ox, but with the point to the opposite side. The last two are positions similar to the Plow, again both inside and outside.

It is important to note that to whichever side the opponent's sword is bound, our point should be directed to that side. If the opponent wishes to push against or break the position we have formed, the angle of the weapon will guide their blade toward our Strong. This also prevents the opponent from seeking the weakest part of the blade to the side it has been bound, lest the opponent further removes their point from the Center.

Strong Overbinds

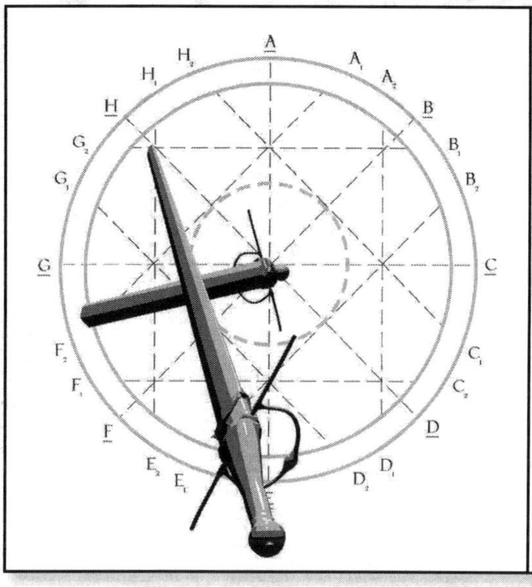

Above: Our sword is creating a strong Overbind on the left in Left Iron Gate, directing the point to H. The end of a diagonal cut from the right (Defense Stroke from the right)

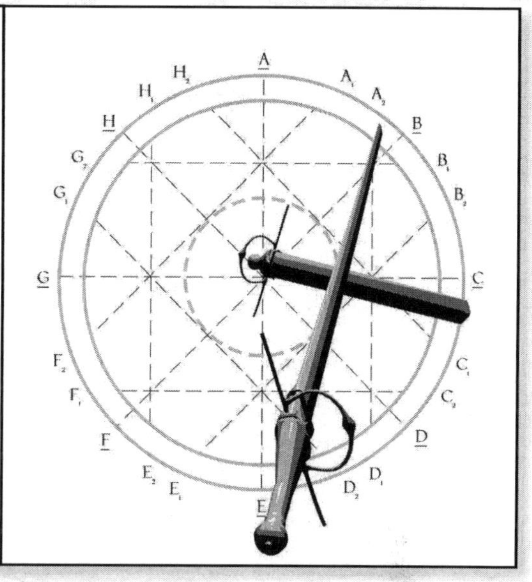

Above: Our sword is creating a strong Overbind on the right in Right Iron Gate, directing the point to B. The end of a diagonal cut from the left (Defense Stroke from the left)

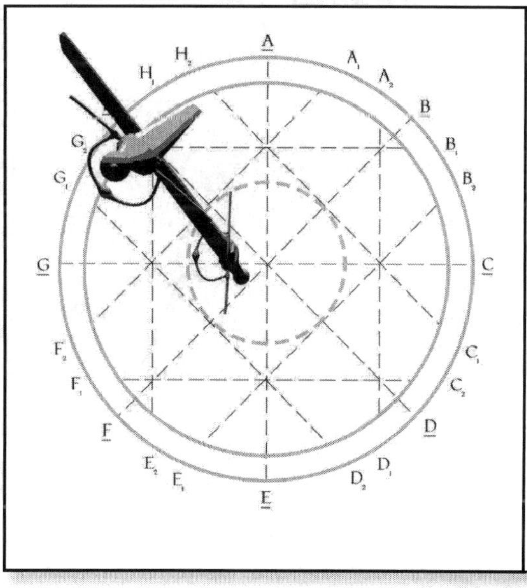

Above: Our sword is creating a strong Overbind on the left in the Left Ox, directing the point to H_2. End of a Low Cut from the right

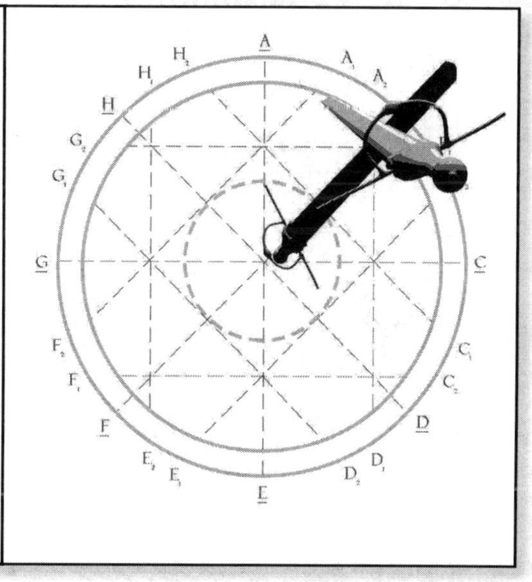

Above: Our sword is creating a strong Overbind on the right in the Right Ox, directing the point to A_1. End of a Low Cut from the left

Note: All four of the above binds are made on top of the opponent's weapon and fortify the position for a thrust. However, because the low binds are formed with the low guards (Iron Gate), they are more suited for defense, and more secure in their position.

Strong Underbinds -hanging points

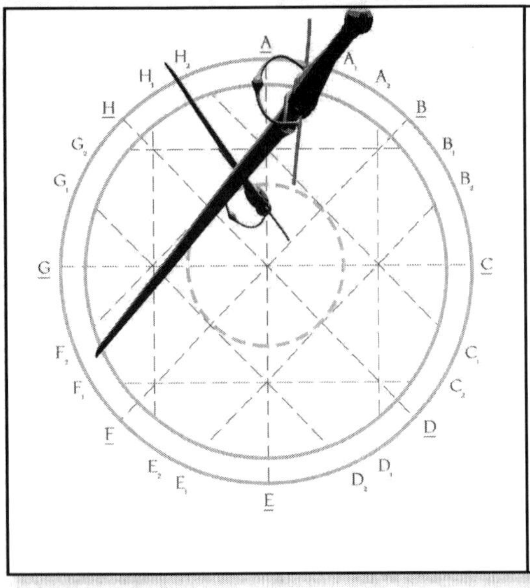

Above: A strong Underbind on the left in a left hanging (similar to Right Ox but with the point sloped to the left), directing the point to F_2

Above: A strong Underbind on the right in a right hanging (similar to Left Ox but with the point sloped to the right), directing the point to C_1

Above: A strong Underbind on the left, directing the point to F_1 similar to a Plow on the Left (with the point low)

Above: A strong Underbind on the right, directing the point to C_2 similar to a Plow on the Right (with the point low)

Establishing the Overbind

Establishing the Overbind is a matter of putting the point of our sword to the side we are binding the opponent's weapon from above. This is accomplished by the forceful transition from one guard to another, into and through the position of the opponent's weapon — cutting. This can be done by cutting to the Center with the long-edge or the short. When cutting with the long-edge, the point slightly lags behind the hand, meaning that at the point of contact, the blade will have a more difficult time crossing over the opponent's, and thus might end in a position of parity (neither weapon having an advantage). If, however, the cut is made with the short-edge, or at least finishes with the short-edge as it passes through the Center, then the point will somewhat precede the hand, allowing the blade to cross over the opponent's, thus creating an Overbind.

This advice lays the ground work for what each edge's functions are. The long-edge is primarily used to strike in the cut while acting as a barrier between our body and our opponent's sword, while the short-edge is primarily used for establishing a crossing while in the bind (both offensively and defensively).

The cuts that bring us to the Middle, originating from the Onset, can begin from wide guards. However, once in the Middle, the same cuts can be made from narrow guard to narrow guard, without the point leaving the confines of the circle, in order to further gain and keep the Overbind, wherever the opponent's weapon may travel.

The subset of actions that one can perform while in the bind, Meyer refers to as the 'work,' often repeating the phrase, 'work from the bind.' From each of the eight crossings exist a specific set of actions. It is important to Instantly know, as soon as the bind has been established, what sort of actions each fencer has at their disposal, dually ours as well as theirs. Generally, actions following out of an Overbind are thrusts (primary for an art that deals with point attacks), while those from the Underbind are cuts.

When [Straight-Parrying] is adopted, at once bind below and above. But a bind above will always be more useful than one below.[39] *-MS.I.33*

This insight will give us an edge as we plan the next stages of the fight. These actions boil down into a binary choice, recited in the Anonymous Commentaries of the early 15th century: "test no more than the two courses, that is, whether he is soft or hard in his course when he binds on your sword. Only after you have felt this, wind and work..."[40] In short, the verse is telling us, if the opponent acts strongly, Immediately respond with weakness. If the opponent is weak, Immediately act with strength.

The mental and physical process in determining these pressures is 'Feeling.'

"Feeling" and the word "Instantly" are the greatest and best of the art of the sword[41] -Anonymous 15th century German author

Feeling is the ability to gauge the effectiveness of the bind (or lack thereof), and what actions are appropriate from it. With the correct placement of the point in the bind, Feeling is a matter of sensing the opponent's ability to displace our point from the position we have placed it, or else their attempt to leave the bind when they can not break through.

The strength of the sword should be a function of the placement of the blade, not of the brawn of the arm or wrist. If you operate according to this advice, you will be more ready to take advantage of any opportunity[42]
-Salvator Fabris, 1606

Overbind to the Inside -Option 1

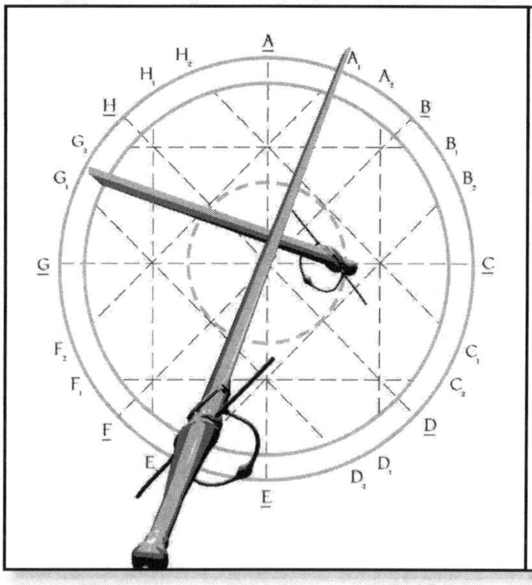

1. 'Parity,' with neither weapon having an advantage over the other, arriving here through a long-edge cut from the right

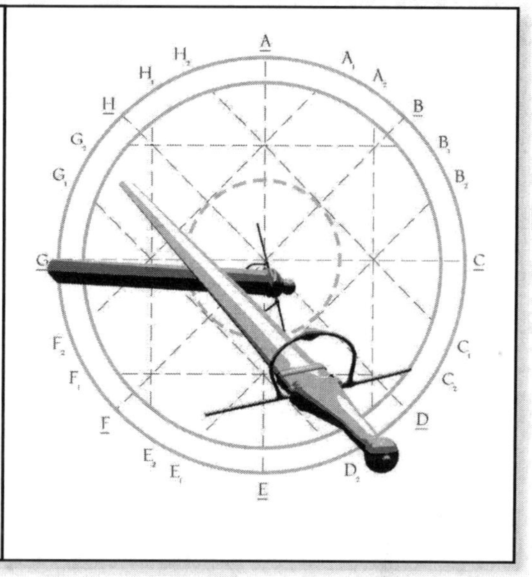

2. from the bind, or just before it, the hand rotates palm down, turning the short-edge to the inside (this can also be done with the inside flat)

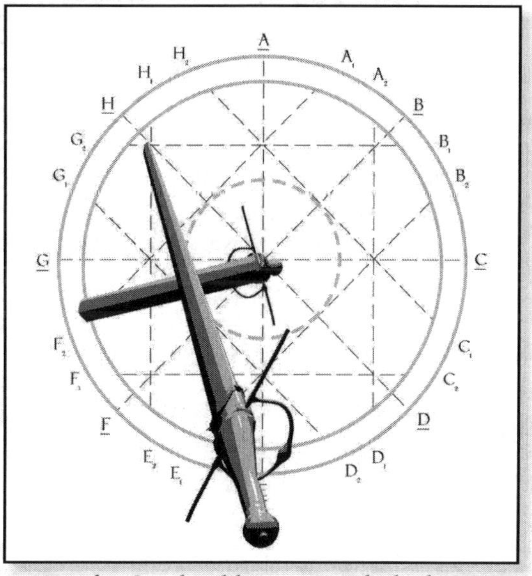

3. once the Overbind has occurred, the long-edge turns back to the opponent's weapon, maintaining the Overbind

In this example, the short-edge is brought to face the Center as the point is directed towards G. This action is a Middle Cut with the short-edge from right to left. It can also be made with the long-edge but crossing the point over becomes more difficult and will require a stronger cut to displace the opponent's weapon. Once the point has traveled through the Center, the long-edge is turned to secure the Overbind.

Overbind to the Inside -Option 2

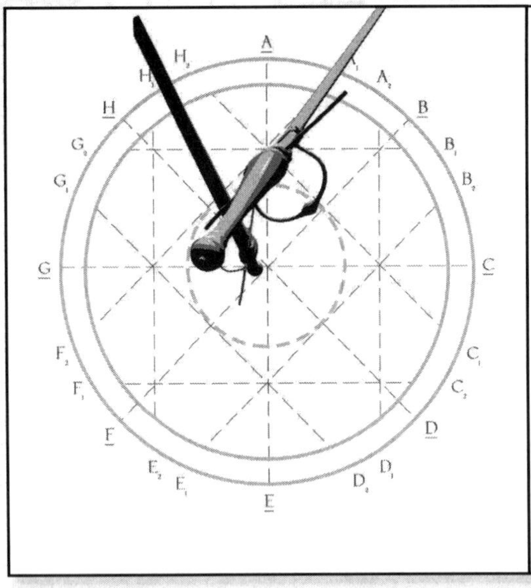

1. Just before the blades come to the bind...

2. the hand rotates clock-wise, turning the short-edge over the opponent's weapon (*Schielhauw*).

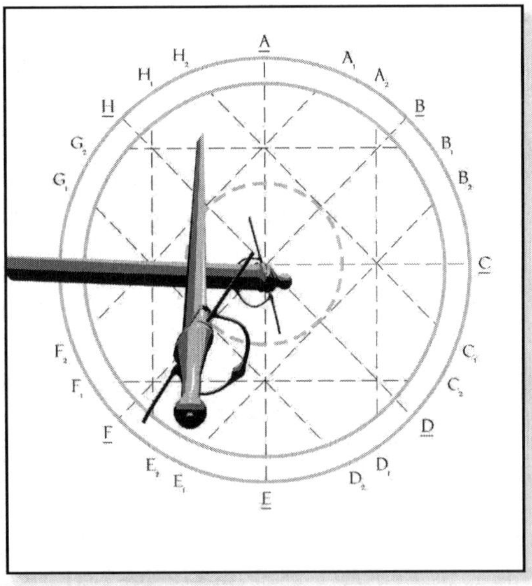

3. from here, the long-edge turns back into the blade

In this example, the short-edge is brought to face the Center as a descending, short-edge cut – a *Schielhauw*. This manner of cutting allows the point to cross the opponent's weapon while leaving the point within the bounds of the Center. It is a more difficult action to perform due to the over rotation of the wrist, but done with the proper turns of the body, is sufficient in gaining the Overbind to the inside.

Overbind to the Outside

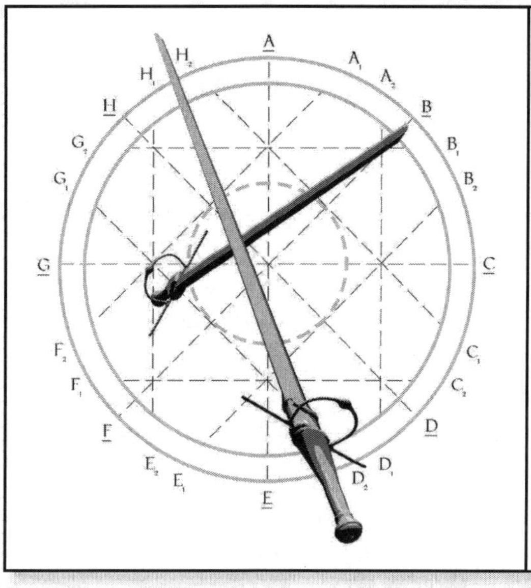

1. 'Parity' to the outside, arriving here by making a long-edge cut from the left

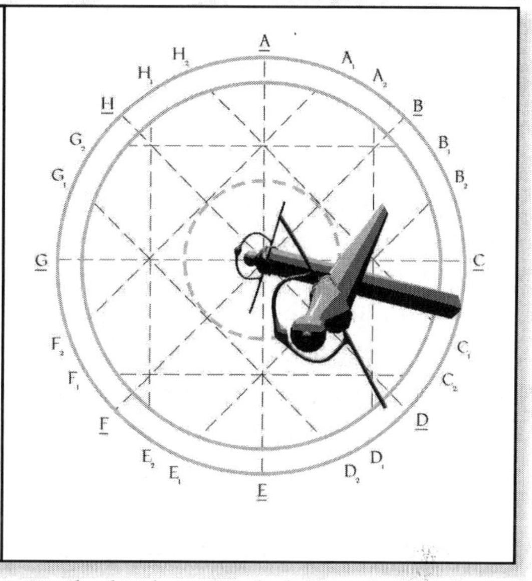

2. in the bind, or just before it, the hand is rotated clock-wise, bringing the short-edge into the opponent's weapon, the same action as before, but to the outside (*Krumphauw)*

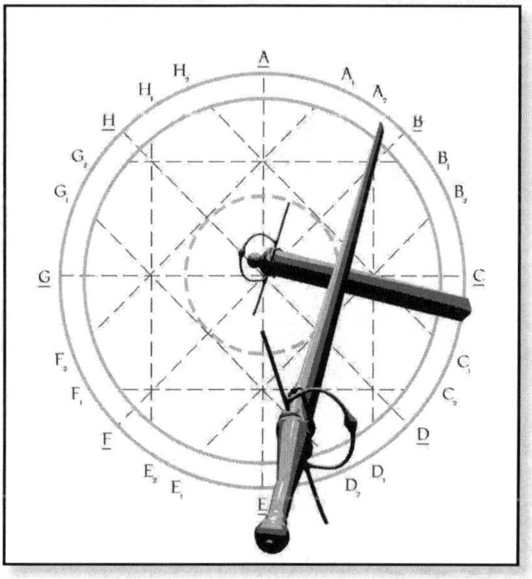

3. once the Overbind has occurred, the long-edge turns back to the opponent's weapon, maintaining the Overbind

In this example, the short-edge is brought to face the Center as the point is directed towards B. This action is a *Krumphauw,* descending from the left to right.

To gain the Overbind is a matter of placing the point across that of the opponent's. The cut is a forceful means to secure this position, as long as the cut ends with the point within the bounds of the outer circle, but far enough to the other side to secure the crossing.

Actions from the Overbind
when the opponent is soft

The most basic action in Meyer's rapier system is delivering a thrust from the Overbind. If the point of our sword is within the bounds of the outer circle but still across the Center to maintain the Overbind, then we should 'wind' the sword against the opponent's sword while putting the point to their face or chest. The act of winding the sword is a technique meant to 'remain' in the bind (to continue to occupy the opponent's weapon) while simultaneously acting as a barrier against their sword, feeding the point to the desired target. To the inside, with the blades crossed to each other's left, the arm should extend while the hand rotates up and to the left, through the guard of the Left Ox. Then, with the strongest part of our blade against the weakest part of theirs, the point comes over to strike a target on the same side on which we have bound their weapon. This is in order to maintain the Overbind throughout the wind and thrust. This can be done to the inside through Left Ox, and to the outside, binding on the right, through Right Ox.

Winding (*winden*)

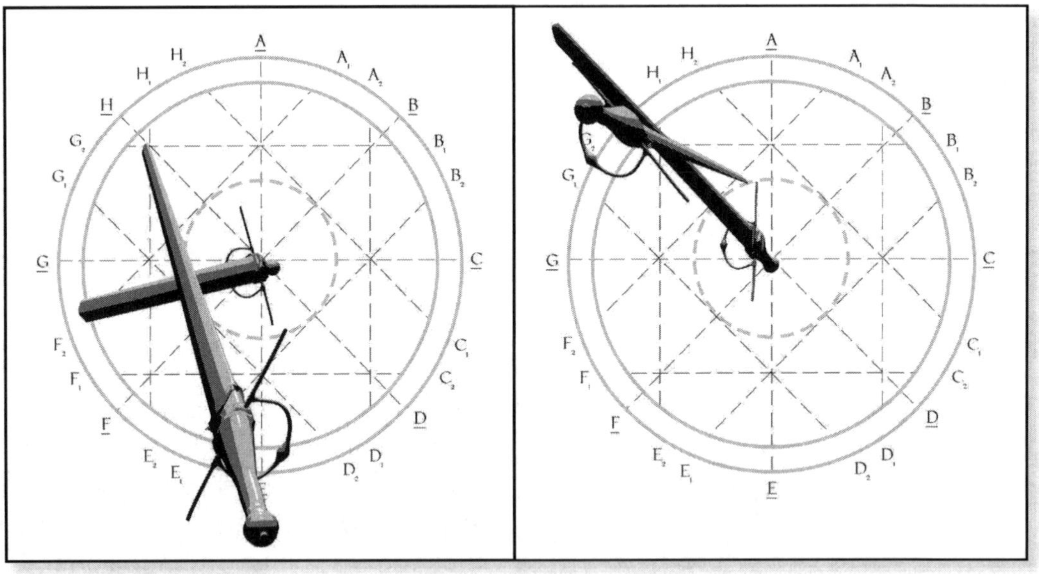

1. Overbind created to the inside, directing the point towards H

2. Hand is turned up through the Left Ox, Strong to Weak, while point turns into the opponent's face or chest to the left side of the vertical line AE (High Thrust on the left)

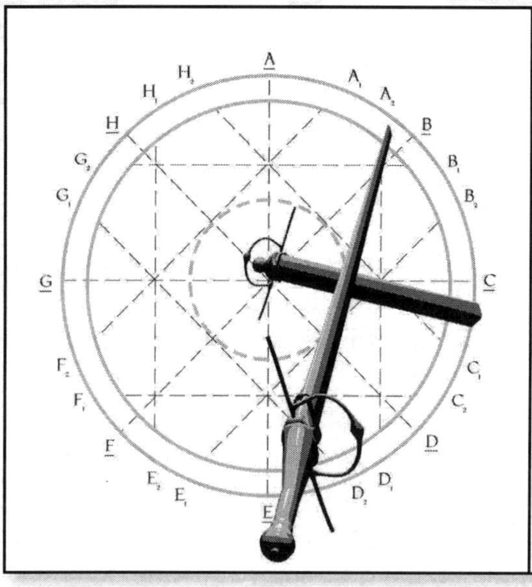

1. Overbind created to the outside, directing the point towards <u>B</u>

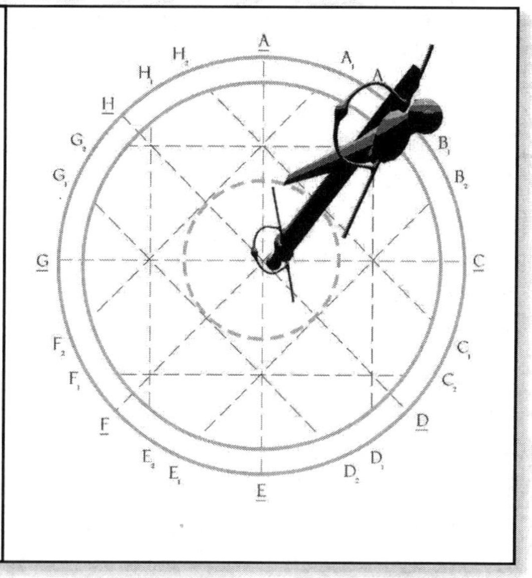

2. Hand is turned up through the Right Ox, Strong to Weak, while point turns into the opponent's face or chest, to the right side of the vertical line <u>AE</u> (High Thrust on the right)

The degree to which we assume Ox as the position to wind into is predicated on the amount of pressure the opponent pushes back on our weapon throughout the winding. It is assumed that the opponent will attempt to stay in the bind and displace the point as it becomes a threat; the guard of the Ox will make this as difficult for the opponent as possible. However, if the opponent does not apply any pressure in the bind, then our weapon does not need to raise all the way to Ox, but rather can stay lower in the Iron Gate.

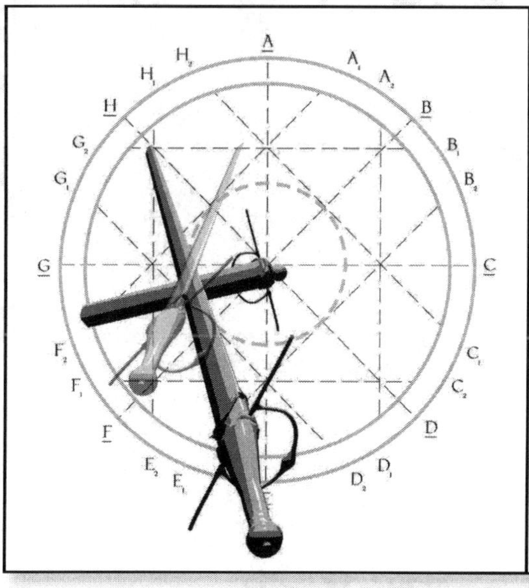

The opponent does not resist the bind, so the hand stays low, extending the hilt to the Weak of the opponent's blade as the point is brought toward the Center, left of <u>AE</u>

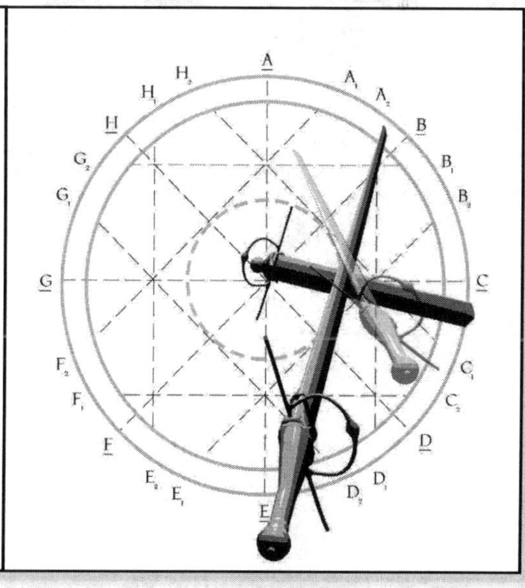

The opponent does not resist the bind, so the hand stays low, extending the hilt to the Weak of the opponent's blade as the point is brought toward the Center, right of <u>AE</u>

Actions from the Overbind

when the opponent is hard

When an Overbind has been established and the opponent Immediately recognizes it and starts to push back, with sufficient pressure to displace our point from the Center, we should Instantly act weakly with the sword. The sword should no longer be used as a barrier but rather cede to the pressure and strike. Take the previous example where the opponent was weak in the bind and thus we wound the sword into the Left Ox: if they are now strong, the sword winds the opposite direction through the Right Ox. By making this 'Outer Winding' we release the pressure in the bind and collect both the sword and its pressure to the opposite side.

Similar to the Outer Winding, Doubling is the same action, derived from the same circumstances. However, instead of ending in a thrust, the action is a cut. From an Overbind to the inside, as soon as the opponent starts to apply pressure, attempting to put their point to the other side in order to establish their own Overbind, our palm should turn down, reversing the edges of the sword so that the long-edge cuts into their right temple (along the line of G_2 - B_1).

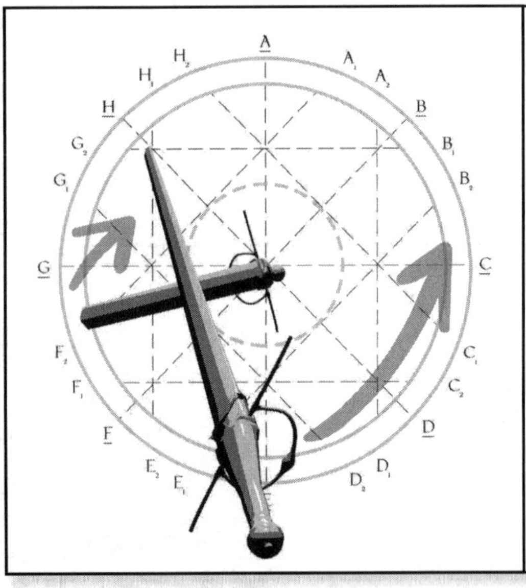

1. Overbind created to the inside, directing the point towards H

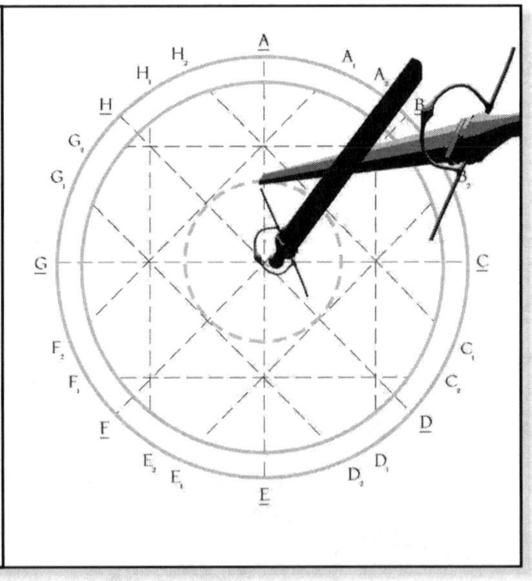

2. Opponent resists the Overbind, and creates an Overbind on their left (our right). We yield to the pressure, turning the hand, palm out and away, to Right Ox, pushing the point forward, towards the Center

Actions from the Underbind

to reestablish an Overbind

If we are losing the Overbind and our strong position, we should Immediately act weak and seek the Overbind on the opposite side of their sword. This can be done in two ways: going under or over their blade. Going under their blade is done in two manners. First, **Changing-Through** (*durchwechslen*) is the process of lowering our point below their sword and reestablishing an Overbind on the opposite side; while **Winding-Through** (*durchwinden*) is going under their blade with the hilt. The act of going over their blade can also be done in two ways: **Changing-Around** (*umbwechslen*) and **Snapping** (*schnappen*).

Recognizing when to go Over or Under

> *Note first: if he falls on the weak, [change] around on his blade, if he falls on the strong, jerk his weapon around on the other side. If he falls on the middle, then let it run through, and fall back on it with suppressing, and work at once to the opening.*[43] *-Meyer*

Meyer's phrasing here is sufficient in giving us a clear distinction that depending on how they attempt to Overbind our sword, or rather where they attempt to Overbind our sword, will determine how we respond. Firstly, if they fall on top of our Weak, we should Change-Through beneath their weapon (or over) and bind on top of it to the other side. Because they have bound our blade from above on the weakest part, do not resist this strength but simply slip the weapon.

Secondly, if they Overbind on our Strong, they are in fact in a weaker position and thus have made a weak Overbind. From here, pull up with the short-edge then turn the long-edge against their blade, bringing their weapon to the other side while thrusting in.

Lastly, if they have bound in the Middle, that is to say not on the Weak or the Strong, winding strongly on their blade from the Underbind will not be possible and Changing-Through underneath will be a longer action in comparison to before when they were on our Weak. From an Underbind on the Middle of the blade, release the pressure by raising the hand and dropping the point, allowing their weapon to run-off of our own, then finish by cutting back on top of their blade (or to them) to the other side. If they begin to raise their sword after we have let it run-off, thus making a re-Overbind difficult, we can oppose their blade with the Ox through the act of Snapping.

Changing-Through (*durchwechslen*)

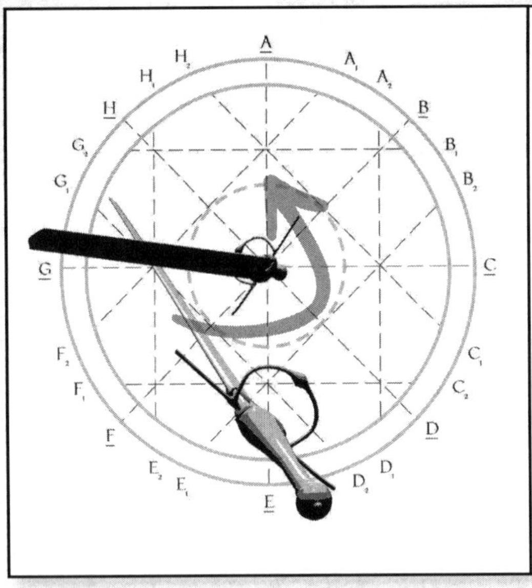

1. From an Underbind on the left when the opponent has bound the Weak, the point drops under...

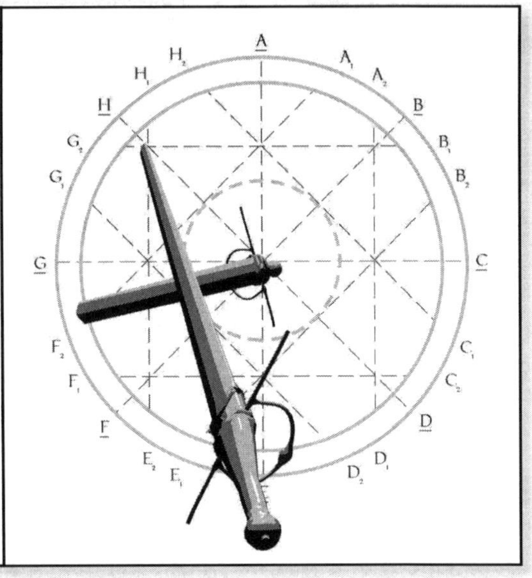

2. and cuts back on top of the opponent's weapon to the opposite side, creating an Overbind on the left (*durchwesln)*. The long-edge (or short-edge with the palm down) can be employed when creating the Overbind

Changing-Around (*umbwechslen*)

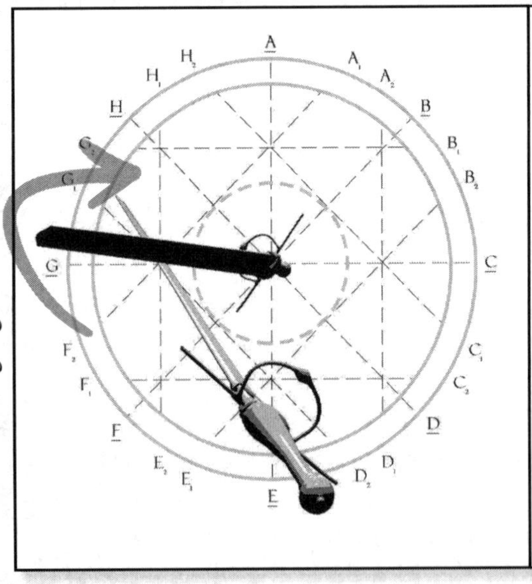

1. From an Underbind on the left when the opponent has bound the Weak, the point slides up along their blade, then...

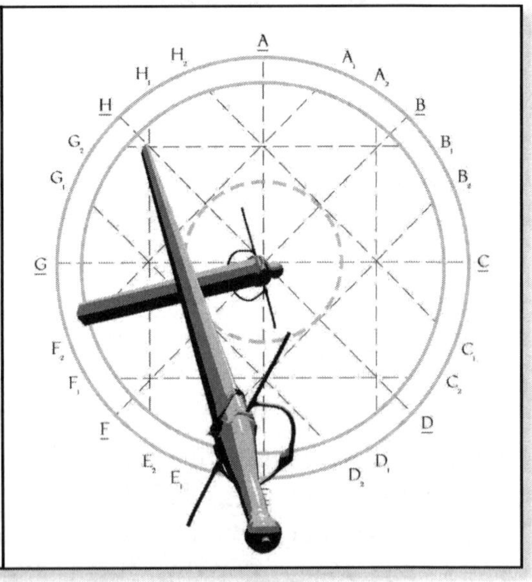

2. cuts back on top of the opponent's weapon to the opposite side, creating an Overbind on the left (*umbschlagen)*. The long-edge or short-edge (*Schielhauw* on the left*)* can be employed when creating the Overbind

Wrenching (*aufßreissen*)

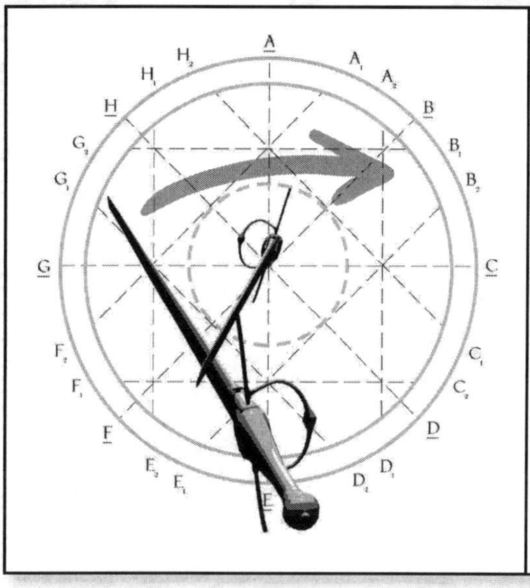

1. Opponent has Overbound on our Strong. Though they are above, our blade has a leverage advantage. First we resist with the short-edge, then...

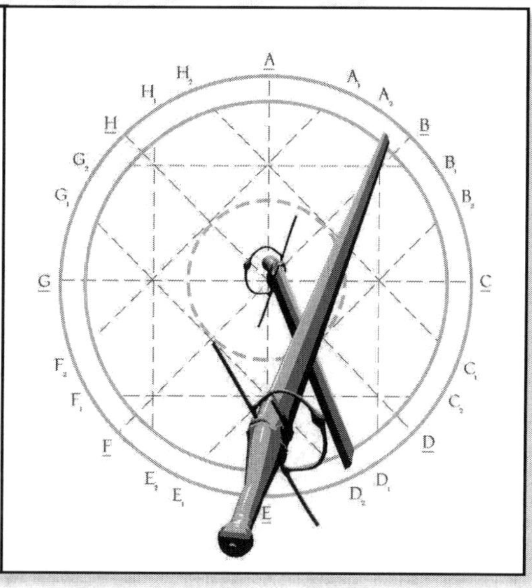

2. our point cuts to the right, creating an Overbind on the right while the long-edge is turned into their blade, directing the point to B

Winding-Through (*durchwinden*)

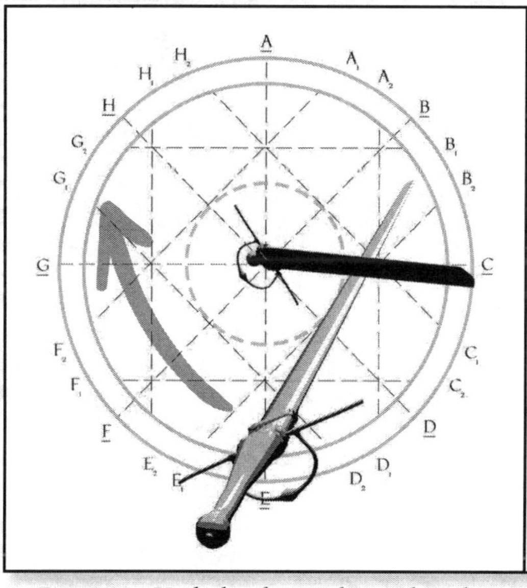

1. From an Underbind on the right, the opponent has bound the middle of our weapon

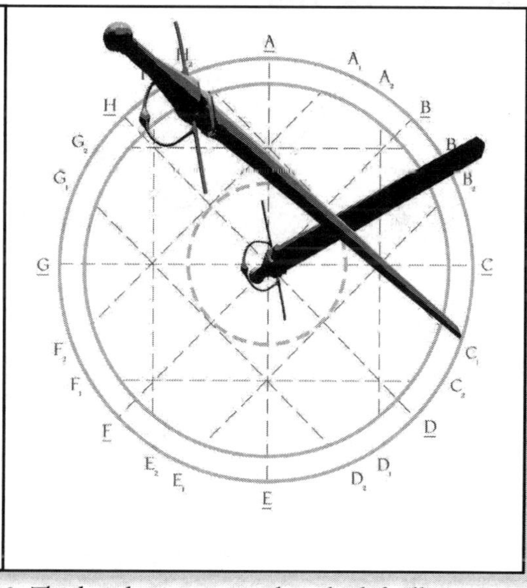

2. The hand raises up and to the left allowing the point to hang to the right. Our sword yields to the opponent's pressure allowing their blade to run-off

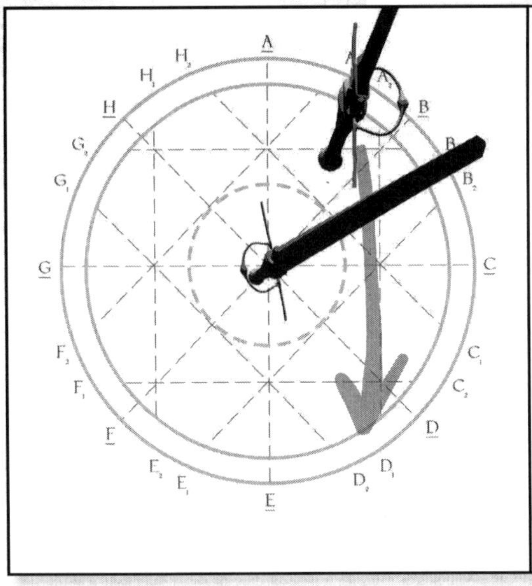

3. As the point lowers to the right, it travels behind and back up to the Right Ox for the Cut

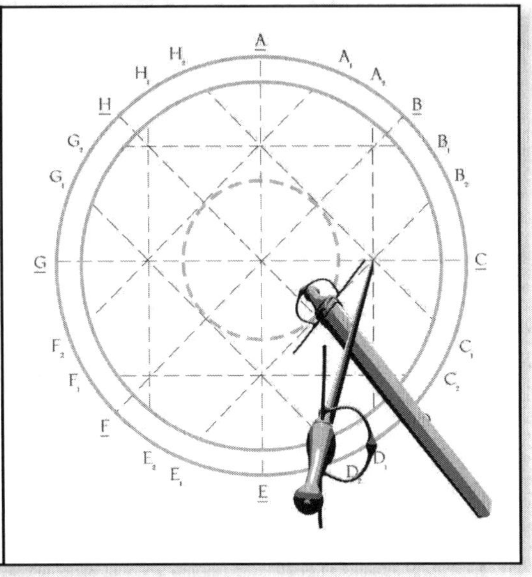

4. From here, we deliver a Suppressing Cut through the right (A_2 to D_1). Or a Squinting Cut (*Schielhauw*) on the right could also be made to achieve an Overbind to the inside

Snapping (*schnappen*)

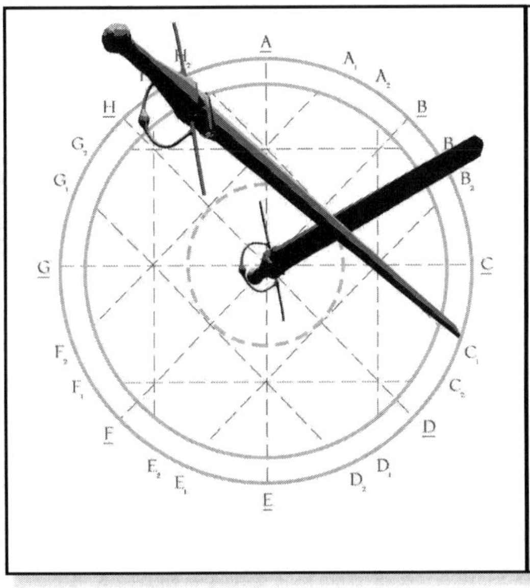

2a. From the previous position in figure 2

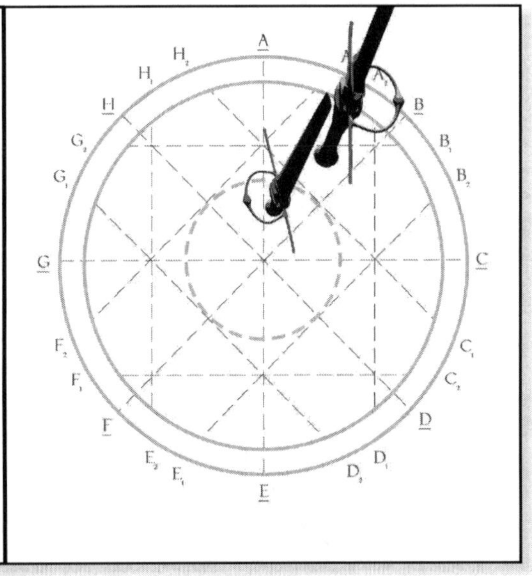

3a. If the opponent begins to bring their weapon back up against our own as it raises through Right Ox for the Cut, making a Suppressing difficult...

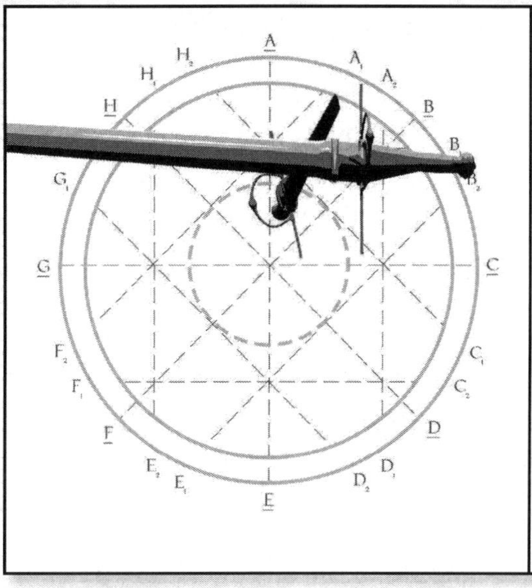

4a. the point should then swing to the left, making a Middle Cut from left to right (with the inside-flat)...

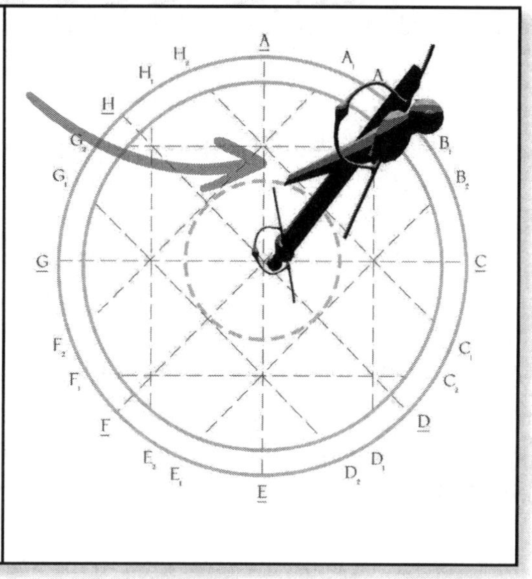

5a. as the inside-flat is brought to the Center, the action finishes as a High Thrust on the right

Strong Bind

- Point into the direction of the bind
- Strong occupies opponent's Weak
- Placement of body to resist pressure

Weak Bind

- Point directed away from the bind
- Opponent's Strong occupies our Weak
- Placement of body to remove the sword from the bind

The strong binds should be understood as engagements that force the opponent's weapon out of the Center, keeping the opponent in the *Nach*, thus making any attempt to act *Indes,* longer. The weak binds, in contrast, allow the opponent to seize the *Vor* more easily by allowing their actions to work through the bind without hinderance. The actions that follow from strong binds are ones that work through the Center while weak binds are forced to work around it.

To make use of the actions that follow from this binary course, means to always put the sword into a position/bind that allows the *point* to move freely. This allows us to thrust when we need to thrust, and to find a new position when that is required of us.

Leaving the Bind & Chasing (*nachreisen*)

But when you have come so near one another that both blades bind in the middle, then you must not cut around, nor go away from his blade without particular opportunity, for as soon as you go away from his blade, he can rush upon you with chasing. But be mindful of the techniques that can be executed on his blade, and if he over commits to a cut or else makes himself open, be sure to crowd after him.[44] *-Meyer*

Meyer advises that when the blades can reach each other at their middles we should bind (*binden*), remain bound (*bleiben*), feel the pressure while in the bind (*fülen*) and act Instantly from it (*indes*). All four of these concepts together are required to keep ourselves safe and react properly to our opponent's intentions.

But, as we saw in the previous section, reestablishing an advantageous position requires us to temporarily leave the bind (unless they have bound our Strong), which allows the opponent to apply the concept of 'chasing.' The fencer who will succeed in the Middle while in the bind is the fencer who is better able to keep their sword closer to the Center with control over the other's weapon. The following techniques illustrate this concept.

In this first example, by creating an Overbind on the left, we intend to keep their weapon as far into the outer circle as possible while keeping our point close to the Center. If the opponent senses this disadvantage and seeks to escape this position by Changing-Through, they must temporarily leave the bind. To counter their action we keep our point close the Center while tracking their blade with our long-edge while Simultaneously striking, or 'chasing' towards the opening.

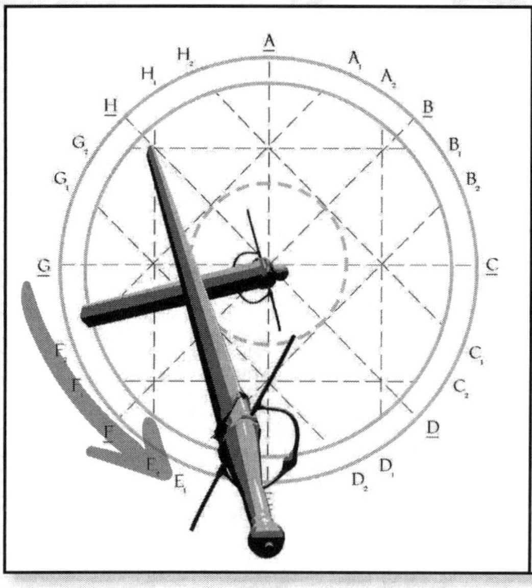

1. From our Overbind on the left, the opponent escapes this engagement by Changing-Through

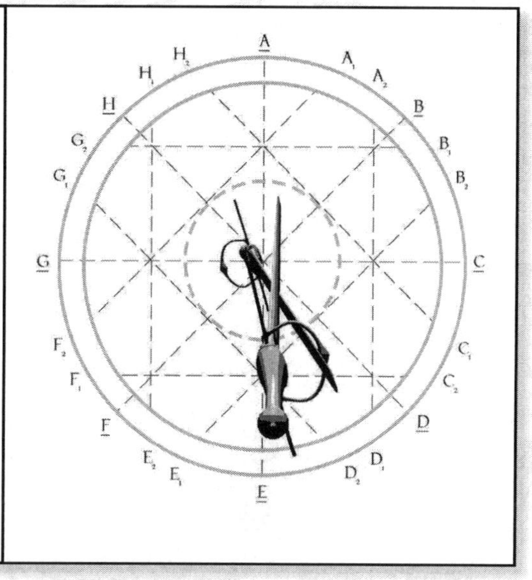

2. Feeling their blade leave ours, our long-edge tracks theirs while we extend the sword forward for the thrust, Immediately denying them the Overbind

In the second example we can combine several techniques, each showing different points at which the opponent may need to leave the bind, thus making them susceptible to 'chasing.' In each instance we will succeed because our sword stayed closer to the Center while keeping control over the opponent's weapon.

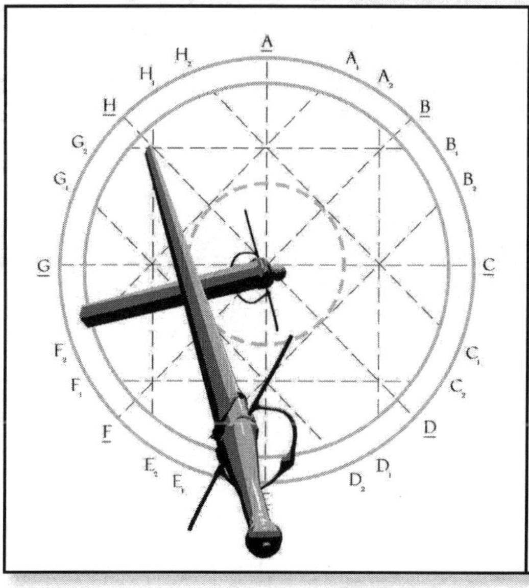

1. From our Overbind on the left, the opponent escapes this position by Changing-Around

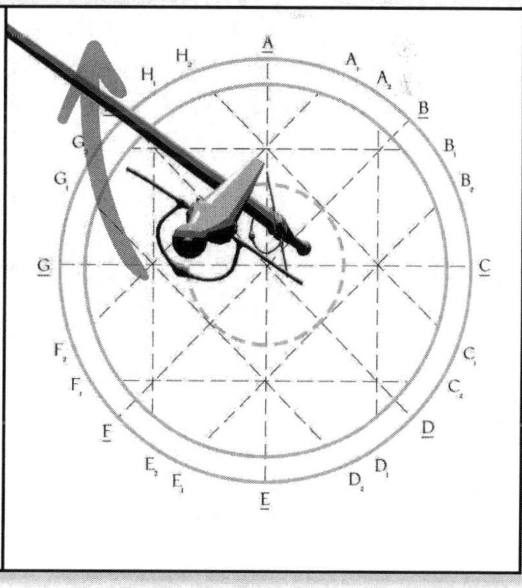

2. As the opponent pulls their sword back in an attempt to cut around our blade, we follow their weapon in, tracking it with the long-edge while delivering the point to the face

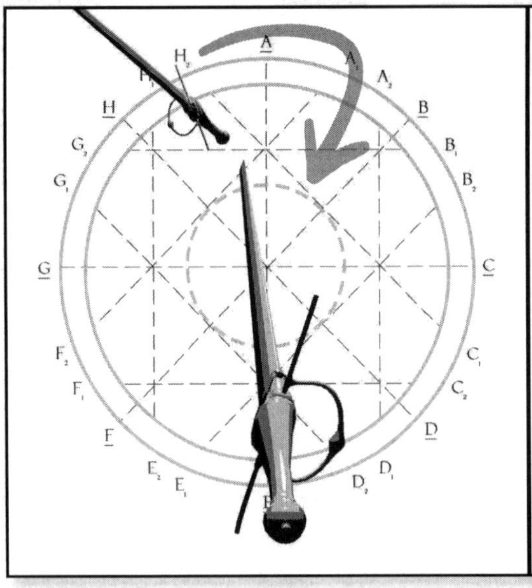

2a. Here the opponent has successfully pulled away from our sword and begins to Change-Around

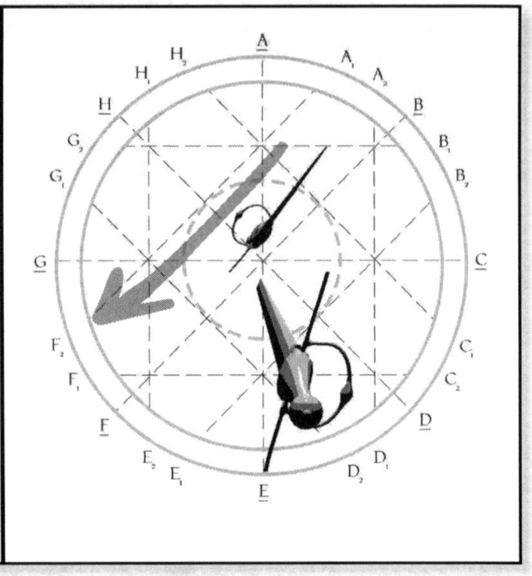

3. As the opponent's weapon seeks to Overbind our sword to the outside, by cutting to the opposite side, we lower our point by Changing-Through

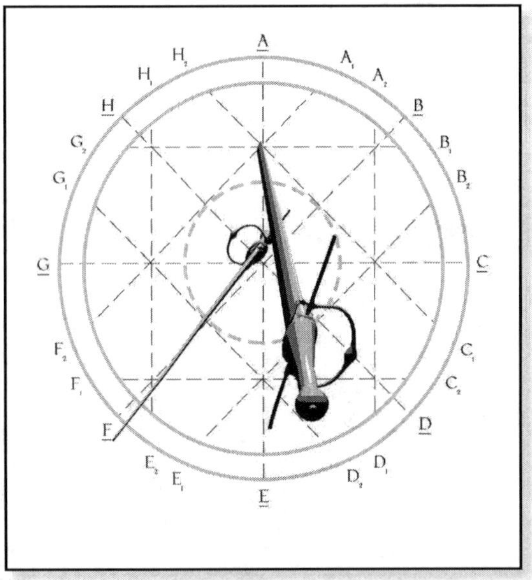

4. Expecting to meet our blade, but missing, the opponent's sword falls away, as our point is raised and thrusts forward towards their face

In this last example we will use a technique that Meyer does not give any specific name to, but Joachim Köppe (an early 17th-century German author on the art) refers to as 'reverting.'[45] This action begins as a Changing-Through, but as soon as we perceive the opponent moving to counter it (like we saw in the first example) we 'return' to the same side, 'chasing' to the opening they have just created.

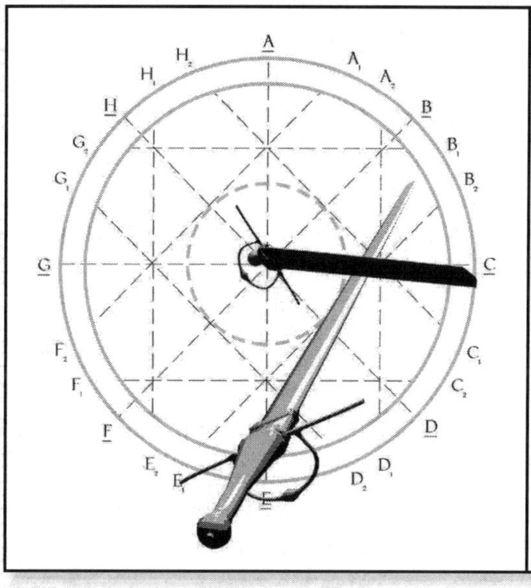

1. Here we find ourselves in an Underbind on the right

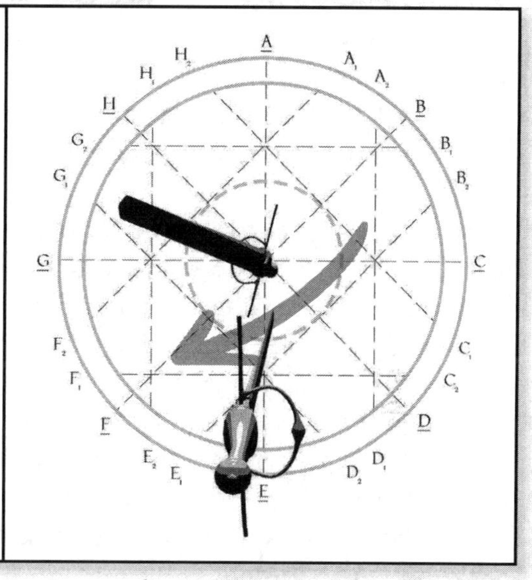

2. As we begin to Change-Through, the opponent preemptively brings their sword to our left seeking to create an Overbind there

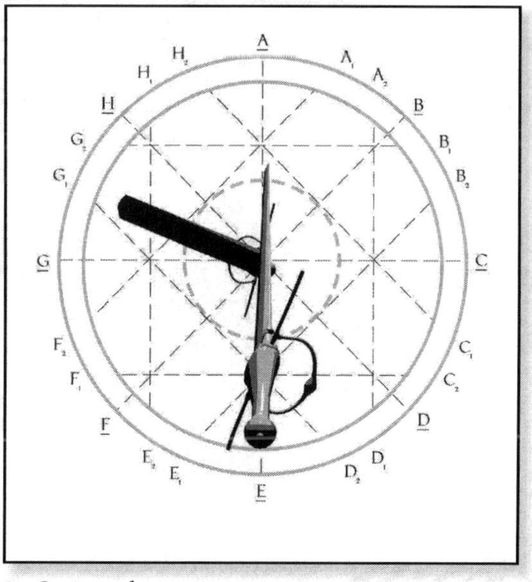

3. Seeing the opponent move to create an Overbind on the left, we 'return' (or Change-Through short) to the same side, 'chasing' towards the opening they have created

Though we were the ones leaving the bind in this instance, because our point stayed close to the Center while our opponent's point swung further in the outer circle (seeking to bind our blade and making them open to our right) our action was shorter and thus arrived sooner.

Turning the Body in the Bind

Meyer is somewhat silent when it comes to how he wants us to position or turn the body when performing various actions, leaving small clues like "and in this cutting turn your right side well after the cut"[46] and "turn your right side well toward your left after the hilt."[47] These small notes along with the illustrations, give us a precious insight on how the body turns with each action. An Overbind to the left can be made by positioning the sword in its proper place, but it becomes immensely more powerful when the weight of the fencer fortifies its position by the nature of the body being exponentially heavier than the sword.

Because the Takings are just the cuts and thrusts applied to the opponent's weapon, the rules surrounding how the body should be used to strengthen the position of the sword are identical to how they have been described in Part III. To fortify the inside bind, the body should rotate to the left from the hips (counter-clockwise if the fencer is viewed from above). The body turns the opposite direction to fortify the bind to the outside. These turns not only strengthen the position in the bind, they power the actions into those binds. For example, if the fencer wishes to create a strong Overbind on the left, they might start this by delivering a Defense Stroke from the right into the opponent's sword. The sword begins its action, then the body starts to rotate to the left, in the direction of the cut. This turn of the body pulls the dominant shoulder and thus the arm through the space with more vigor and speed. Once the Overbind is made, the hips and body are turned into the crossing, adding weight behind the relatively light sword.

From Right Ox for the Cut, the right side is forward, but with the chest and left shoulder somewhat square to the opponent

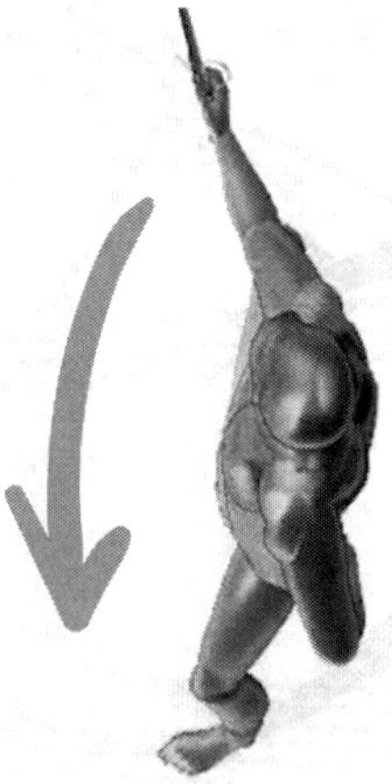

Making a descending, diagonal cut from right to left into Left Iron Gate, the body rotates counter-clockwise, hiding the left shoulder behind the right

From the Left Ox for the Cut, the left shoulder starts behind the right

Making a descending, diagonal cut from left to right into Right Iron Gate, the body rotates clockwise, bringing the left shoulder forward and chest more square

The turns of the body to either side also hide the body behind the weapon. If any part of the body were to show on the side the bind was taking place, the opponent's sword will still be a threat. Meyer repeats the phrases: "turn your right side well after the cut"[48] and "turn your right side well toward your left",[49] emphasizing just this concept.

The body not only turns when making a strong bind to either side, it also turns the opposite way when yielding or acting weak in the bind. In this situation the body does not turn to add force behind the action because the sword is being used less as a barrier between us and the opponent. Instead, it turns to allow the sword to both work around the opponent's while also moving the body away from it.

From Iron Gate, receiving and yielding to pressure from the left

The body turns clock-wise to release the pressure in the bind, allowing the opponent's sword to continue to the right, away from the body, while allowing our sword to yield around theirs

Forming a Strong Bind on the Left

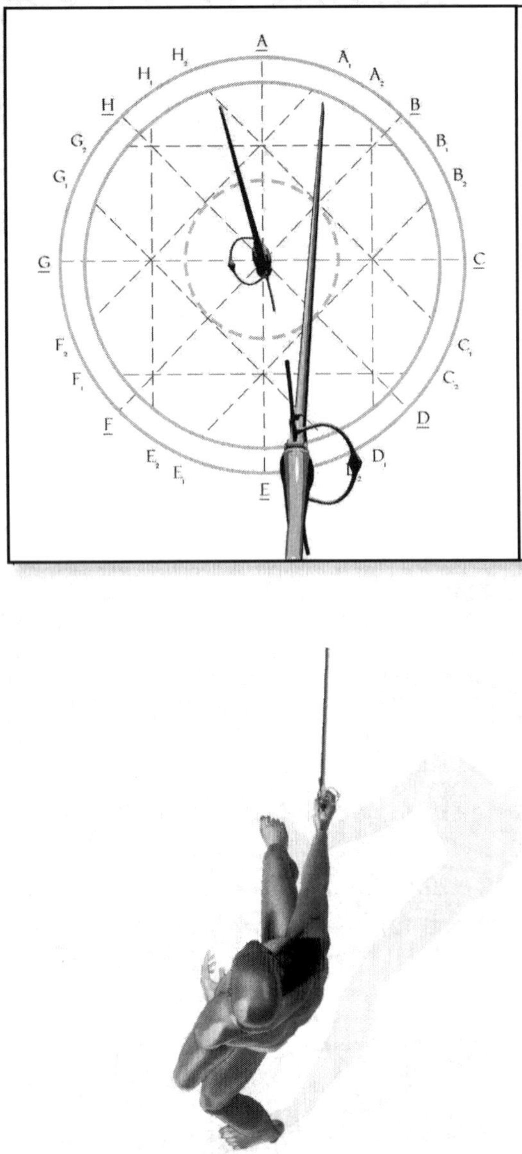

1. Without the swords in the bind

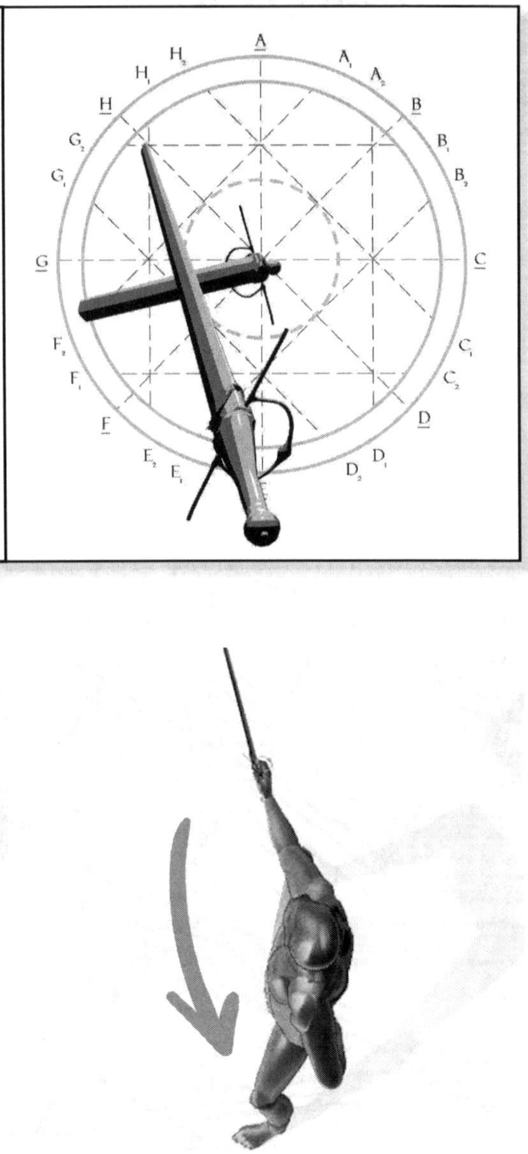

2. Making a strong bind to the left, turning the body into the bind, moving the left hip back

Forming a Strong Bind on the Right

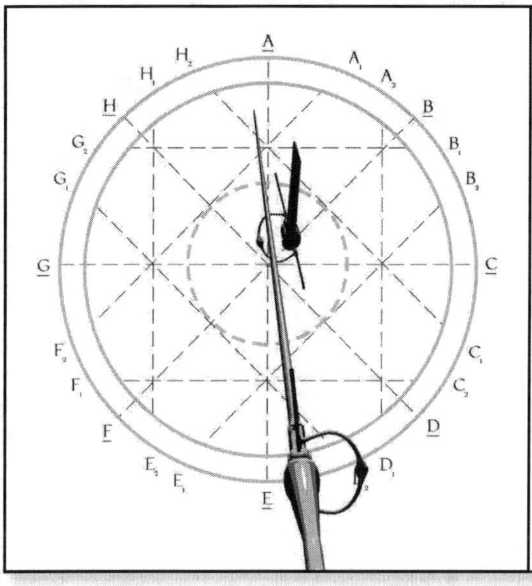

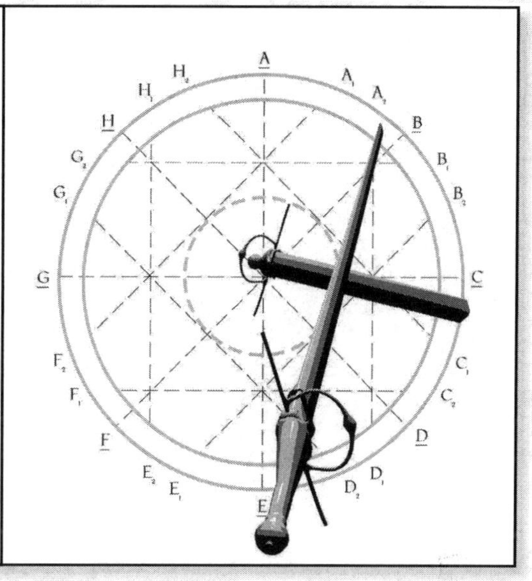

1. Without the swords in the bind

2. Making a strong bind to the right, turning the body into the bind, moving the left hip forward

Ceding to Pressure on the Left

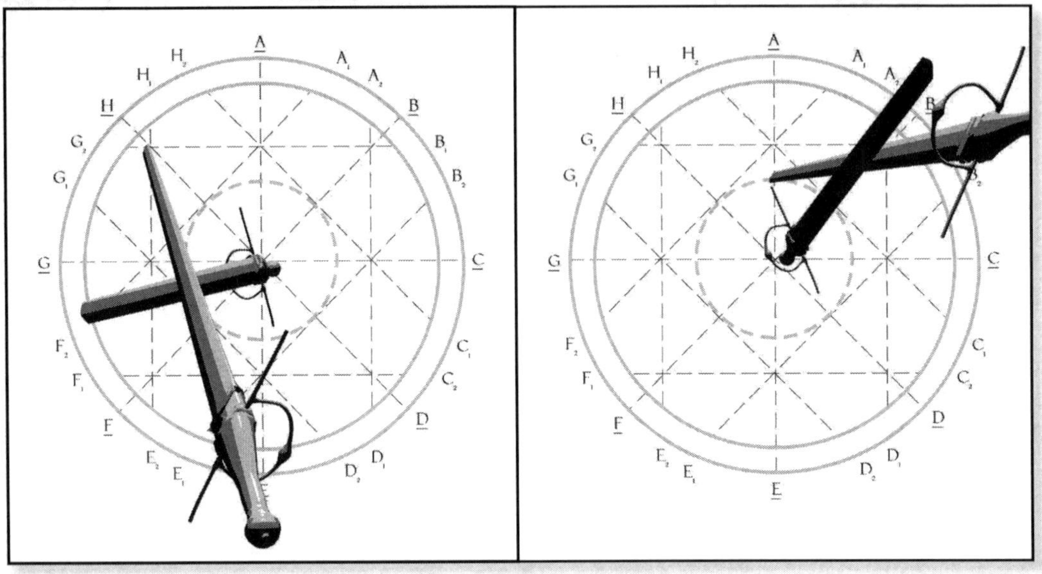

2. From the previous bind on the left, the opponent pushes back against our blade

3. We yield to the pressure turning the body the opposite direction

Ceding to Pressure on the Right

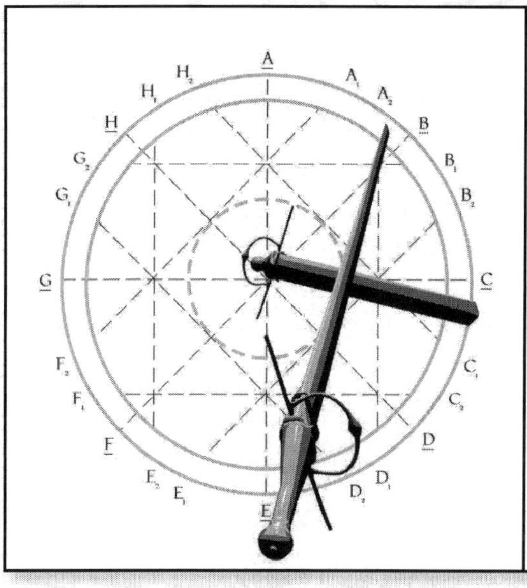

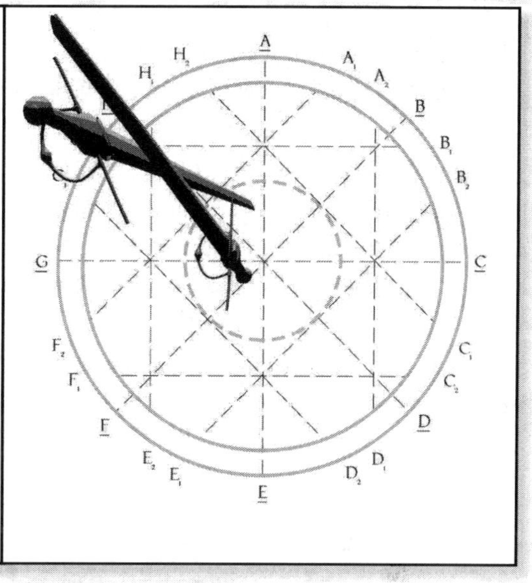

2. From the previous bind on the right, the opponent pushes back against our blade

3. We yield to the pressure turning the body the opposite direction

Stepping in the Bind

The turns of the body can be further reinforced when the feet turn and step in accordance with the actions of sword and body together. For example, when turning the body to the left, the rear foot should step to the right to allow the body to fully turn into the bind in order to further strengthen the bind to that side. The converse is true when turning into a bind on the right; the rear foot steps to the left allowing the body to turn into the bind to that side. The simplest way to picture these actions is to place the weight of the body on the forward foot then start turning the body to either side. At some point, the rear foot will want to now follow the turn of the body once the body has turned as far as it can without stepping.

However, there are many ways in which the swords can bind (as we saw in the previous section) and very little time to think about how we step when in the bind, especially because we will only be here for just a moment. The majority of the time, we can follow this simple rule: step away from the pressure in the bind. This means that if we are applying pressure, step away from it. If our opponent is applying pressure, step away from their pressure. Meyer repeats the phrase "with this stepping out that you have been taught..."[50] to remind us that every bind has its step.

Strong Bind

- body rotates into the pressure
- rear foot steps away from the pressure
- body is removed as a target to that side
- body and sword are moved to where the opponent is now exposed
- body and feet are in a straight line with the sword, fortifying its position

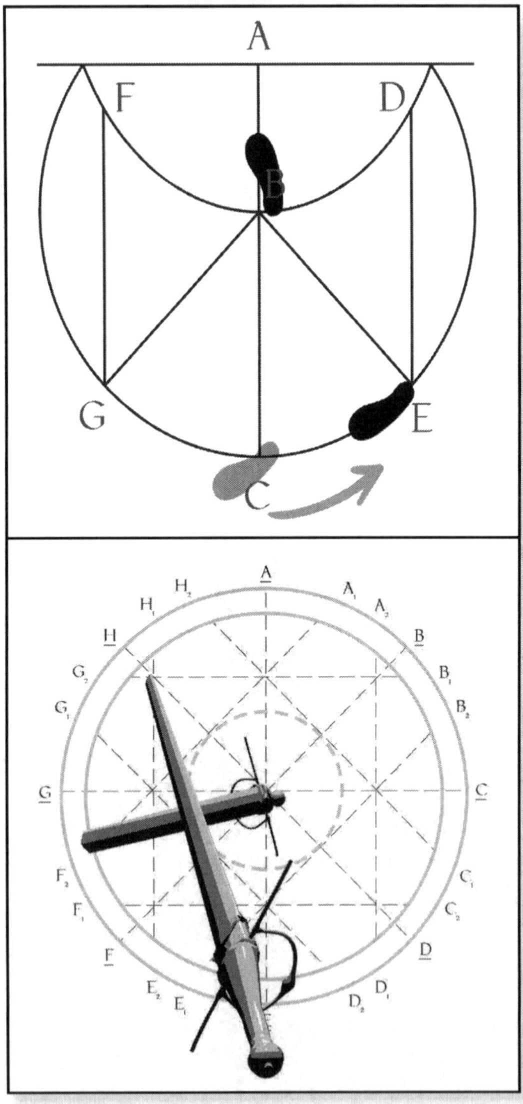

Above: a triangle-step is made to the right, stepping left behind right (from C to E)

Below: Overbind on the left

When we are weak in the bind or wish to cede to pressure from the opponent, again the advice is to step away from the side their pressure is going. This is not to be confused with the side their pressure is coming from. For instance, if the opponent has bound our sword to the inside and is applying strength to our right, we should step to our left. We have already covered several actions of the sword when they are creating strong pressure by Overbinding our sword on the inside, and each of them should be accompanied with a step to the our left. This is sometimes done with the right foot and sometimes with the left foot, depending on the action that follows and the circumstances of the fight. Conversely, if they are Overbinding and applying pressure on our sword from the outside, we should step out to the right. To recap when we are weak in the bind:

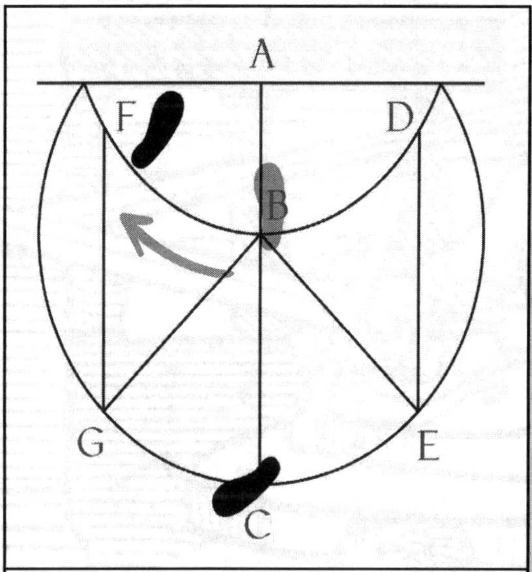

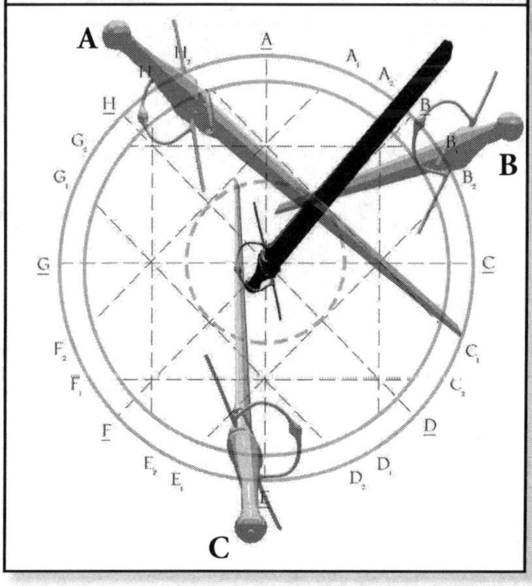

Weak Bind

- body rotates away from the pressure
- either foot steps away from the direction the force is being applied
- body moves away from the opponent's sword
- body and sword are moved to where the opponent is now exposed

Above: the right foot steps to the opponent's right from B to F

Below: Opponent makes on Overbind on the inside, **A**) the sword Winds-Through **B**) makes an Outer-Winding **C**) Changes-Through

Parries

Taking in the Nach

The parries in Meyer's system are nothing more than the Takings in the *Nach*. That is to say, if we are receiving an attack from the opponent, our sword should move to intercept theirs, and Immediately work from the bind. Meyer describes seven parries (really 8) which are various ways in which the bind can develop when receiving an attack. Three parries are Overbind Takings; three displace their sword from an Underbind, and two deal with the low-line (when the attack is beneath our sword).

Recommended Guard

Lund 1568: Straight-Parrying & Iron Gate

Setting-Off (*absetzen*)

Setting-off is the first parry presented in Meyers art, and is his preferred defense. At the core of this parry is the use of the long-edge of the sword to create a barrier between us and the opponent's blade. This parry can be made from any of the four quadrants by first extending the sword and turning the long-edge into the attack, whether that attack be a cut or thrust. As the sword extends and turns, the point should move across the opponent's creating an Overbind the moment the blades come to the bind. The body should rotate to the side the opposition is being made, pulling the rear foot with it, stepping to the opposite side of the parry.

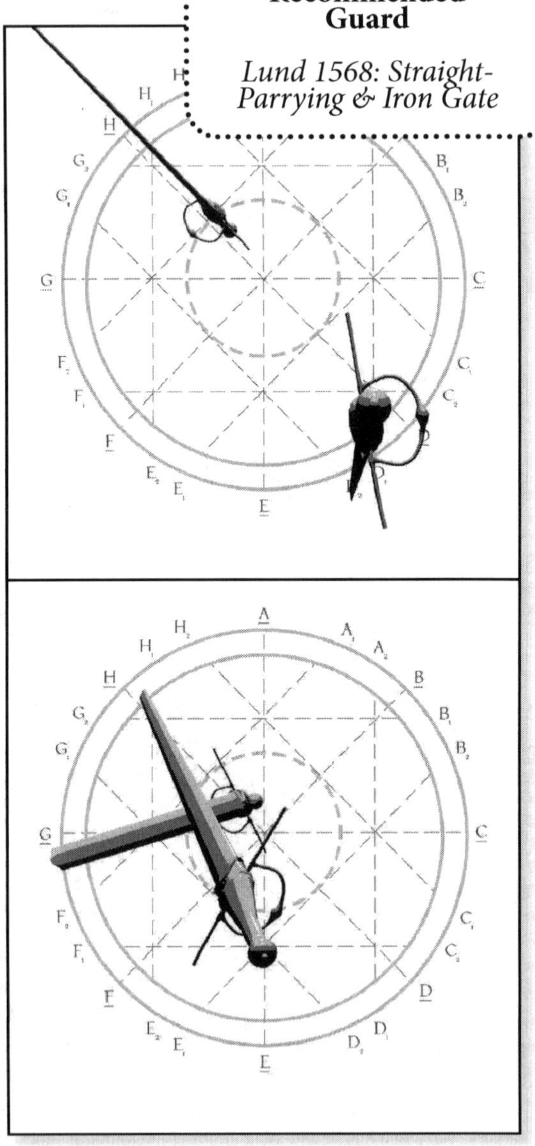

Above: Possible setup for this parry is we start in Low Right and receive an attack from above at our left

Below: As the attack comes to the Middle, our long-edge turns into the attack while seeking an Overbind.

This position could have originated by receiving a cut (lateral pressure to the Center) or a thrust (receiving the point on the Center). Either attack will result in this position when a Setting-Off is made.

see Appendix E, Plate F

Just as the blades come to the bind on the inside, and the body turns counter-clockwise for the reasons stated earlier, the rear foot makes a triangle-step to the right from C to E. As mentioned, this step of the rear foot to the right supports the turn of the body, further removes the body from the threat of the sword, moves us closer to the side on which they are now exposed, but also moves the rear foot somewhat forward along the straight line (as indicated by the dashed line). This allows the front foot to step further than it could before when the left foot rested at position C.

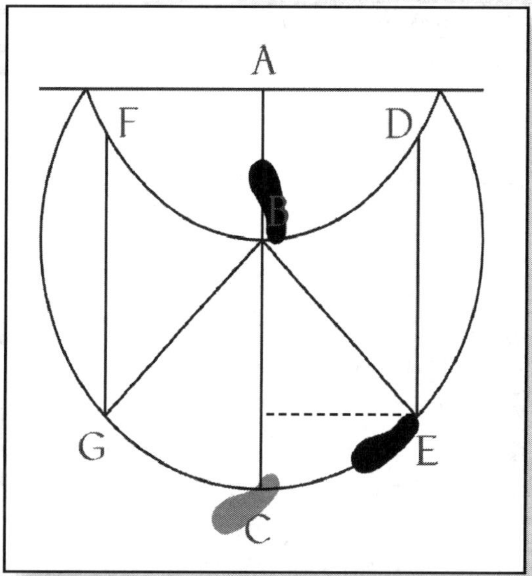

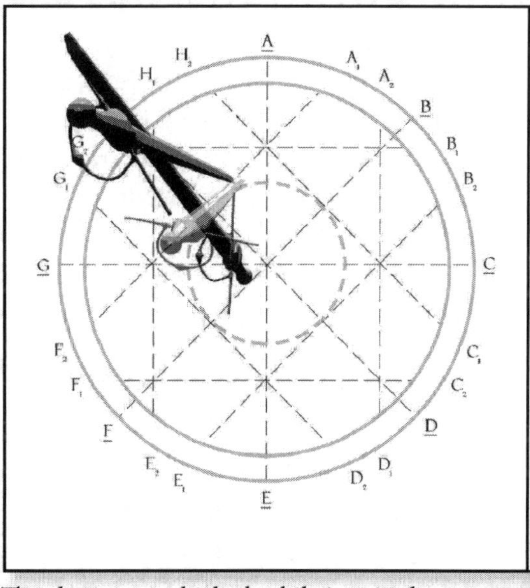

The degree to which the hilt is raised as we wind is dependent on the opposition required, Left Ox being the fullest extent of the wind.

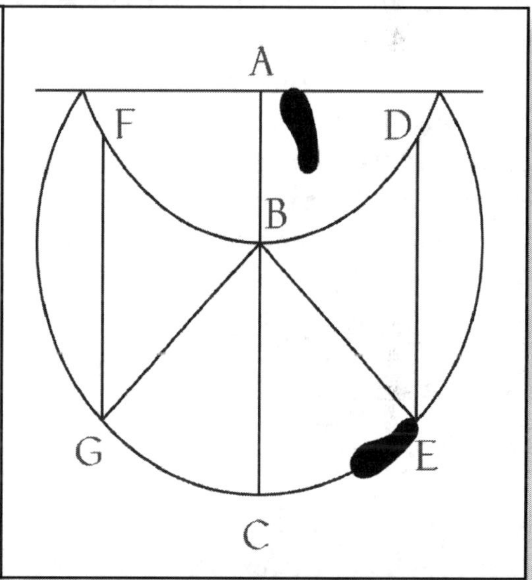

After the parry has been made with a triangle step to the right, the right foot steps to the opponent carrying the body and sword forward

As soon as the blades come to the bind and the rear foot has stepped, we wind the long-edge fully into the opponent's weapon as the point is brought to the left side of the Center in order to keep the Overbind as the strike is made.[51] This winding of the sword is accompanied with a small step of the front foot equal to the distance the rear foot moved along the straight line (top illustration). If the opponent is already retreating when we have begun our attack, this step will close that distance. Both actions, the Overbind and wind, should occur in a single, continuous action without interruption.

Setting-Off
to the outside

In Meyer's description of Setting-Off he states this parry can begin from any of the four guards (meaning Right and Left Ox, and Right and Left Low Guard). Setting-Off from these four positions gives us room to make each one of the required actions with enough time to make them successful (extending the sword, turning the edge and Overbinding their sword). However, Meyer would also like us to set-off from his preferred guard, the Straight-Parrying. Setting-Off from the Straight Parrying to the inside (blades meeting in a bind on the left) is still performed as prescribed. When two right-handed fencers face each other, their right shoulders are on opposite sides of the circle and thus there is space to work to the inside. However, if the same two fencers meet on the outside (blades meeting in a bind on the right), their right shoulders are now in-line and the space to work is significantly reduced. This outside-bind limits the room in which our sword is able to make an Overbind to that side. The technique on 2,75r.1 of *Kunst des Fechtens* (dealing with making a Setting-Off from Straight-Parrying against a cut to our right) Meyer has us withdraw the arm as soon as the blades come to the bind. Besides "gather[ing] for a powerful thrust,"[52] the act of withdrawing the arm (which is only described in this particular engagement of the blades) allows the Strong of our sword to track the Weak of our opponent's, allowing for a straight sword to make an Overbind on the right. If the arm were not to withdraw, the opponent would too easily suppress our

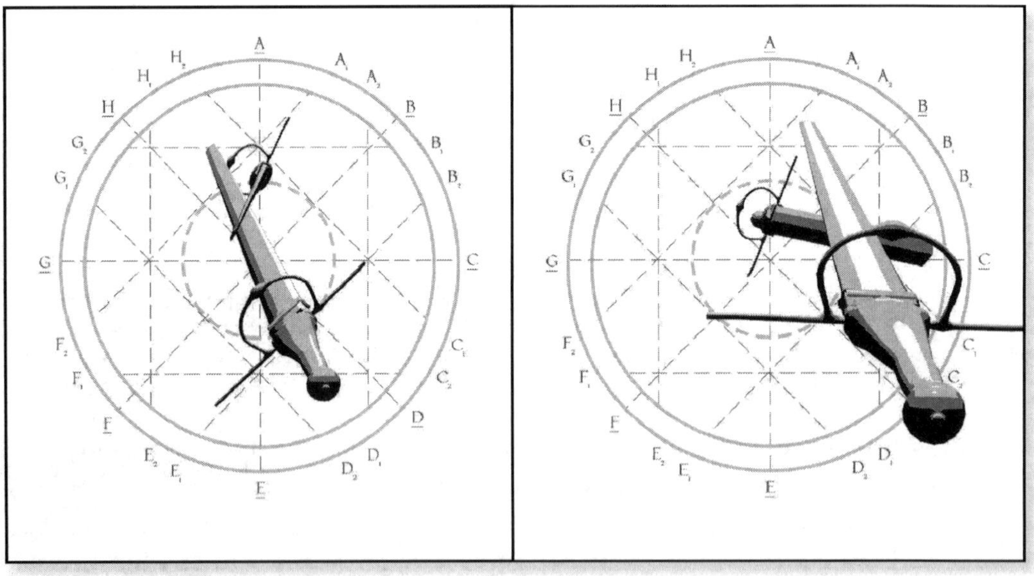

From Straight-Parrying, the opponent's cut to our right will quickly envelope our sword, making an Overbind difficult for us

By pulling the arm and sword back, we can track the Weak of their sword, align the wrist to our forearm and create an Overbind while keeping the threat of the point

sword to that side. There are also two other factors to consider when making this outside Setting-Off. First, it is more difficult for the wrist to make this outside rotation in order for the long-edge to track their sword with the arm straight and extended. Second, the opponent, through the delivery of their cut from their left, will be more covered than if they were cutting from their right. All of these factors promote the exception of

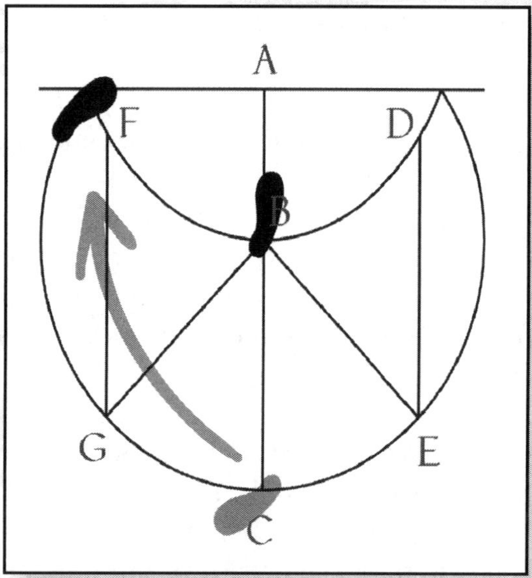

1. A full step of the rear foot to F, moves away from the attack while bringing the left side forward

withdrawing the arm in this particular instance. Because the arm must necessarily withdraw in this manner, it is important for the body to move past the point of the opponent's sword. Instead of making a simple triangle-step to the left, the left foot should move all the way around the left arc bringing the body in a full rotation to the right side (left shoulder forward).

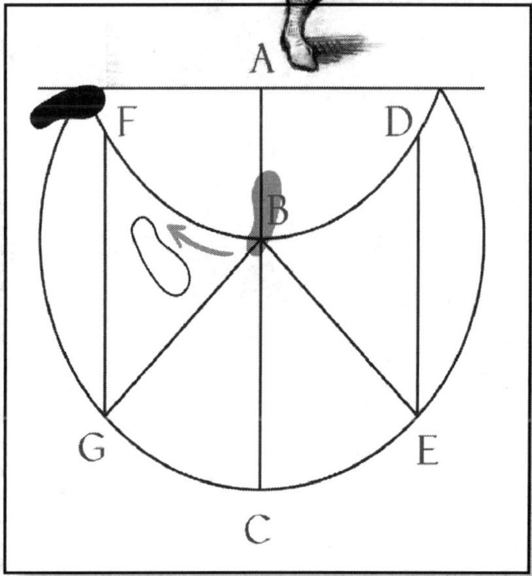

2. After the step of the rear foot has concluded with the parry, the right foot lifts and rotates back, fully turning the body and is ready to step forward with for a powerful thrust

In this position, the right hand still resides above the right foot, but with the left foot somewhat ahead of the right. From this point, after the parry has been made and arm withdrawn, the arm again extends, turning the long-edge upwards locking the opponent's sword in the cross. The body then begins to uncoil itself while the right foot is raised for the step as it carries the arm and body forward for the strike.[53]

Slicing-Off (*abschneiden*)

Recommended Guard

Lund 1568: from all guards

Slicing-Off, the second parry Meyer lists, is the act of gaining an Overbind position by making a diagonal cut or slice through the opponent's attack. Unlike Setting-Off, where we seek an Overbind through an extension or thrusting like action, Slicing-Off will gain the Overbind slightly later through the completion of its cutting motion. The moment the blades come to the bind, they will be temporarily in parity. Meyer tells us to prepare our parry (our cut) the moment they prepares theirs. As they cut down, we cut down.

What makes our cut succeed and theirs fail is two-fold. The opponent is seeking to strike us (Hitter) while our cut is short, through Iron Gate, striking to the space between us (Taker). The more extended their action, the weaker their sword is lateral to the Center. Second, our opponent steps 'on' the line (straight towards us) while we step 'off' the line. Once the swords come to the bind, we continue our cut, lowering the hand to the level of the knee and allowing the point to slice all the way to the opposite low guard. If we prepared our cut/parry into the High Guard on the Right, then we would end in the Low Guard on the Left, and vice-versa. Stepping in this parry is the same for the Setting-Off to the inside, and can be more conservative to the outside, moving the rear foot to G instead of all the way to F. After the Slice-Off has been made, the sword should Immediately cut back up the same path to the most expedient target.

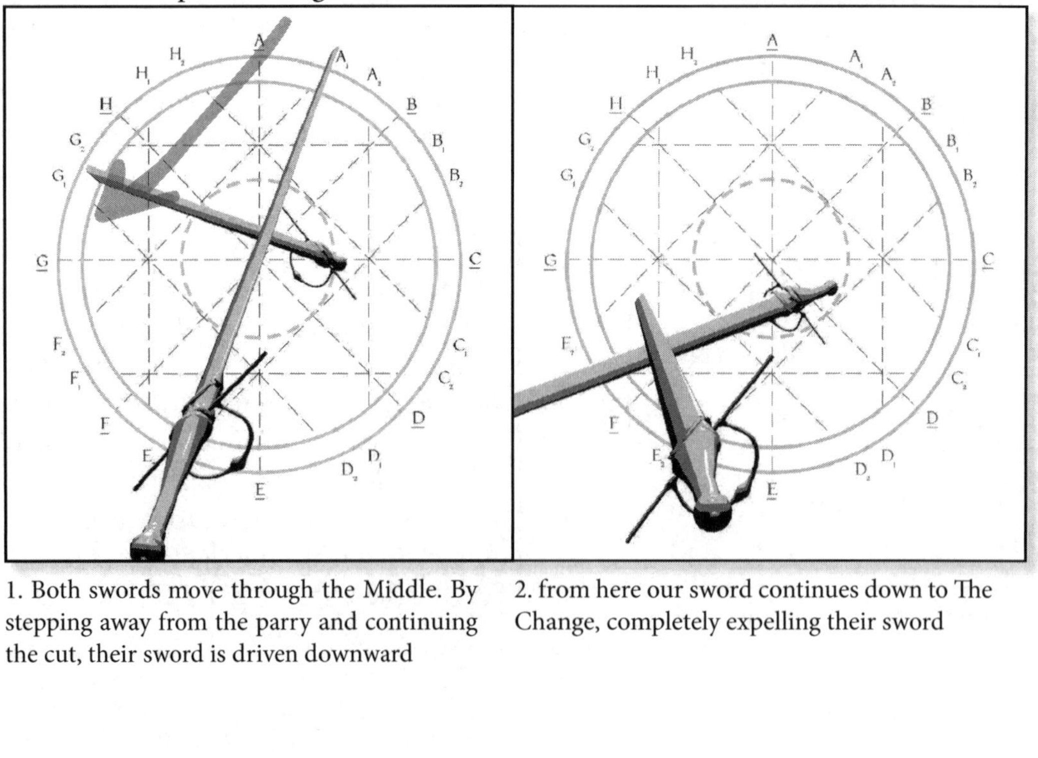

1. Both swords move through the Middle. By stepping away from the parry and continuing the cut, their sword is driven downward

2. from here our sword continues down to The Change, completely expelling their sword

Suppressing (*dempffen*)

> **Recommended Guard**
>
> *Lund 1568: from all guards*

The third parry, Suppressing, is similar to the second in that it is a parry through a cutting motion, but also like the first because we seek the Overbind early in the action. A suppressing cut/parry will always happen down the vertical line through the opponent's shoulder that they are cutting from. If they cut from their left, our Suppressing will be a vertical cut through their left shoulder, and opposite shoulder if they cut from their right. By making the cut vertically through the shoulder, we constrain their blade to that side Immediately Overbinding it and driving it downward. It does not matter if their cut comes from above or below, by driving our sword through the space their

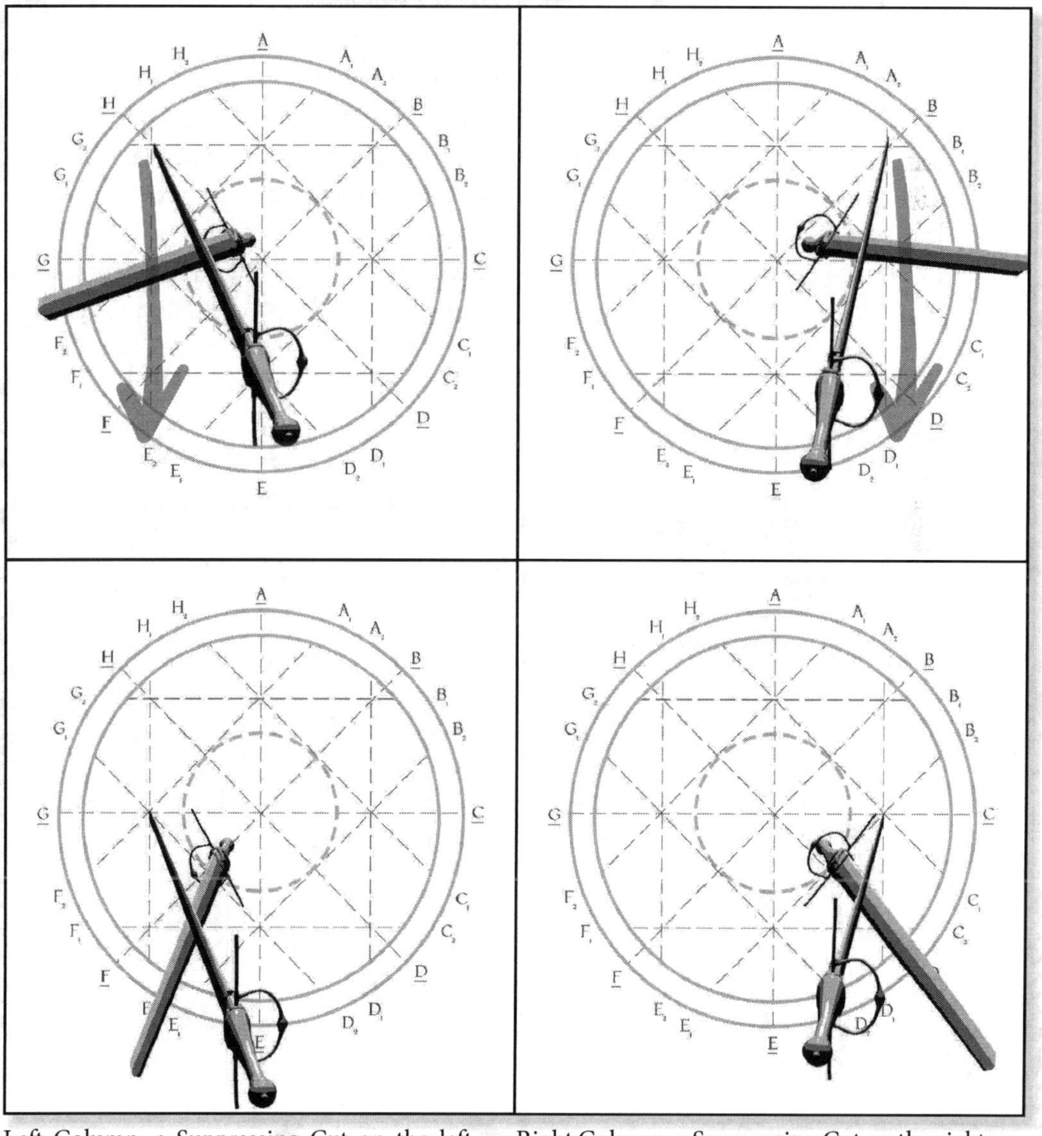

Left Column: a Suppressing Cut on the left. The sword follows the vertical line through the opponent's right shoulder

Right Column: a Suppressing Cut on the right. The sword follows the vertical line through the opponent's left shoulder

sword wished to occupy, we 'suppress' the blade to that side. Similarly to the first two parries, Meyer has us step to the opposite side of the bind. However, when we Suppress, he wants us to take a double step, or double-triangle away. The reason for this is due to the nature of the vertical cut ending with our weapon fairly central, with our Weak on their Strong. Normally this crossing would be weak from above, but due to the impetus of the downward cut, it creates strong pressure from above, driving their point away. The body is also completely removed from the side of the parrying by making this double step, adding an extra degree of safety.

After the Suppressing has been made, the point should Immediately extend to the target on the same side of the Center that we Suppressed through.

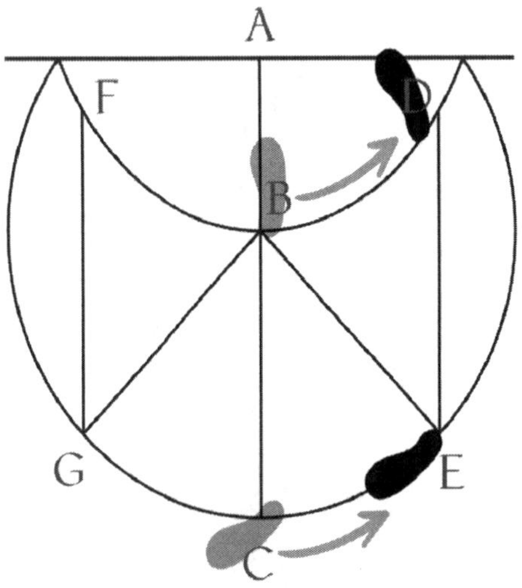

Above: Double Triangle-Step to the right. The front foot starts then the left foot immediately follows

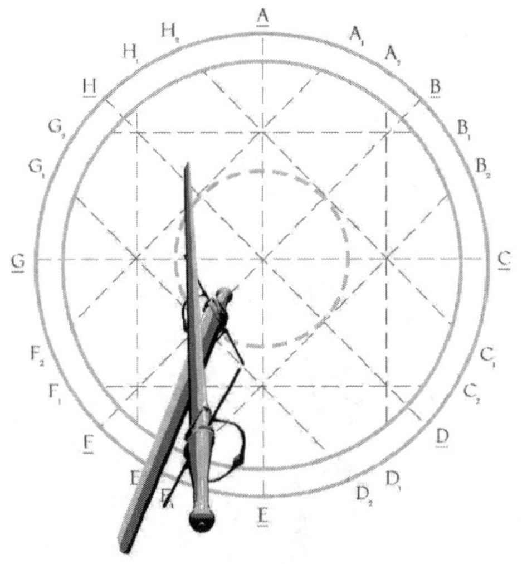

Right: After the Suppressing Cut to our left (their right) the point extends to a target left of AE

see Appendix E, Plate G

Going Through (*durchgehn*)

Recommended Guard

Lund 1568: Iron Gate, Side Guard & Right-Ox

Going-Through is a combination of two techniques. First, sensing the opponent will be strong in the bind (but before the bind develops) we Change-Through (*durchwechslen*) and then Sett-Off or Slice-Off to the opposite side. In fact, this parry is just a method of completing either the first or second parry on the side the opponent is cutting from rather than the side they are cutting to. Because we are moving to the side they are cutting from, our sword will move in behind theirs and continue the momentum of their attack away from the intended target.

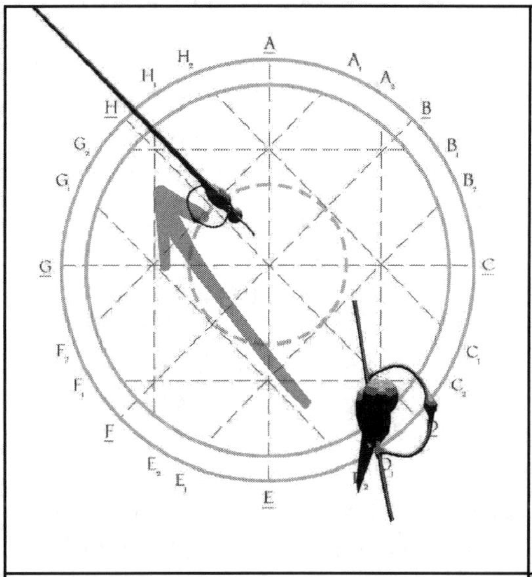

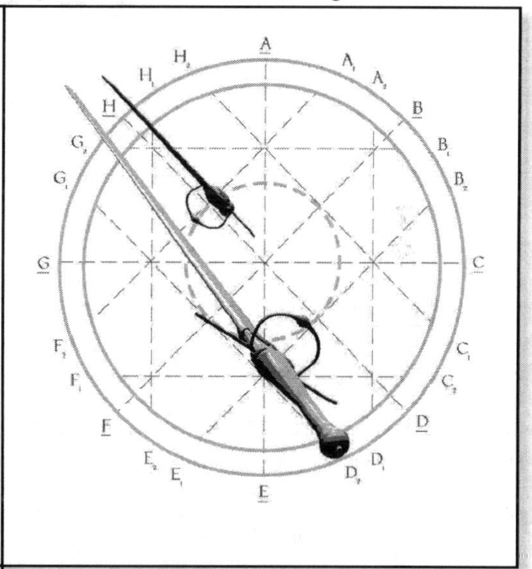

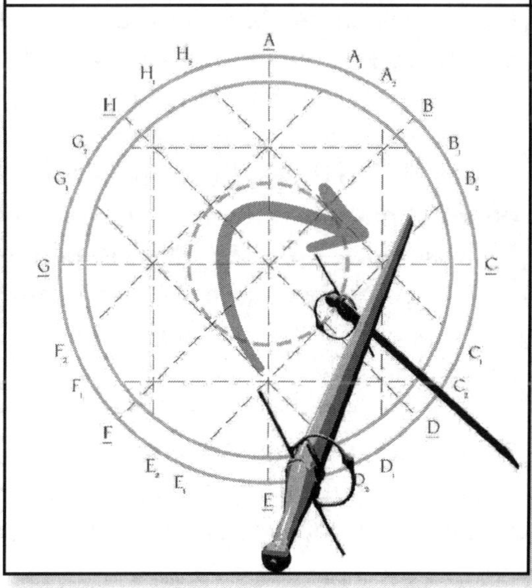

Top Left: from the Low-Right Guard, the point moves to the left to reach under their cut

Top Right: the long-edge starts to turn up against their sword to make a temporary barrier

Left: as soon as the blades comes to an Underbind on the left, the point moves over and across their blade, continuing its momentum off and away to the right

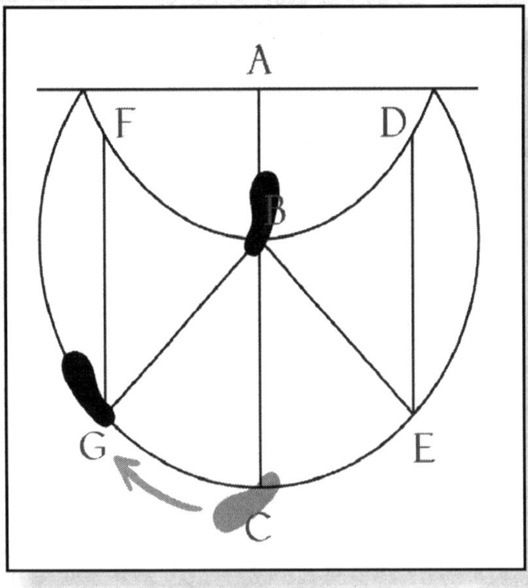

Simple triangle step to the left

Though the parry begins on the right, the bind does not conclude on the left like a standard Setting-Off or Slicing-Off, but instead on the right because of the initial Changing-Through. Thus, the step must be made to the left, rotating the body clock-wise. The danger of this parry is that one could bring the opponent's sword into their own face because it is being transported to the opposite side. To avoid this, as the sword is brought through under the opponent's blade, the long-edge should turn up into it in order to make a temporary barrier while it reaches behind and slices it off to the same side it started.

Hanging (*verhengen*)

> **Recommended Guard**
>
> *Lund 1568: Iron Gate, Side Guard & Right-Ox*

Hanging is the first parry done into an Underbind. This action uses the strength of the Strong of the blade and the flat of the sword to deflect the incoming attack. Hanging is more expedient from the low guards; It does not require any further motion aside from raising the hand. As the hand is raised the point is left to fall and 'hang' in front of us. With the blade hanging in this fashion it tends to cover the head behind the Strong with the rest of the blade covering the upper body, offering more cover than the previous parries. Following the stepping advice from previous parries, a triangle-step away from the side of the bind should be made.

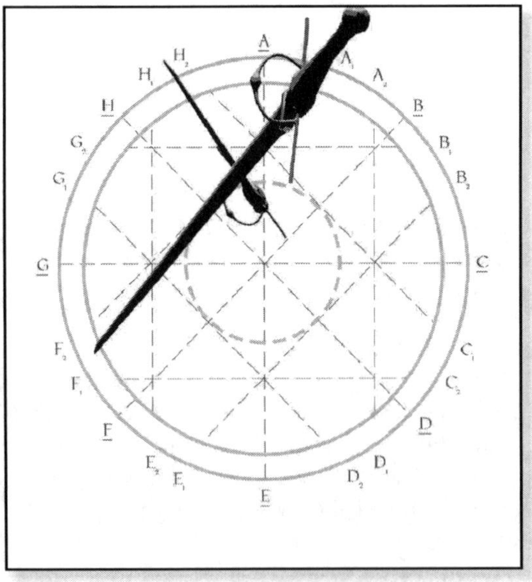

1. An inside Hanging using a position similar to Right-Ox to create a barrier to the left

Meyer admits Hanging is more naturally done from right to left, as making this parry to the opposite side requires the

see Appendix E, Plate E

1a. An outside Hanging using a position similar to Left-Ox to create a barrier to the right

hand to lift into a quasi-Left Ox position with the point dropped to the opposite side, a much weaker action. This position is more effective as a Winding-Through in response to a strong bind, as opposed to an action meant to keep the opponent's weapon out of the Center. Though this position satisfies all of the requirements of a strong Underbind, it is difficult for the arm and body to be situated in such a manner to strengthen its position, making it relatively weak in contrast to the other strong binds.

As the sword moves into the parry, it should continue along the path, over the head, and strike the opponent from the opposite side.*

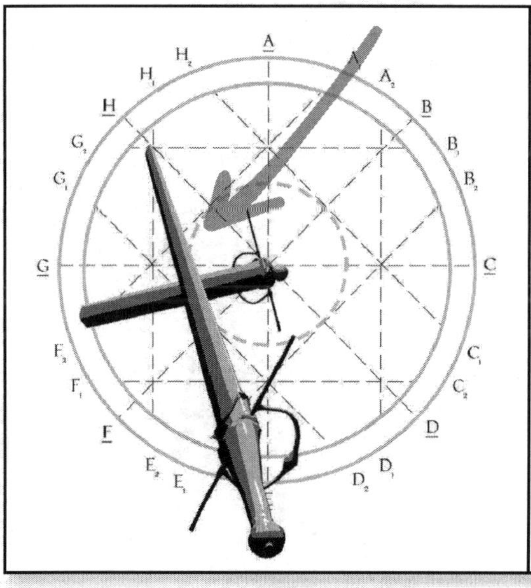

2. From the inside Hanging (figure 1), the point continues to drop to the left as it loops behind the body and back up to the right, delivering a Wrath Cut from right to left, or Defense Stroke back into their blade, and then working further from the bind

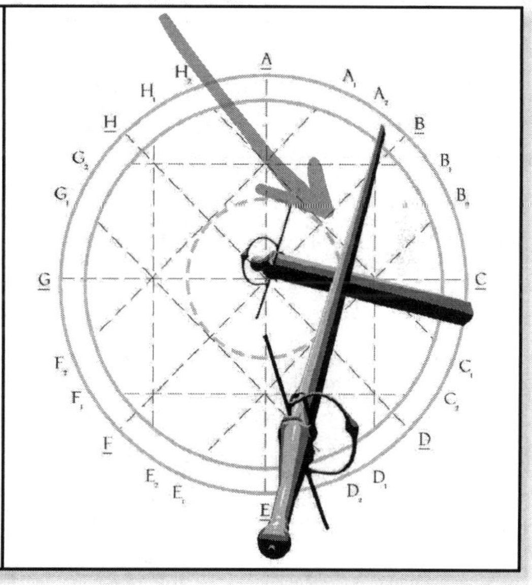

2a. From the outside Hanging (figure 1a), the point continues to drop to the right as it loops behind the body and back up to the left, delivering a Wrath Cut from left to right, or Defense Stroke back into their blade, and then working further from the bind

*It is also possible to respond with a thrust after making an inside Hanging (see Appendix D).

Barring (*sperren*)

Meyer consistently refers to any position where the point is lower that the hilt as a "hanging blade," including when he wants us to 'Bar.' The Barring is a parry specifically used to defend targets lower than the sword hand. While in Hanging the hilt is held above head level, Barring is held with the hilt at shoulder height with the point dropped towards the ground to create a barrier for the low targets. Though technically this is a strong Underbind, it shares all of the same qualities as an Overbind, just with the crossing to the low-line instead of the high-line. The same triangle-step is used in this parry as well, with the rear foot always moving to the opposite side of the bind.

1. The opponent cuts to our leg against our right (from their left). We turn the palm down and lower the point, directing it towards D.

The most common response from this parry is to turn the point back towards the right side of the Center and thrust under the opponent's weapon.

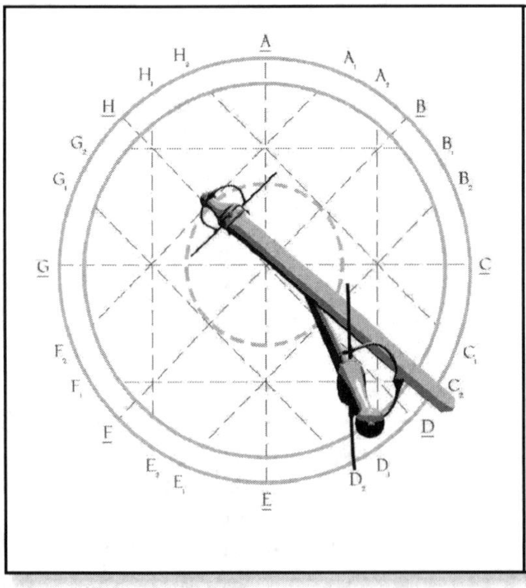

2. After the parry has been made, the short-edge can be turned up, lowering the hand, thrusting the point forward (Groin Thrust)

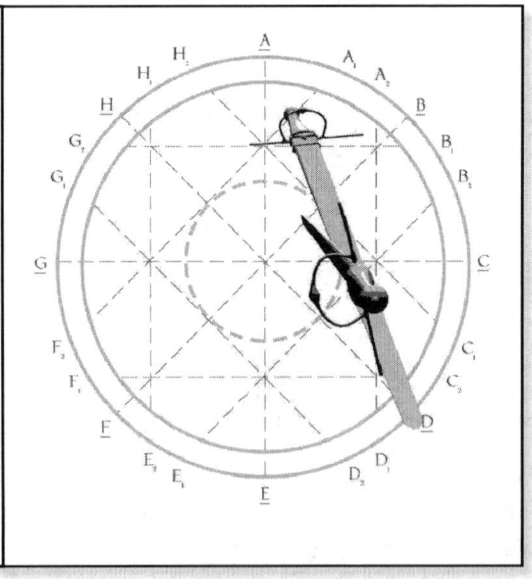

2a. It is also possible to oppose with the short-edge or inside-flat if the opponent's hilt remains high with their point also hanging (Reversed Thrust: see Appendix E, Image C)

Striking Out (*außschlagen*)

Striking-Out is the same action as Barring, except this parry is used to send the opponent's sword through the Center, similar to Going-Through, but to the low-line. As the opponent begins their attack, we should raise the sword, then come in behind it to strike it out with the long-edge. Because there is no forceful binding of the blades, the front foot must necessarily be refused or gathered back to avoid drawing the sword into our own leg.

This action is more commonly used against thrusts under our blade or against an opponent who stands with the weapon extended under ours.

The response from this parry is the same as with Barring.

Above: The opponent cuts at our leg against our left (from their right). We drop the point over it, initially directed towards F_2, then transport the engagement to the right to D

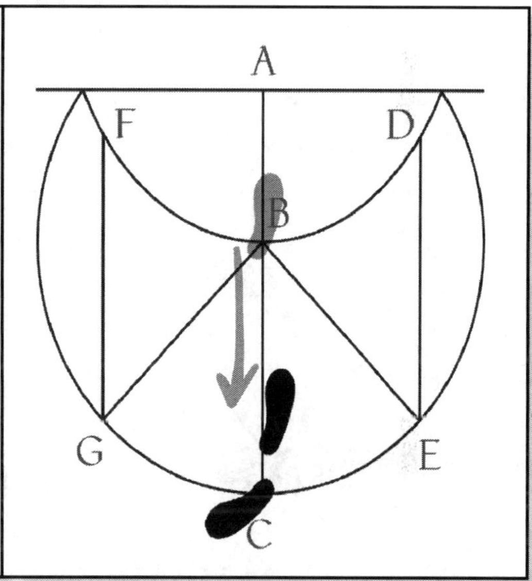

Because there is no hard meeting of the blades, and the opponent's cut is transported through the Center, the front foot is slipped back to remove the lower targets

*Note: both Barring and Striking Out are not listed as parries in the Lund (MS A.4°.2), 1568 manuscript

Taking Out (*außnemen*)

Taking-Out can be done with the long-edge or short-edge. This parry is similar to the Slicing-Off, but originates from either Low Guard. Taking-Out with the short-edge is only done from The Change (Low Guard on the Left).

Long Edge

Recommended Guard

Lund 1568: Long-Edge: The Change & Side Guard

The Taking Out with the long-edge is the Low Cut as a parry. From either Low Guard, the short-edge is initially directed to the Center, so we must first turn the long-edge toward the incoming attack. From there, we make a slicing or cutting action through the middle of the opponent's sword. A Taking-Out from Low Left will end in Right Ox for the Thrust. Conversely, a Taking-Out from the Low Right will end in Left Ox for the Thrust.

After the parry with the long-edge, a High Thrust should be made, directing the point to the same side of the Center the parry occurred.

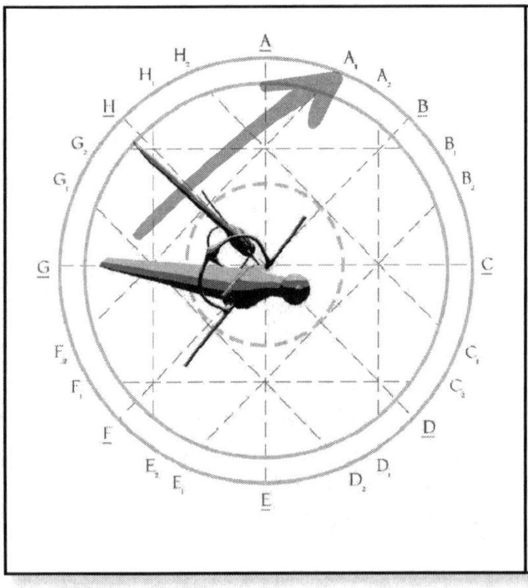

1. A long-edge cut is made to drive the opponent's cut out from below

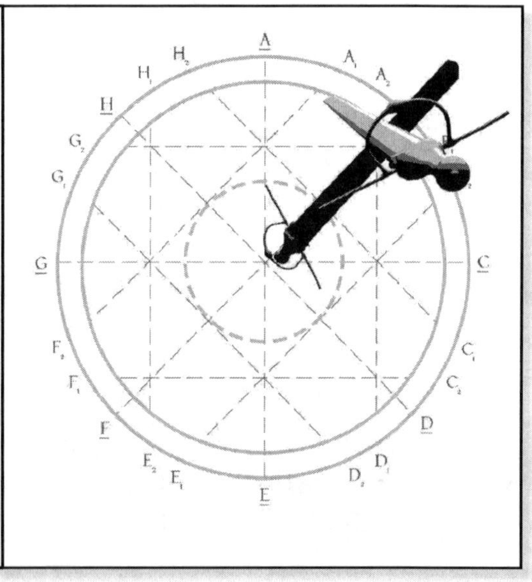

2. The point of our sword must end in an Overbind position or else it will end up as a Hanging parry

Short Edge

> **Recommended Guard**
>
> *Lund 1568: Short-Edge: The Change*

Taking-Out with the short-edge follows the same cutting path as its long-edge equivalent (a reversed low-cut), but the nature of the bind is somewhat different. The parry with the long-edge uses the impetus of the cut to drive away the opponent's sword while also providing a barrier. Using the short-edge creates an Overbind more easily against a sword in the same instant the blades meet (even though the action begins from below). This short-edge opposition, which Meyer only performs from left to right, expels their blade while also controlling it from above.

At the end of the parry, if the point is still within the circle, the long-edge turns against the opponent's blade while delivering a High Thrust from the right. If the parry has been made wider, then a cut back down the same path is the quicker alternative.

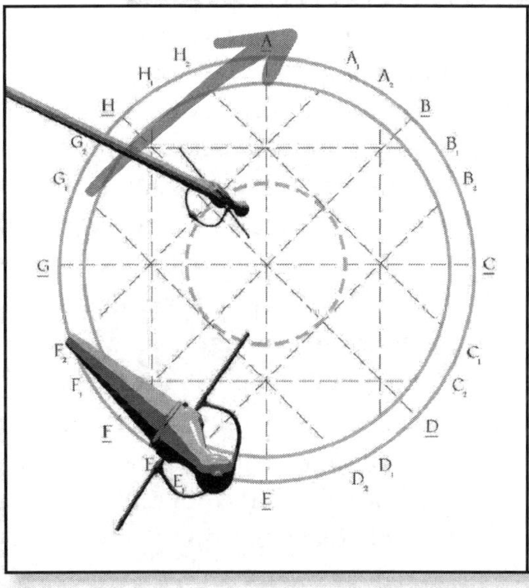

1. The same action as the previous, except the short-edge it used to cut away the opponent's blade

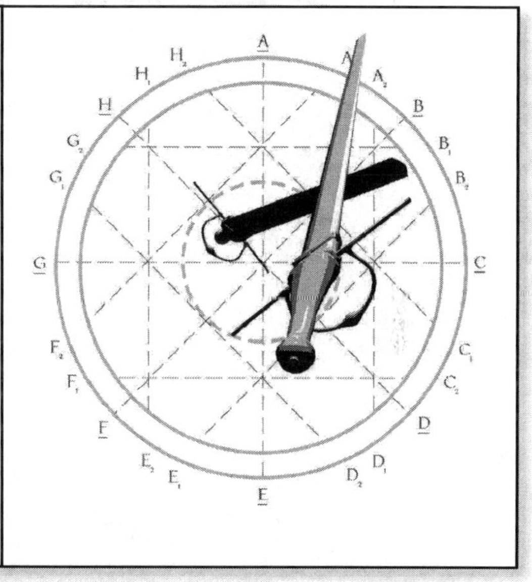

2. Because the short-edge can more easily make an Overbind, it is easier to use the short edge to Strike Out

Parries

The Common Parry

> *is when you parry without any particular advantage in the common fashion only out of fear, in which you do nothing but catch the strokes that come from your opponent by holding your weapon against him, and you do not seek to injure him, but are content to get away from him without injury*[54] *-Meyer*

In those times when we are overcome with opponents' attacks and need to buy ourselves time to compose our thoughts and plan our next action, the basic or 'common' way of parrying can be used. To employ it, we simply stick our sword out in front of us to ward off their blow while stepping back. This 'parry' is not an action that Meyer advocates nor lists in his seven parries, but acknowledges its place within the fight: an action from fear but at the very least defends us as we get away.

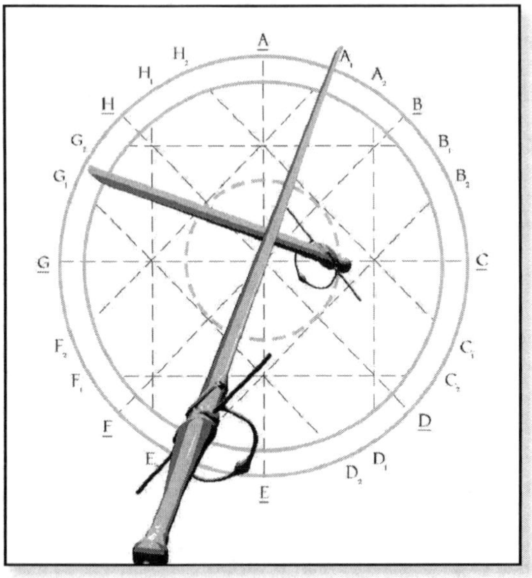

The Common Parry creates a barrier by moving to intercept their blade, quite often creating a 'Parity' bind

While the other parries are made as cuts (excluding the first parry, Setting-Off), the Common Parry moves to catch the opponent's attack simply by turning the blade against it. In fact, the Common Parry shares many elements with Straight-Parrying with one major difference: the Straight-Parry keeps the point within the Center by creating the Overbind, while the Common Parry does not. In fact, Meyer quite often calls the Straight-Parry the 'Common Straight-Parry' while differentiating it from simply the 'Common Parry.'

Note: Other authors in the 16th century, such as Angelo Viggiani, also describe the Common Parry (a *mandritto* with the point high and pommel low) while decrying its tactical deficiencies.

Concluding Taking/Parrying

Once all of the subtleties of the bind are understood, it is important to note the tactical implications of coming to the bind or of relying on the bind as a matter of necessity over choice (both in the *Vor* and the *Nach*). Whenever we come to and remain in the bind we gain certain information through Feeling, but so does the opponent, and it is possible to unwittingly give them information we want to keep from them. Before we get to a point in the fight where the blades could bind, we should have already established a position where the bind will be in our favor and of our own making.

You should also not let him touch or bind your blade, unless you want to intercept, catch, or take his blade. For whenever the blades touch and hit in the bind, you should have a sure opening, otherwise your art is false.[55] *-Meyer*

Meyer says that if they wish to bind your blade, make sure they can not, and if you wish to bind theirs, make sure we Immediately have a way to strike. This same advice is given when we use the Takings in order to parry, when declared in the verses:

Guard yourself from parrying;
if need befalls you, it will cause you trouble[56] *-Meyer quoting Liechtenauer's verses*

Meyer means that if you are forced to bind their blade to protect yourself, you have succumb to their plan out of a sense of fear and obedience.[57] This is not to say that one should not defend ones self, but that the smart fencer seeks to strike their opponent in the same Instant the opponent sought to strike them and always in a manner as to remain safe. This approach to defense is summarized when Meyer glosses the verses:

A true combatant doesn't parry, but when the opponent cuts, then he cuts too; when the opponent steps, then he steps too; when the opponent thrusts, then he thrusts too.[58] *-Meyer*

In fact, Meyer specifies later on in his text, that the 'true parrying'[59] is the *absetzen* or Setting-Off, which at its core is a thrust into their attack, designed to parry while Simultaneously (or as close to it as possible) thrusting to their body.

From whichever side he sends his cut in, catch and parry his cut, and cut or thrust in at him to the same side from which he has sent in his cut, before he has entirely finished it[60] *-Meyer*

part VI provoking

Creating Opportunities in the Onset

You must thus incite and provoke him out of his advantage, since you cannot attack without some opportunity, for you must worry that he will overreach or catch you in your own device. Therefore you must see how you can bring him out of his advantage.

We learn the bind not to seek it, but to understand how to avoid it, or at a minimum how to dominate it if it becomes a necessity. The method of controlling the bind, and the means to move through it and past it, is encompassed by the concept of Provocation.

In the Onset, with the weapons crossing at the Weaks, we should seek to form positions to pass through the Middle in the most advantageous way possible. When we are the first to commit our weapon forward, we should position our blade as it arrives in the Middle in a way that entices the opponent to move their weapon to a place where we can dominate it or move past it. We seek to deceive our opponent by acting as if we are doing one thing, when in fact we do another: to draw them out of the Center, giving us an opportunity, in both space and time, to strike.

If we see Taking as the method to remove the opponent's weapon from the Center by force, then Provoking is the method employed to remove it through coercion.

Provocation by Deception

Deceiving is when I send in my stroke at an opening, and then see that he goes against it to parry it, so that this cut becomes useless to me, so I let it run past without hitting, and quickly pull it in the same motion to the nearest opening elsewhere[61] *-Meyer*

The initial action from the Onset that brings us through the Middle can be a cut or thrust. From the Middle, a subsequent cut or thrust is made to Hit the opponent. This means that all deceptions preceded by our earnest attack can be any permutation of the transformation of cuts and thrusts:

1: Provoke with a cut, Hit with a cut
2: Provoke with a cut, Hit with a thrust
3: Provoke with a thrust, Hit with a cut
4: Provoke with a thrust, Hit with a thrust

How the opponent responds to the initial action (the Provocation), will determine with which action we Hit. Let us first start with deceptions by cut.

Provocation by Deception: Cut into a Cut

The first named cut that Meyer presents to us is the Scalp Cut (*scheidelhauw*).[62] This technique is a combination of two vertical cuts through the Center. The first is meant to Provoke the opponent to parry the deception while the second is intended to Hit them in the Instant they thought they were parrying the first.

Scalp Cut (*Scheidelhauw*)

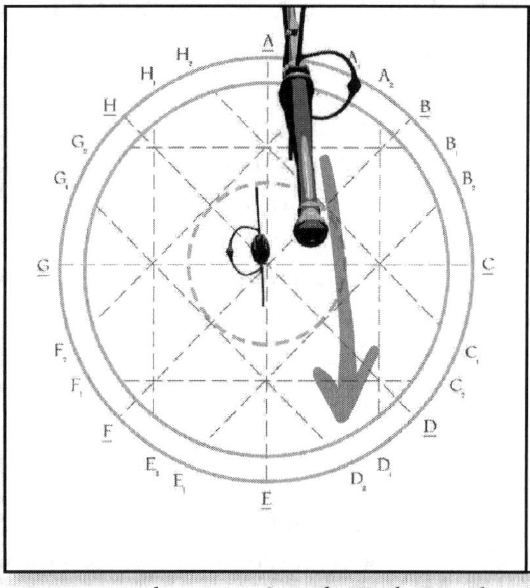

1. Preparing the cut in Straight High Guard against Straight-Parrying (or Iron Gate)

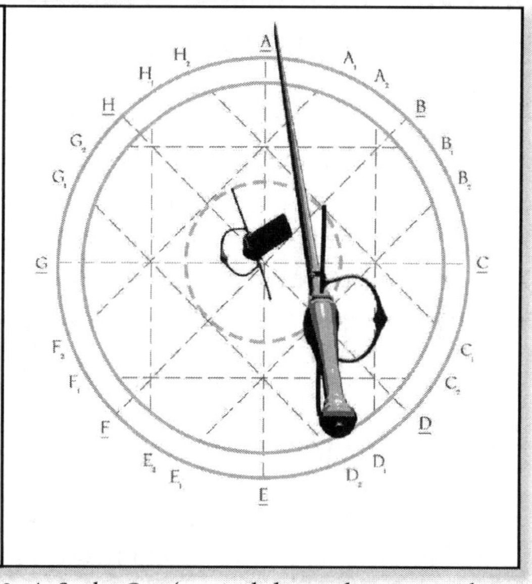

2. A Scalp Cut (vertical descending cut with the long-edge)

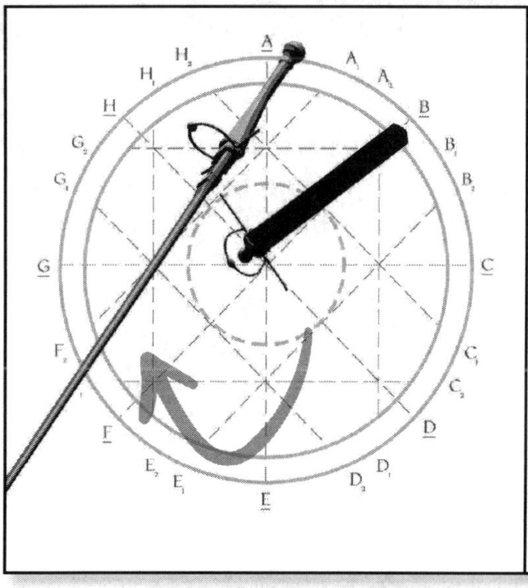

3. As the opponent moves to Overbind or else parry the Provoker, our sword is pulled away from the bind and prepares for a new cut

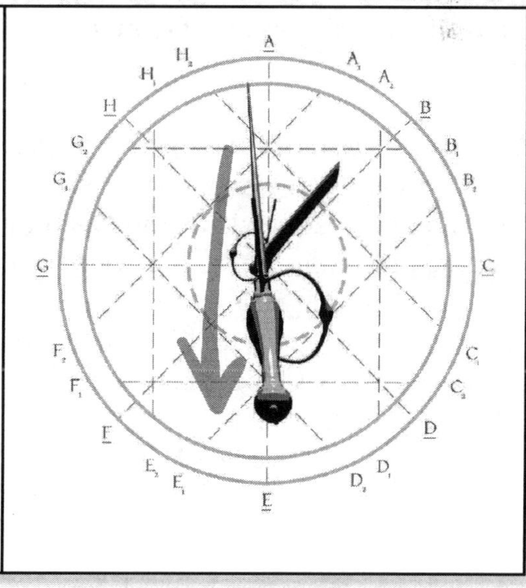

4. As the opponent moves to parry the cut to their left/inside, our cut is pulled, prepared and begins anew to the opposite side (their right/outside)

How the opponent responds to the vertical cut should be taken into careful consideration. If the opponent seeks to parry the cut by Overbinding the sword, we should Immediately start to avoid their parry by allowing the sword to drop in front of their hilt as the sword is brought around to the opposite side. Because the opponent initially resided in a guard that threatened with the point and protected the Center, the goal is to remove their sword from that position by enticing them to bring the sword slightly to our right by threatening a cut to that side. As the opponent obliges us in this action, we Immediately strike to the opposite side. Because the opponent made a motion intended to make an Overbind against our incoming cut, it prompted us to finish the sequence with another cut.

This succeeded because we did not stop our sword in the Middle, Feel the bind, and then react. We rather saw the bind as it was developing, and Immediately moved onto the next action Before our opponent was able to gather information from the impending bind. The benefit of making two vertical cuts is that the momentum of each cut is maintained through the conservation of momentum by allowing the sword to make two circles from the wrist along the vertical plane.

Hip Cut (*Hüffthauw*)

A provocation by a deceptive cut can be made in other ways besides two vertical cuts. For instance, a vertical cut made with the short-edge descending can turn into a diagonal cut. The threat the opponent will see from a descending short-edge cut is that the sword will angle over the top of their guard, forcing a stronger Overbind of our blade, allowing us to cut around their blade more easily, even if they are inclined to leave their point in the Center.

As the initial vertical cut is made with the long-edge, the short-edge is turned downward by rotating the hand clock-wise, making it a Squinting Cut. As the opponent moves to parry or make an Overbind against this action, the cut Immediately falls away from the bind to our right or outside and comes over the head to make a descending long-edge cut through the middle-diagonal cross (their right hip). This second cut could easily be made through the upper-cross (their face) but if the opponent is keeping their parries small, they might already perceive the second action coming from above and move to parry it. If this is the case, the cut will fall below their parry through the middle-cross (as shown).

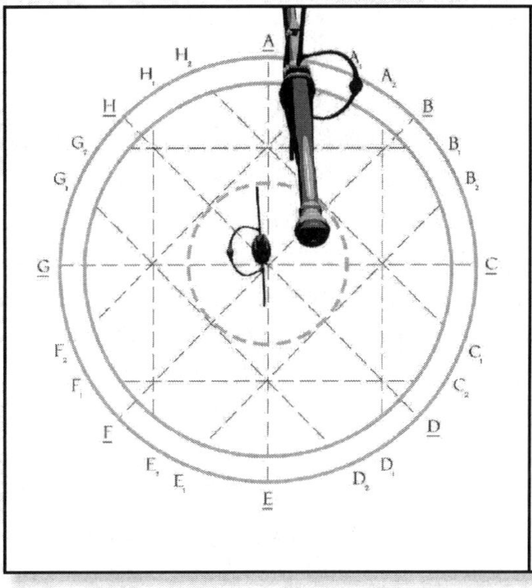

1. Same setup as the previous action

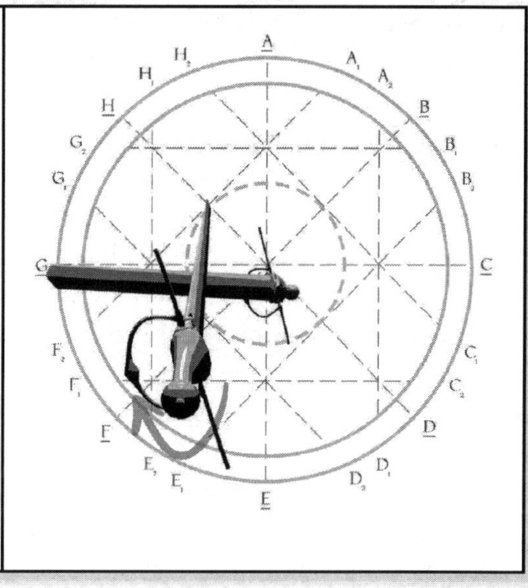

2. Here the short-edge is turned downward (clock-wise) making a Squinting Cut on the left, creating a strong opposition to the inside

3. As the opponent moves to parry, we let their sword run-off as we pull the sword up to the left to create a barrier/hanging as we prepare the second cut

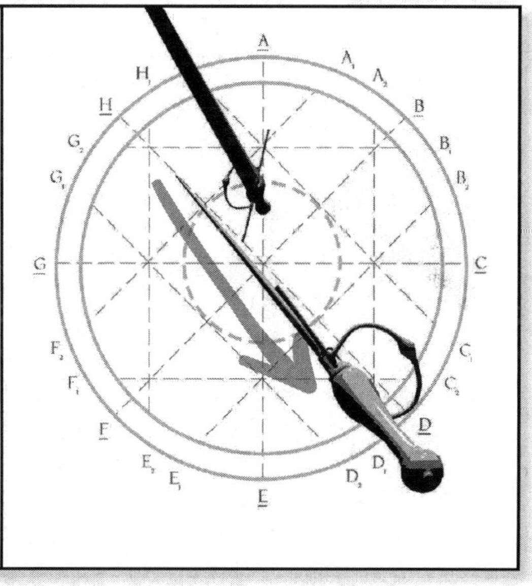

4. If the opponent moves to parry the second cut, we avoid their blade cutting through the middle-cross at their hip

Round Stroke (*Rundstreich*)

The same concept can be applied to any cut where the opponent will give a predictable response: to parry the initial cut. If the opponent is Provoked into a defensive position, i.e. a parry, then it does not matter what the initial strike is, only that it threatens an exposed target. In the first two examples a vertical cut is made (first with the long-edge then with the short) that drew a parry from the opponent. In this example, a Middle Cut to the upper target is made from left to right. When the opponent goes to defend themselves by means of a parry or Taking, then we abandon that strike and transform it into another; in this instance a cut from the right to left through the lower opening.

It is important that the opponent does not bind the Provoking action when one Provokes through a deceptive attack. If they were to do so, we would be giving the opponent a particular cue, through Feeling, that they had parried the attack and they would Immediately begin their answer to it. The goal here is to force the opponent to reach for the parry in the widest possible position to draw them further from our intended target, in this case, a Middle Cut through the leg.

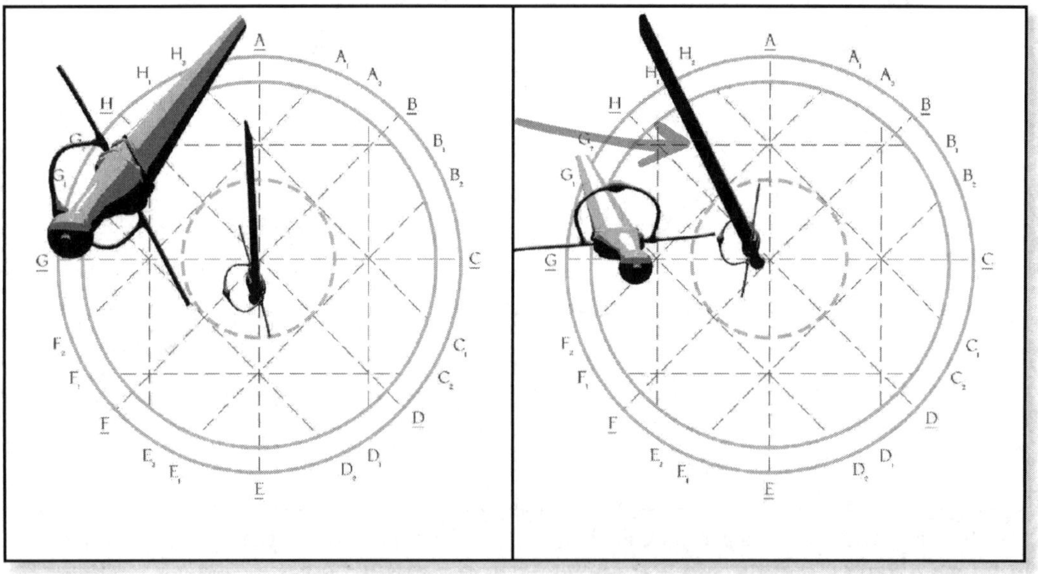

1. From Iron Gate, the sword is pulled back to Left-Ox, then the point goes back to Left-Ox for the cut to prepare the first action

2. A middle cut through the high cross to draw a parry. Before binding their blade, our sword is pulled away, going over theirs to our right

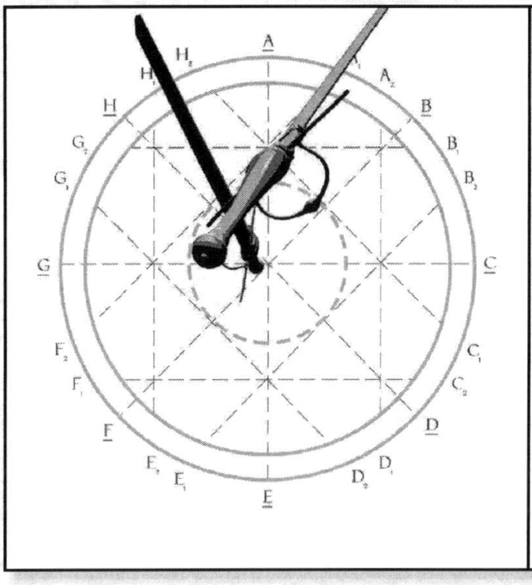

3. As the weapon is brought over to the right side...

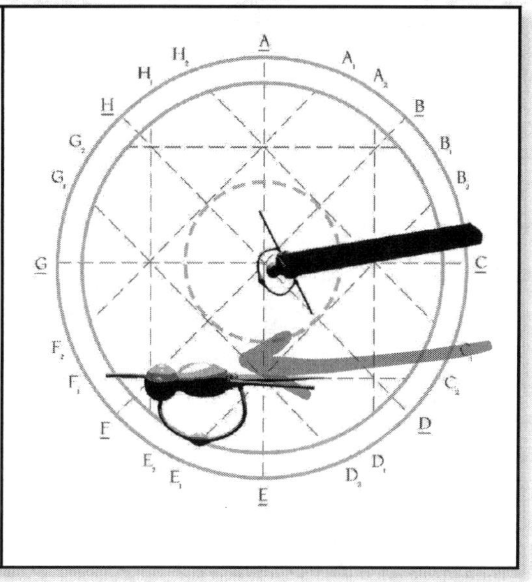

4. the point drops making the second action, a Middle Cut through the low cross (their leg)

Provocation by Deception: Cut into a Thrust

Transforming a cut into a thrust is more subtle and requires a better read of how the opponent is moving their sword just before the weapons come to a bind in the Middle. Where as the previous transformations of a cuts into cuts, all that is required is the opponent to move to parry, and just before the blades clash, we begin a new cut to the opening as it presents itself. However, if we wish to turn a cut into a thrust, the manner in which they parry will determine how we follow with our thrust. We have already looked at how to thrust from the Middle, and the rules explained there directly apply here, the only difference is that instead of beginning the action from the bind, the action starts at a further distance, in the Onset.

As we begin the Provocation by Cut, the opponent may bind weakly. Our cut (which began with the long-edge directed towards the Center) will now be given a forward momentum, continuing in with the long-edge remaining engaged in the bind. If, however, the opponent, seeing our cut, moves to make a strong bind or an Overbind in order to cover themselves, we should then turn the short-edge into the Center, pushing the sword and point forward.

Wrath Cut into a Thrust

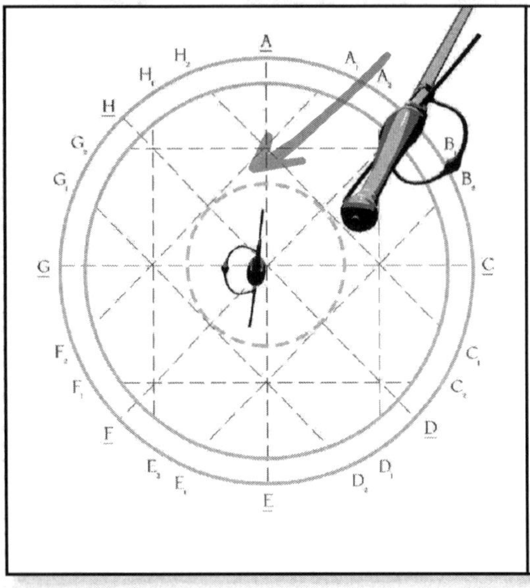

1. Preparing the initial cut into Right Ox for the Cut

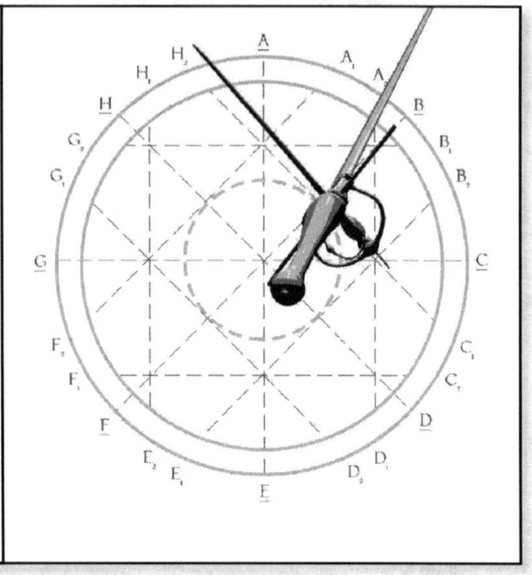

2. The opponent moves to make a 'Common Parry' simply creating a barrier with their sword

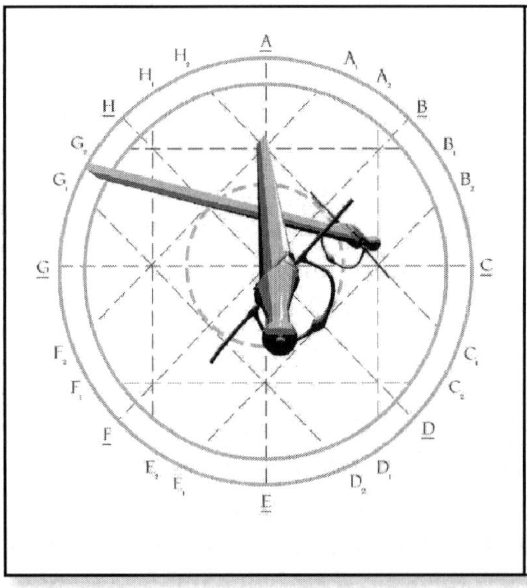

3. As our blade comes to the bind, we create an Overbind, putting the point to their face

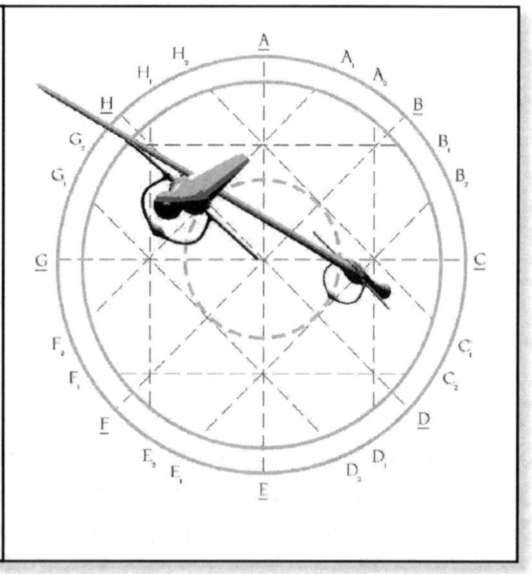

4. The thrust can finish as in the previous illustration with the long-edge down, or if they begin to resist, the sword can wind into the Left Ox

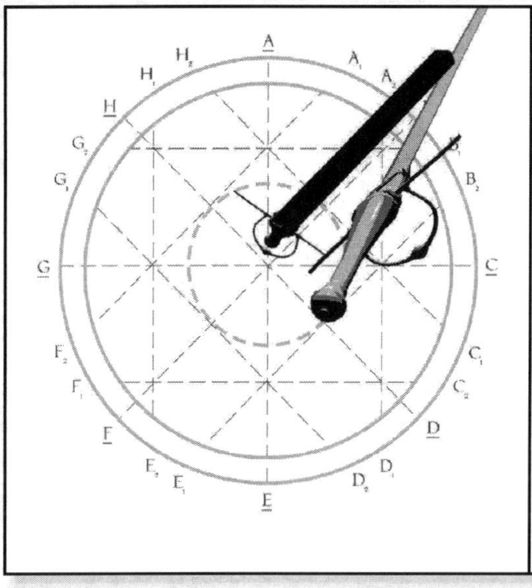

2a. From the same setup as the previous action, instead the opponent moves to Set-Off or otherwise form an Overbind

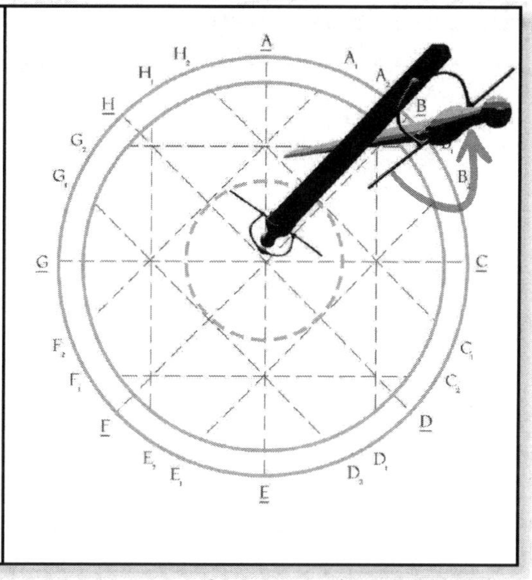

3a. As we perceive the opponent's strong bind, the short-edge is turned into the Center as we make an Outer-Winding through the Right Ox

see Appendix E, Plate G

Provocation by Deception: Thrust into a Cut

Transforming a thrust into a cut or Provoking with a thrust in order to Hit with a cut, follows the same basic principles of changing a cut into a thrust. From the Onset, a thrust is used to threaten a target, drawing a parry from the opponent. While the opponent is busy parrying what they thought was an earnest thrust, that action is pulled into a cut. The most significant cue for going from a thrust to a cut is an Overbind from the opponent as they seek the parry. If they do not Overbind as we extend the Provoking thrust, then we can usually continue the thrust in a different fashion, but not usually as a cut.

From our beginning position, whether it be an Ox for the Thrust or any low, point forward guard (Low Right Guard included), the point should threaten the opponent's exposed position. If they are in a guard on the right, the point should extend to their left, and vice-versa. If they are in a low guard, the point should extend high; low if they are in a high guard. If their sword is in the Center, in Straight-Parrying for example, our initial thrust should not only Provoke but seek to Take as well, in order to remove the threat of their point.

Hip Cut - thrust variation

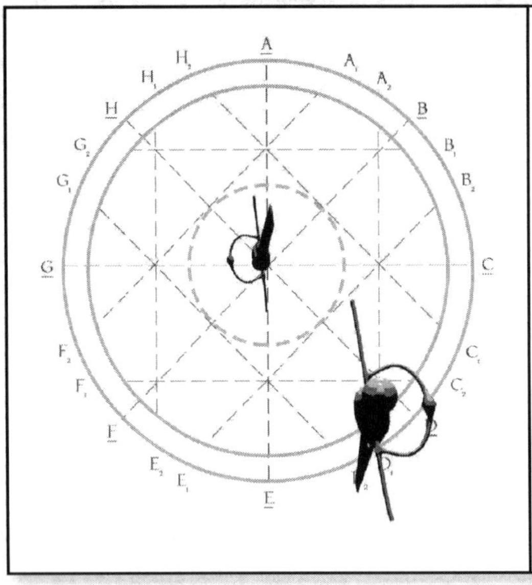

1. From Low Right, or Iron Gate

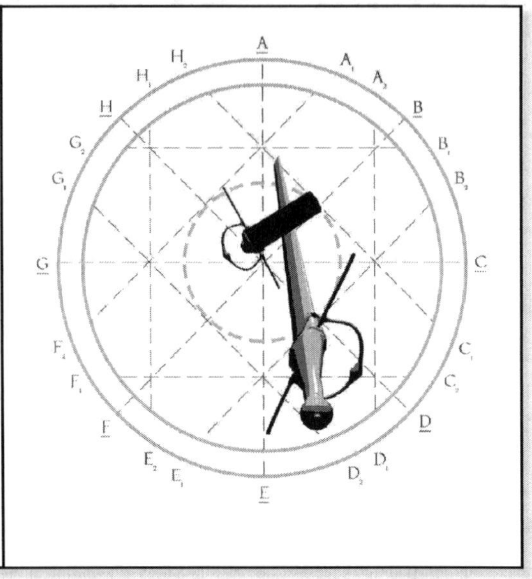

2. The point extends to the opponent's face. If the opponent is in a guard that threatens with the point, this thrust can also move to Take their blade

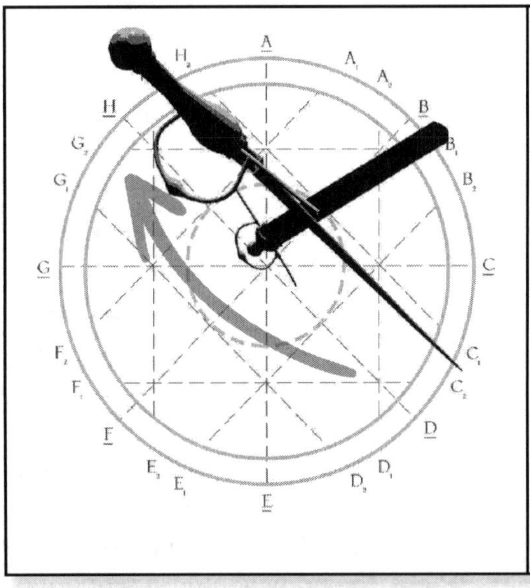

3. As the opponent moves to parry our thrust, the blade is pulled up and to the left, yielding to their strong bind

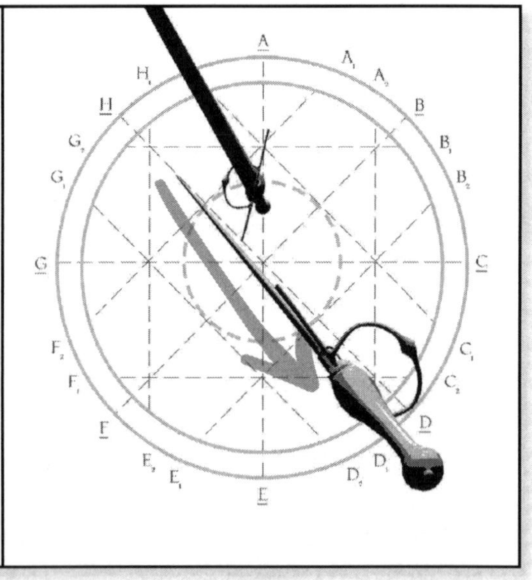

4. As our blade is pulled away from theirs, we prepare a Wrath Cut from left to right by passing through Left Ox for the Cut, cutting under their blade through the middle-cross

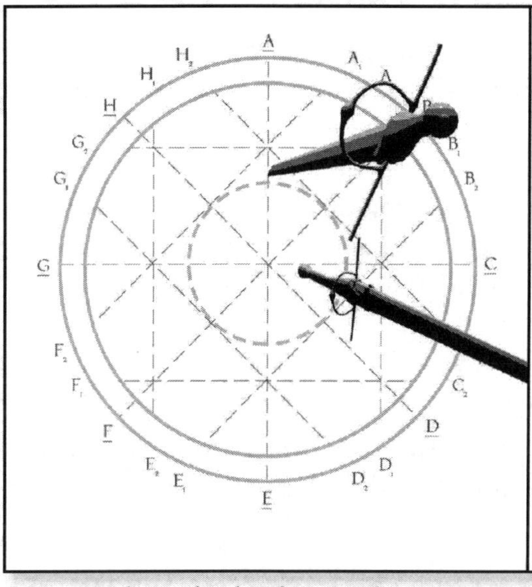

1. From Right Ox for the Thrust and opponent in Low Left/The Change

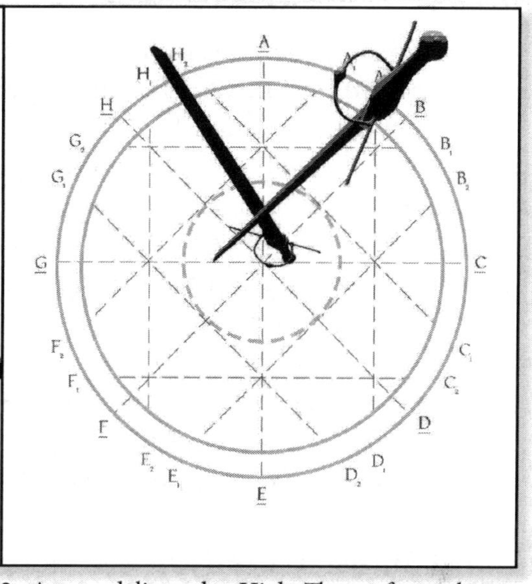

2. As we deliver the High Thrust from the right, the opponent attempts a Taking Out with the short-edge. But before they do, we drop the point to the left and...

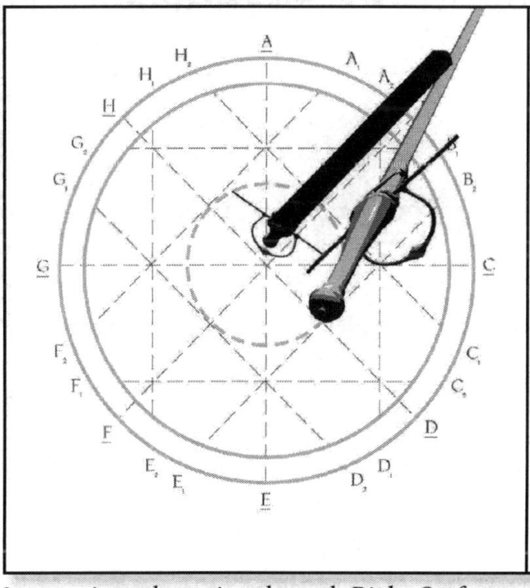

3. ...continue the action through Right Ox for the Cut.

4. As the opponent moves to parry our cut, we drop it below their hilt cutting through the middle-cross

Provocation by Deception: Thrust into a Thrust

There are several methods in changing one thrust into another. First, is to begin our initial action as a thrust, and as the opponent moves to parry it, Change-Through to the other side and finish the thrust there. The second way is by Snapping, where a high thrust through Ox turns in the air and finishes in the opposite Ox. The third and last way is by turning the short-edge into the opponent's blade in response to pressure, which I will refer to as Mutating (to keep in line with earlier German sources). Against an Overbind this action is an 'Outer Winding' and against an Underbind it is the classic Mutating.

The ability to Instantly turn one thrust into another in response to how the opponent reacts to the initial threat is crucial in understanding a point oriented weapon, and Meyer gives us many examples of how this should be done.

Throat Thrust (*Gurgelstich*)

The first method can be explained through an action Meyer calls the Throat Thrust. A thrust is made wide to the opponent's blade to draw their sword away from the location we plan to Hit. As they move to parry, we Instantly Change-Through, Hitting them on the opposite side.

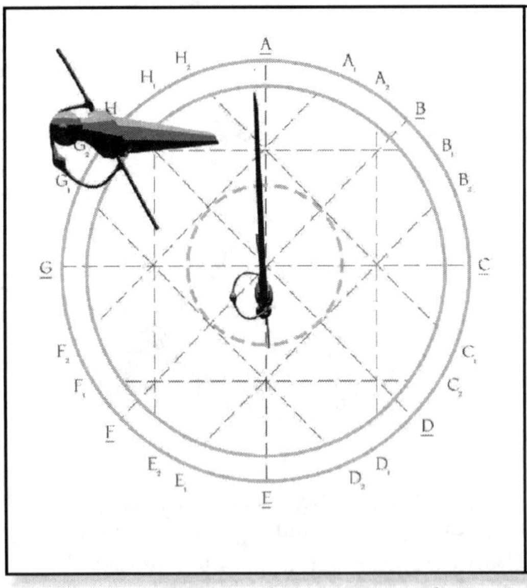

1. With the opponent in Iron Gate, we thrust through Left-Ox

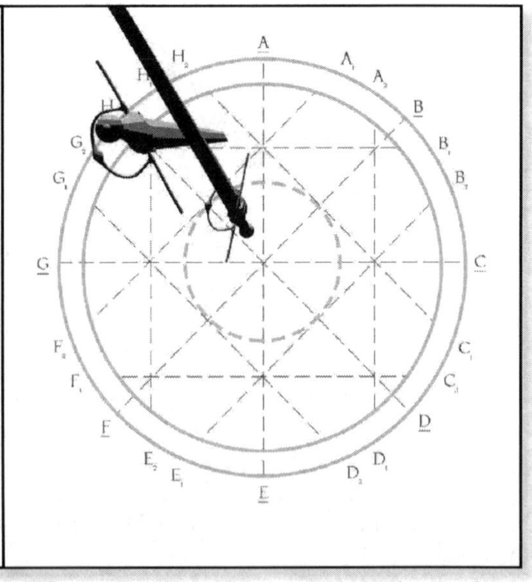

2. The opponent moves to parry the High Thrust on the left

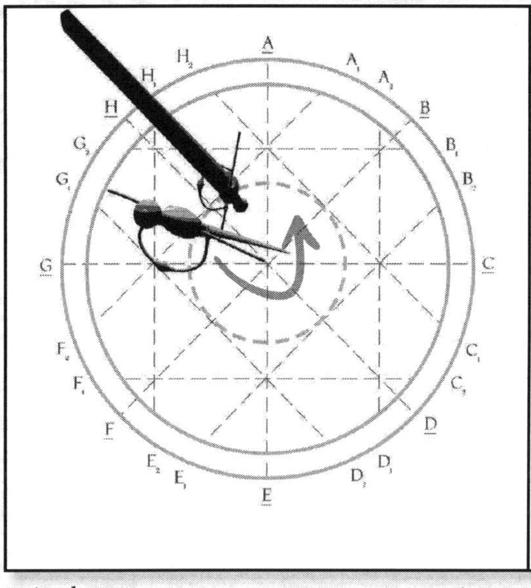

3. As the opponent moves to parry, our point drops under their hilt and moves to strike on the opposite side

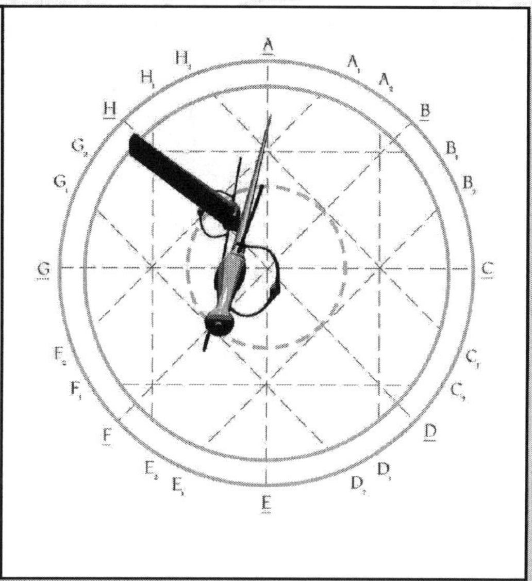

4. Meyer has us turn the long-edge down, extending into Longpoint. Alternatively, the long-edge can stay to the left creating opposition to the inside

Double Thrust -Snapping option (*Doppelstich*)

The second method, Snapping, involves an intermediate cutting action with the flat of the blade. This action is something we have already looked at in the chapter on Taking as a means to respond to pressure by going over their blade, but it is worth mentioning here again as a way to turn one thrust into another. Snapping goes from one Ox to another by turning the wrist, leaving the long-edge up. To the inside, with the blades bound to the left, the sword should travel from Left Ox into Right Ox on the outside. Conversely, with the blades bound to the outside (to the right), the sword should go from Right Ox to Left Ox, finishing on the inside.

In the previous example of the Throat Thrust, because there was a potential outside bind in Left Ox, the sword must necessarily Change-Through because Snapping is impossible from this position due to the wrist not being able to rotate away from the bind. Conversely, the same is true with an inside bind in the Right Ox.

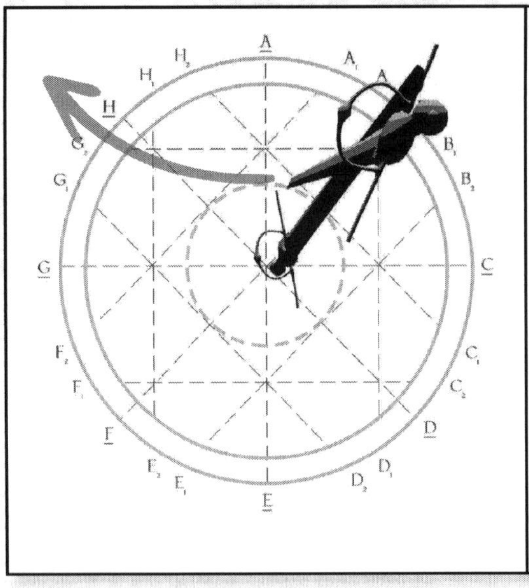

1. A thrust through the Right Ox is made over and outside their blade

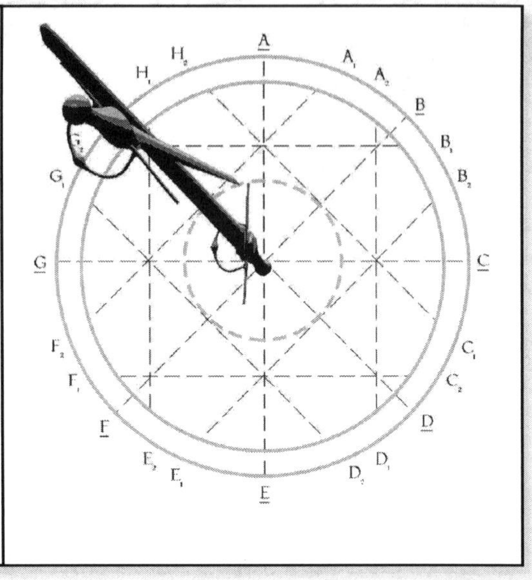

2. Responding to pressure to divert our thrust, the sword travels over our head into the Left Ox where our second thrust is made

Outer Winding and Mutating

Where the first two options in turning one thrust into another involved changing sides (first, by going under; second, by going over or around), the Outer Winding and Mutating are options for Remaining in the bind when turning one thrust into another.

The Outer Winding is an action performed when the opponent moves to create an Overbind as the first thrust is being delivered. Through Feeling the pressure given by the opponent's Overbind, we act weakly against it by winding the short-edge against their blade, staying on the same side as our original thrust while keeping the point directed at its original target.

Mutating can be considered the converse action to the Outer Winding. As we begin to deliver our initial thrust to Overbind against our opponent's weapon, the opponent Immediately releases the pressure in the bind while hanging their blade, attempting to have our weapon run-off theirs. Against this action, we should lower our point so as to Remain on their blade, thrusting to a lower target. Though we need not turn or wind the blade in this action, we end up with the our short-edge Remaining against their long-edge due to the nature of the opponent Hanging against our blade.

Outer Winding (*auswinden*)

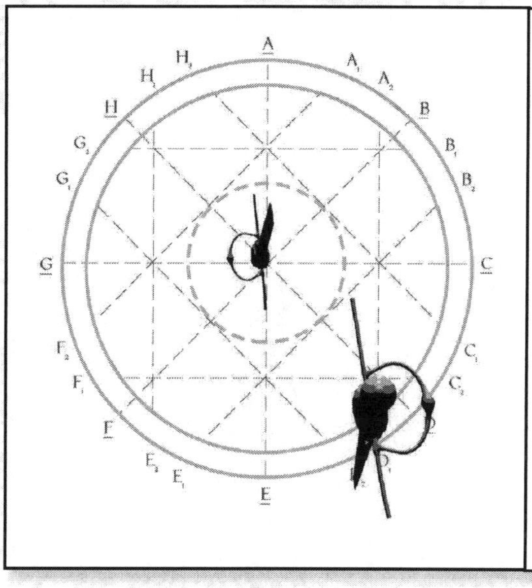

1. From Low Right, or Iron Gate

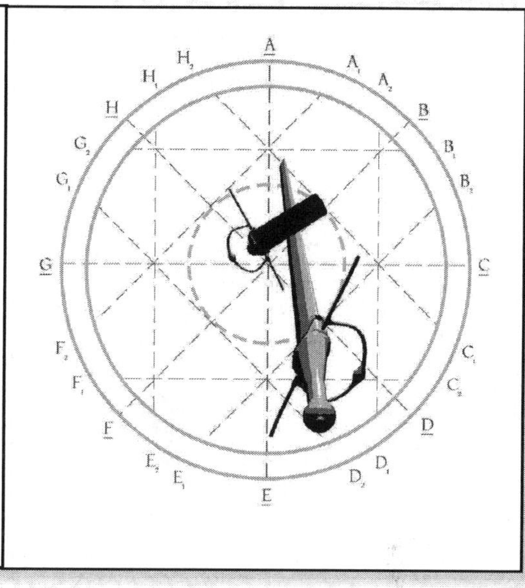

2. As the thrust extends to its target, the opponent moves to parry the thrust by Overbinding it

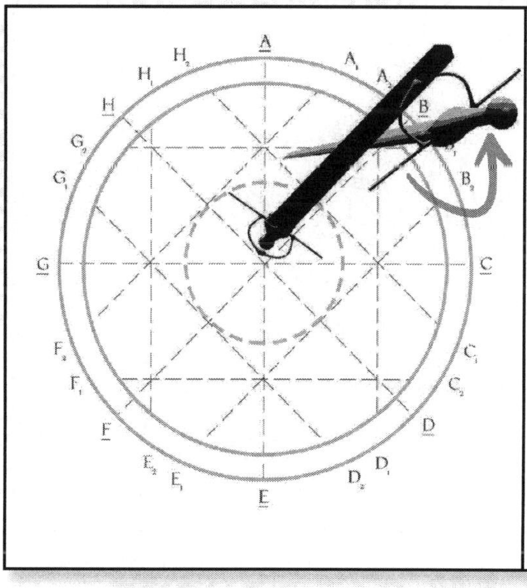

3a. As we perceive the opponent's strong bind, the short-edge is turned into the Center as we make an outer-winding through the Right Ox

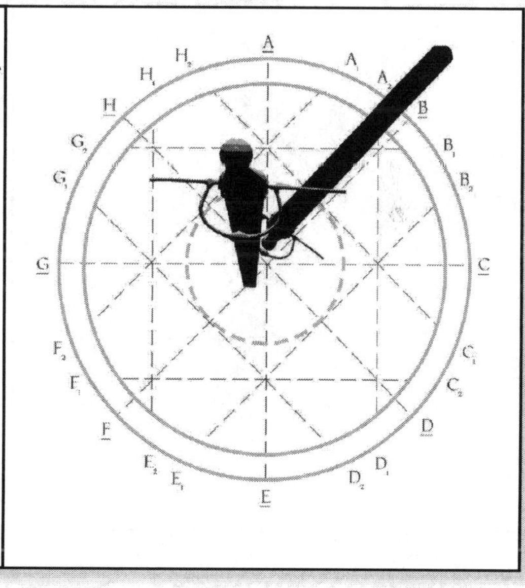

3b. Alternatively, from figure 2. we can drop the point low, raising the hand, leaving the palm up through Left Plow, thrusting outside and under the opponent's parry (a form of *mutieren*)

Mutating (*mutieren*)

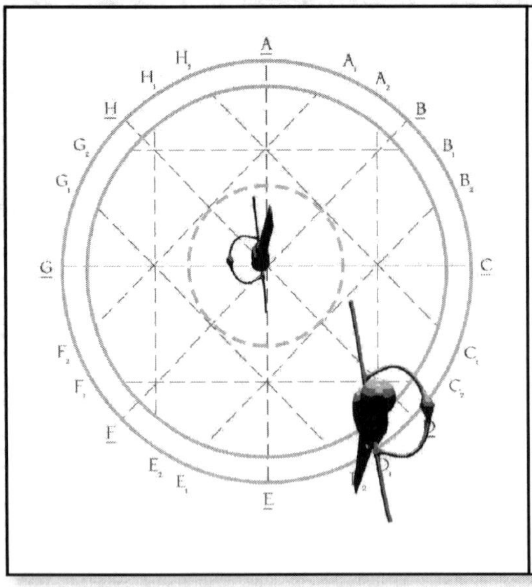

1. From Low Right, or Iron Gate

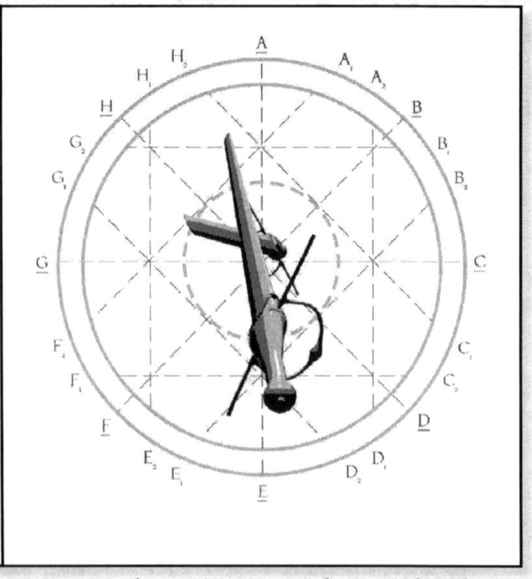

2. As we thrust in, we seek to Take the opponent's blade by making an Overbind against it

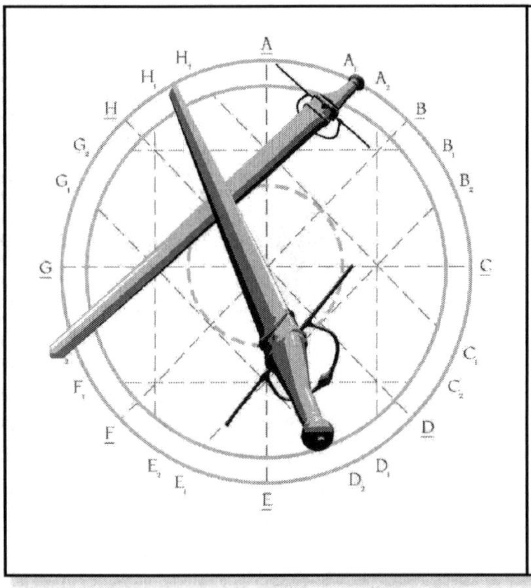

3. As the opponent perceives our Overbind, they seek to displace our thrust from below by hanging their blade

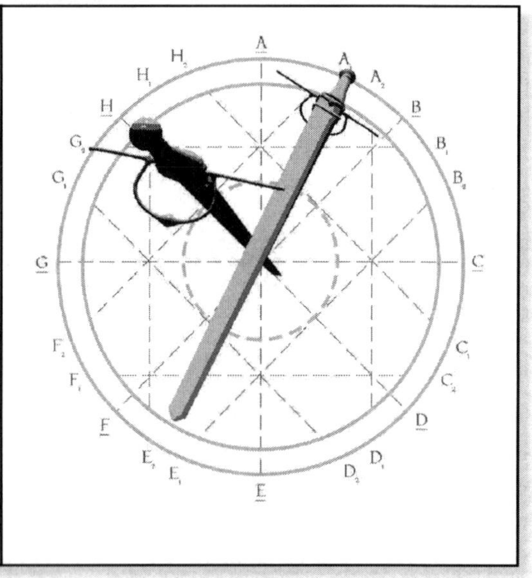

4. As the opponent attempts to slip our blade by letting it run-off, we remain strong on their blade with the short-edge by raising the hand and dropping the point low

Provocation by Invitation

Changing-Off and False Attacks

While Provocations by Deception, or feints, are designed to draw a parry to one side or quadrant so that we are more able to strike to another, Provocations by Invitation are designed to entice the opponent to attack into a specific target we have pre-planned to defend and Immediately counter.

Meyer describes two methods when making an invitation. The first of these invitations draws an attack in the first stage of the fight, the Onset, referred to as Changing-Off. The second invitation provokes an attack in the Middle, called False Attacks or Falsing.

Changing-Off is the act of cutting from one of the four quadrants to the next until the opponent takes the opportunity to strike. For instance, starting in the Right Ox for the Thrust, Meyer Changes-Off into the Low Left. From there, he raises the guard into the Left Ox for the Thrust, and then cuts back down into Low Right. These four postures are used to Change-Off in order to invite an attack because a single Taking can be used to displace any attack the opponent wishes to make from each of these positions. For instance, if we stand in the Right Ox and the opponent decides to attack us, any attack they wish to make will be to the left and below our sword, whether they cut from above or below or deliver a thrust. Because of this, we can use a single, pre-planned action to displace their attack and counter with one of our own.

The fact that our defense, or action in the *Nach*, has been predetermined, independent of their action gives us the advantage and thus is categorized as a Provocation. If we come to a posture where the opponent has multiple avenues to strike, or we are unsure of our defensive action, then we have not gained the advantage and will struggle to alleviate ourselves of the *Nach*, failing to regain the *Vor* and Hit safely.

What is true of Changing-Off into the Right Ox is also true with the other three postures. From Low Left, all attacks the opponent makes will be to the right and above our sword. From Left Ox, all attacks will be to the right and below, and from Low Right, their only avenue is to the left and above our sword. From any of these four postures, any parry already discussed in the previous chapter can be employed to defeat their attack and Immediately respond; however, *Absetzen* is always preferable.

The one bit of important advice Meyer makes when Changing-Off is to make the cuts go through the Center near their hilt or hand.[63] If they decide to attack in the Instant our sword passes though the Center, their hand will be in danger and will likewise be slower in their attack, delaying it until we have arrived in posture, more ready to Take their sword as it extends for the Hit.

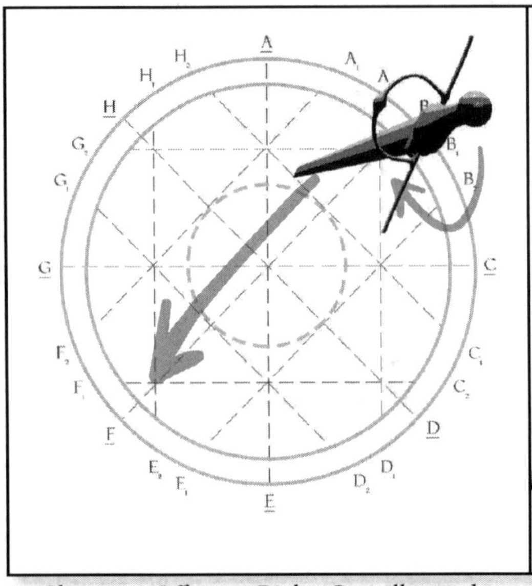

1. Changing-Off into Right Ox, all attacks received will be under and to the left of our sword

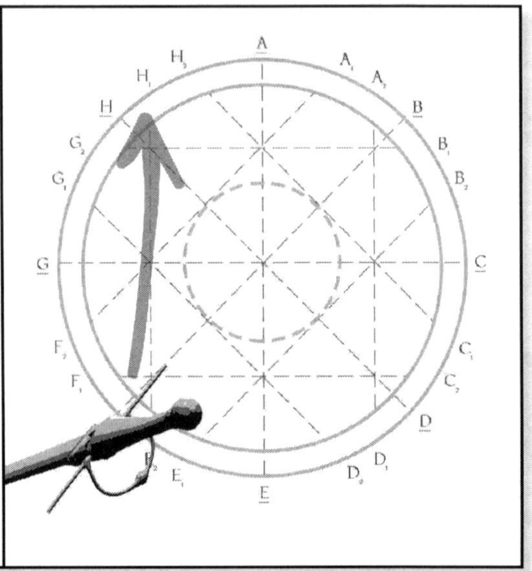

2. Changing-Off into Low Left, all attacks received will be above and to right of our sword

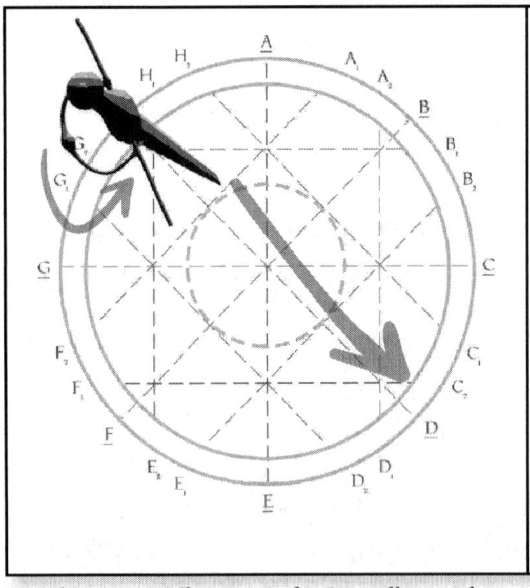

3. Changing-Off into Left Ox, all attacks received will be under and to the right of our sword

4. Changing-Off into Low Right, all attacks received will be above and to left of our sword

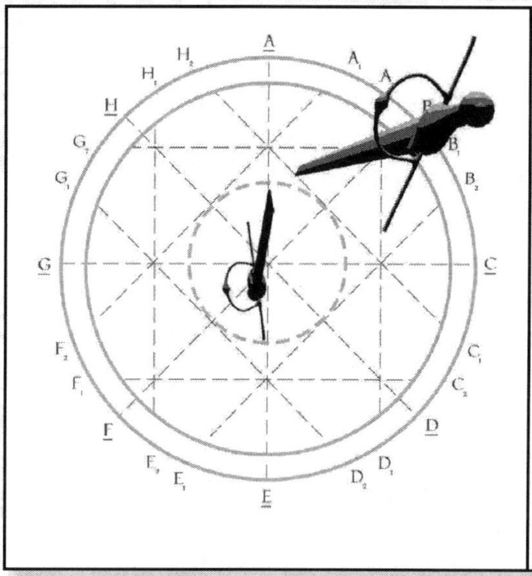

1. Our weapon is in Right Ox for the Thrust while the opponent is in Straight-Parrying or Iron Gate

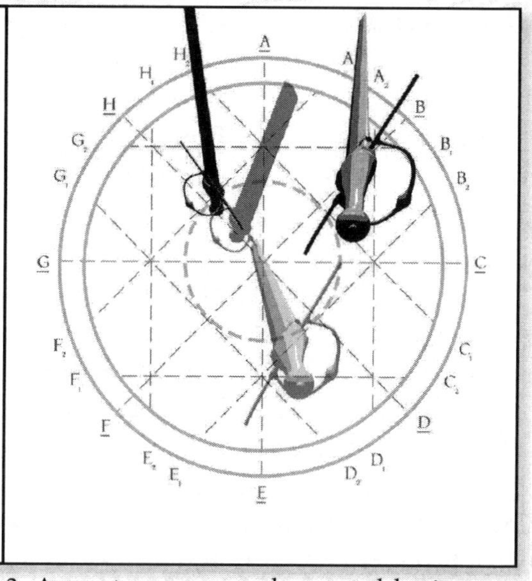

2. As we turn our sword over and begin to Change-Off into Low Left (The Change), the opponent uses this opportunity to cut. Because our action to get to Low Left was a cut through the Center, the opponent's hand is struck

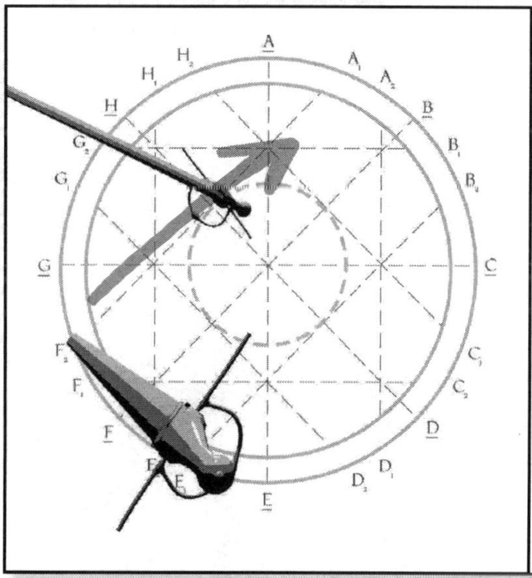

3. If the opponent did not choose to attack in the Instant we cut into Low Left, but rather attacks After we have come to rest in the guard...

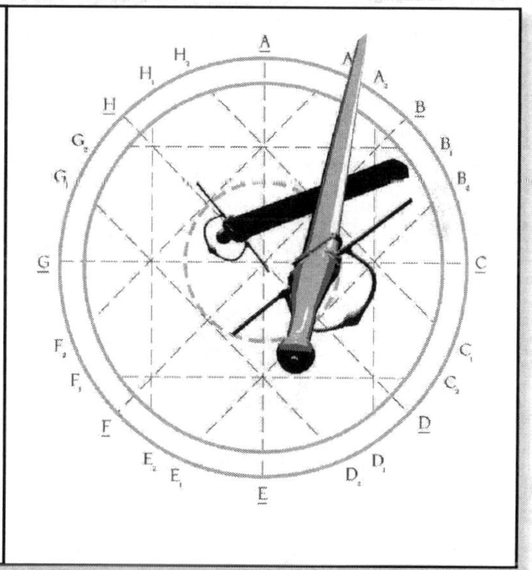

4. then we should use the most convenient Taker/Parry for the guard we find ourselves in (in this case, a Taking-Out with the short-edge)

False Attacks

Where Changing-Off invites an attack in the Onset, using the benefit of distance and space of the bodies, Provocation by Falsing is more aggressive, designed to look as if our action was intended to Hit, but rather settles into a defensive posture, ready to deal with the opponent's counter-attack.

If the opponent hesitates in their attempt to attack in the Onset after we have Changed-Off into several different postures, they might be more inclined to strike if they see an opening being created after a credible attack has been made. The idea here is the same as the Changing-Off but is executed at a later stage in the fight and at a closer distance as to seem more enticing. Because of this, Provocation by Falsing should always occur in either the Low Right[64] or the Low Left,[65] two very defensive postures. Just like the previous Provocation, it is important to prevent the opponent from striking us in the Instant we are moving through the Middle and Center. With Changing-Off this was done by striking towards the opponent's hand; in Falsing (though we do not intend to Hit), if they decide to move forward for a strike as we 'miss,' our weapon should still extend towards a target, actually making contact.

After we have missed and have pulled our weapon into one of the low postures, we should be ready to Immediately Take/Parry and counter with our own Hitter.

The fencer on the left prepares an cut against an opponent in Straight-Parrying

The fencer on the left cuts towards the leg, not quite ending in Low Left, expecting the fencer on the right to strike to a target above their arm

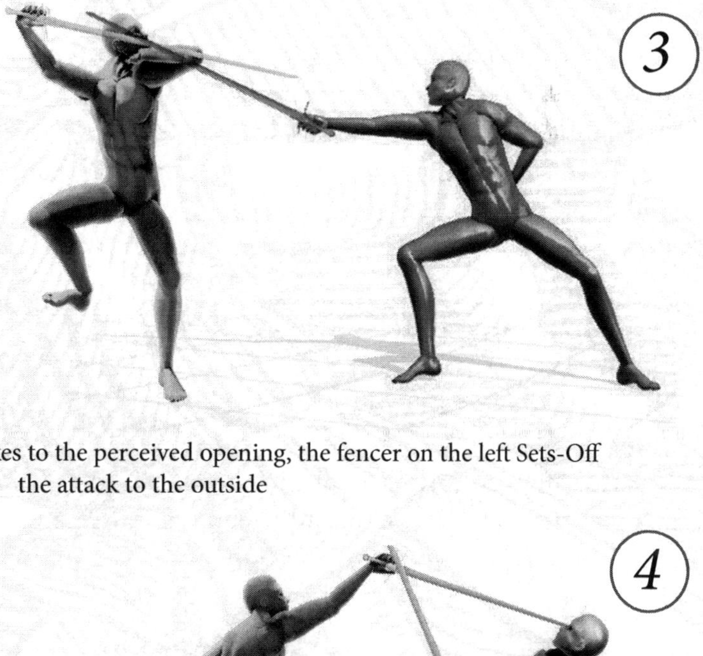

As the fencer on the right strikes to the perceived opening, the fencer on the left Sets-Off the attack to the outside

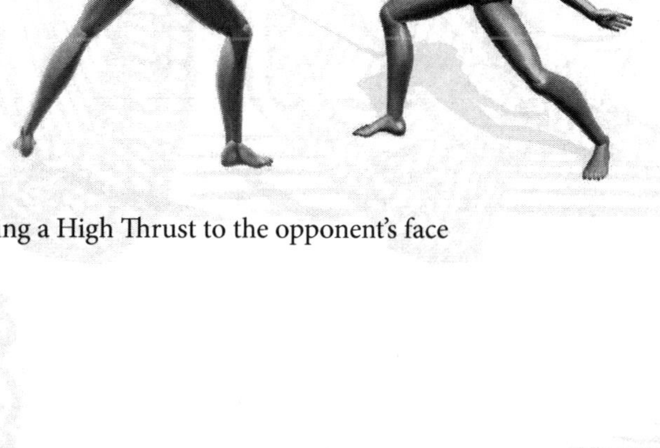

...and finishes the fight by making a High Thrust to the opponent's face

Provoking 'Gleich'

Simultaneous Hitting

Likewise there is another consideration in the countercutting, and another advantage with the cuts that take place at the same time, so that the combatants do not both hit one another, as often happens.[66] *-Meyer*

It occasionally occurs during fencing that both fencers attempt to take the same opportunity or time to strike one another. Often the one who has the better position will Hit safely without being struck themselves, while sometimes they succeed only through luck. However, it is not good enough to rely on luck. To properly strike the opponent in the same Instant they are attempting to strike us, we must know when and how they intend to accomplish their action.[67]

Provoking *gleich* properly requires us to Provoke the opponent to strike towards an opening we have created intentionally, in a longer time than the counter we have pre-planned. When they choose this opportunity to Hit, we will not just parry it (if at all), we will Hit them in return, remembering that a smart fencer attacks as they attack and steps as they step.

Face Thrust (*Gesichtstich*)

The Face Thrust is an early example illustrating the concept of *gleich*. To set up this action, we begin by Changing-Off into Left Ox for the Thrust. Here our opponent uses this opportunity to commit to a thrust into the perceived opening. As their attack is delivered, we avoid it by stepping off-line in the same Instant returning a thrust of our own. We Hit the opponent the very moment they would have Hit us.

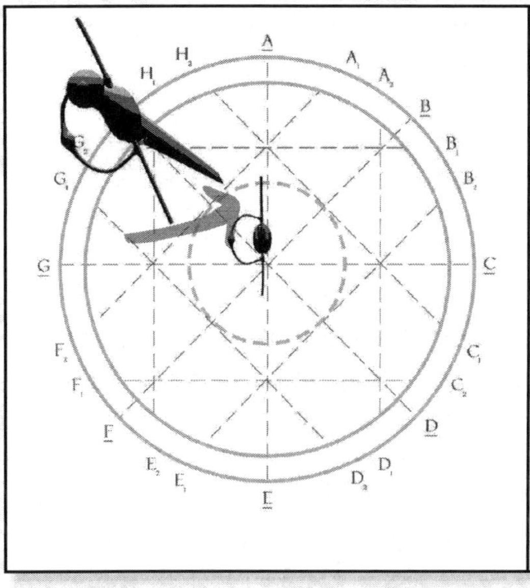

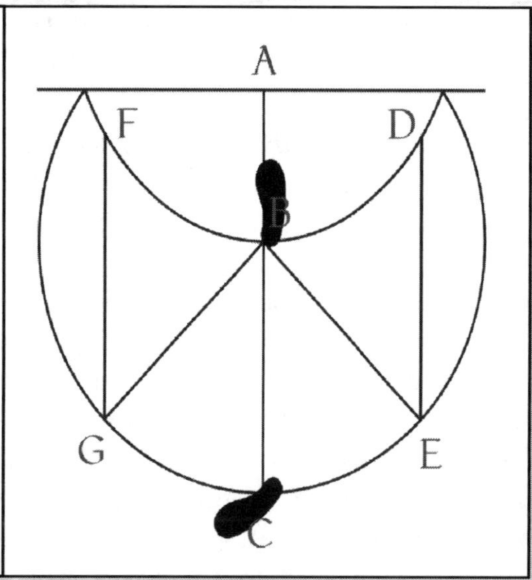

1. Changing-Off into Left Ox, the opponent uses this opportunity to begin their thrust straight in (note: we do not see their sword because it is directed straight ahead)

From the basic stance with the right foot on B and left foot on C

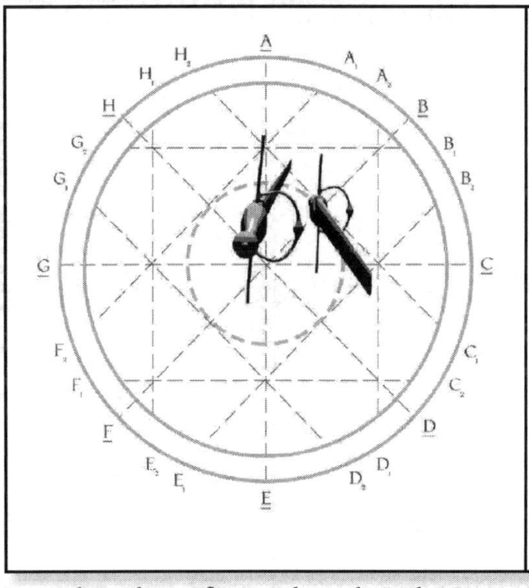

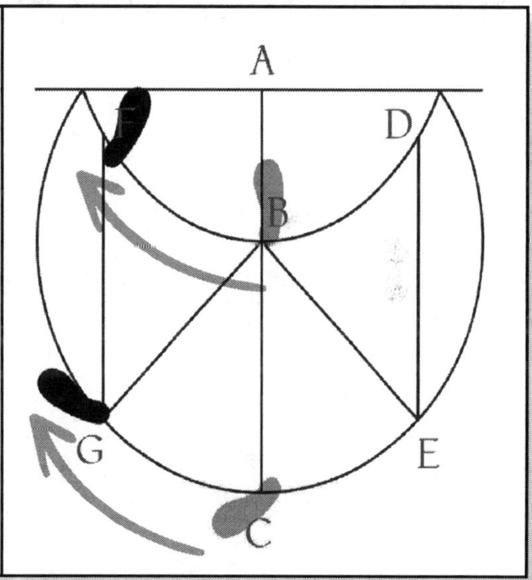

2. As their thrust flies in through Right Ox, we deliver a thrust of our own outside their arm. Note: it would seem their sword has deviated from the Center without any action of our blade, but rather this is due to the circle following our center of mass as we step to the left

As they thrust and we do the same, we make a 'double triangle step' to the left. Either foot can step to the left first, followed by the other

see Appendix E, Plate A

Chasing into a Provocation

Gleich Continued

In all combat you should take heed of the opponent's limbs, for whenever he gathers them you have an opportunity for chasing. Also, in chasing you should change around his hilt, and learn to step correctly for everything.[68] *-Meyer*

Whenever an opponent seeks to strike while preparing their action, whether it be by 'gathering' their sword for a cut or 'gathering' their foot for the step, they are momentarily preoccupied with their current action and thus vulnerable. This is a good opportunity to begin our attack. It is of little importance if they are gathering their sword to Provoke us or seeking to Hit us; as long as their sword goes wide, ours should stay narrow. The most narrow of the guards is the one that resides in the middle of the body, not high or low, nor to the left or right: the Straight-Parrying.

Meyer's true intent for the Straight-Parrying, as a guard, is to threaten the opponent with the point, turning the long-edge into the direction of their sword no matter where it might travel or what its intention might be. For as soon as the opponent makes an action with their blade, ours will shoot straight in, 'planting' the point on them.

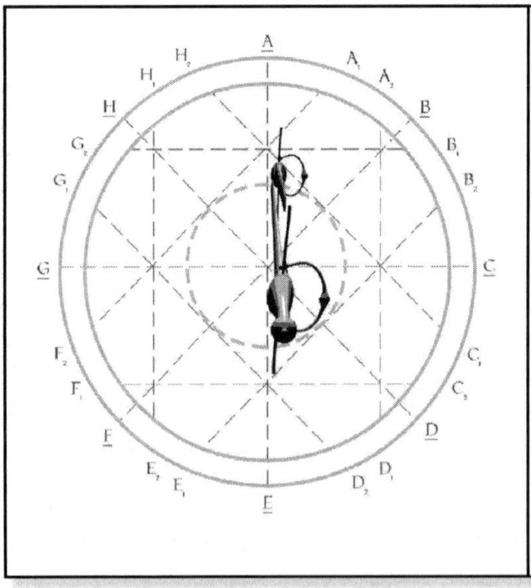

1. In the Onset, both fencers rest in Straight Parrying

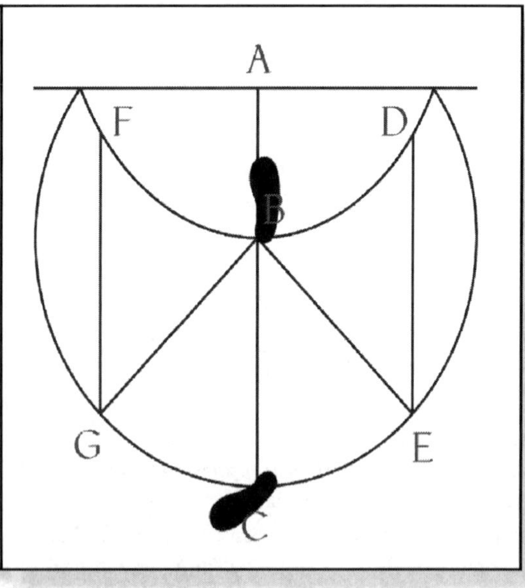

From the basic stance with the right foot on B and left foot on C

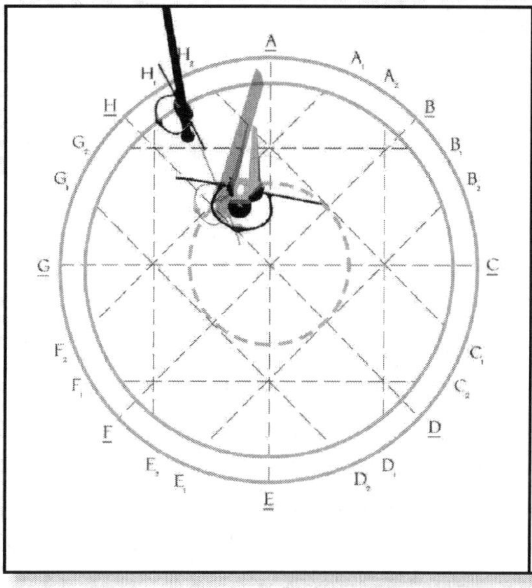

2. As the opponent gathers/prepares their sword for a cut, we Immediately send the point at their face, turning the long-edge toward theirs

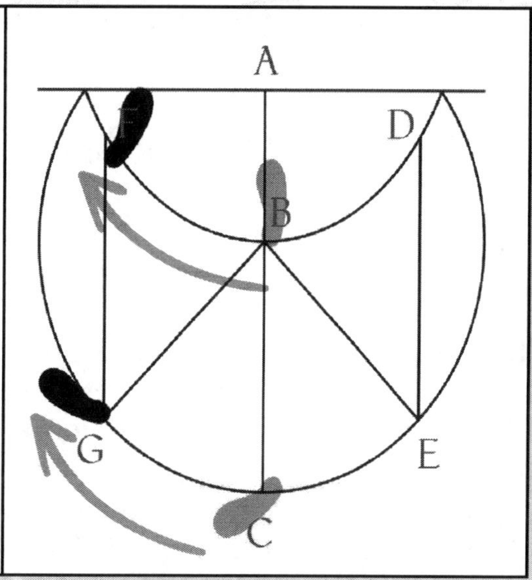

As they gather their sword, we make a 'double-triangle step' to the left. If performed from the Onset, the left foot moves first, followed by the right. If performed from the Middle, the right foot steps first followed by the left

In the example above, the opponent prepares their cut into their high-right quadrant — our sword Immediately follows theirs as if they were tied together. In the same Instant the opponent's sword is gathered back, ours shoots in to their face, all the while the long-edge turns up against it.

As our sword shoots in, we should step to the same side they have gathered their sword. Operating this way constrains the space between the weapons, disallowing them room for further action. The further to their right they gather their sword, the further to our left we should step. If the opponent is able to complete their preparation/gather before our point makes it to its target, and is now descending, their blade will find the long-edge of our hilt, which is high enough to keep their point out of the Center.

Again, in the same Instant they sought to Hit us, we have Hit them, all the while remaining safe. We can defend ourselves from our opponent's attack while Simultaneously Hitting them in two manners: first, by moving out of the way of their attack (voiding) as seen with the Face Thrust; second, by using the sword to parry and strike in a single action with Setting-Off.

STEPPING WITH PROVOCATIONS

Much depends on stepping, therefore see that you give every stroke its step. For when you cut at his opening and do not step with the foot from the side from which you have cut, then the cut is useless. But when you are not really cutting but only threatening to do it, then you should also not really step, but only act as if you were stepping. However, practice will teach you this better.[69] *-Meyer*

There is much buried in this quote from Meyer's longsword section, and it perfectly sums up how one should step when attempting to Hit and when Provoking. What Meyer is saying is that if you wish to Hit the opponent from the Onset, it is necessary for the foot to bring the body forward and close enough to apply the sword to the target. However, if the action of the sword is merely a feint (a Provocation by Deception) where the fencer is not intending to Hit, then the foot should not bring the fencer so close to the opponent.

When you threaten to strike to a place, you can very readily deceive an opponent. To do this, you must as it were take the ground away from him in laying on, and in the [Onset], act as if you were going to take a small and tight step; then before he knows it, step broadly to the attack. Contrarily, first act as if you intend to step broadly; when your opponent perceives this, and hastily tries to meet you in earnest to get there before you, restrain your step, and do it moderately, so that he wears himself out for nothing. Meanwhile look for your advantage, and as soon as you see it, you should be rapidly back upon him with broad stepping.[70] *-Meyer*

We can surmise that the length of the step should be proportional to the commitment of the weapon. If we pull the attack short in order to Provoke, then the foot should also step short. If instead, we wish to Hit the opponent, extending it into Longpoint, then our step should be in accordance and also make its maximum extension.

With two feet to consider in all steppings, we can apply certain functions to each in order to apply the above advice.

Provoking on the Rear Foot

Provoking with the Preparation

In Part IV, we looked at the preparatory actions of the sword and rear foot that bring the fencer into the Middle. If all actions of the sword fall into one of the three categories of Provoker, Take and Hitter, the preparations should be seen as belonging in the first category, the Provoker. The act of preparing an attack is a cue to the opponent that a certain type of attack will follow. This information that we are intentionally feeding the opponent can be exploited.

Though it might be impossible to Hit the opponent with this form of Provocation in its beginning stages, the goal here is to draw the opponent's weapon into a position where we can Take it more easily to one side or the other, or to draw the sword wide so that we may more easily extend an attack to the target without interference.

The 'Provocation by Preparation' can begin as a cut or thrust paired with a step on the rear foot. But, the more the preparation brings the sword wide, the smaller the step should be. The step should be proportional to the threat of the weapon. In other words, as the body is brought forward on the rear foot, the sword should seek to occupy the space between us and the opponent while simultaneously creating a threat.

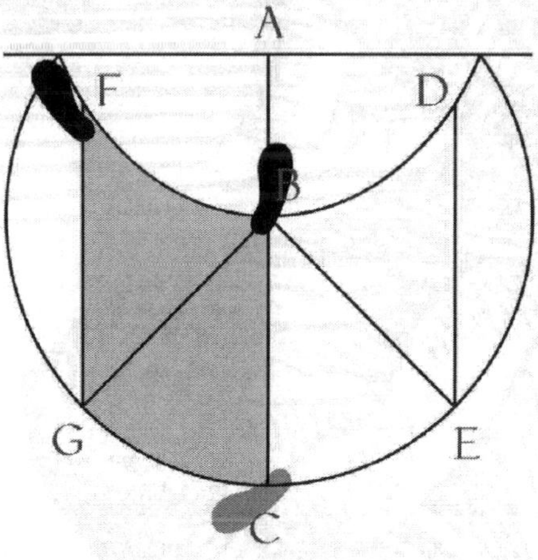

The left foot can step anywhere within the shaded triangles to the left to bring the body and sword further to the left while also preparing the right foot to extend for the Hit

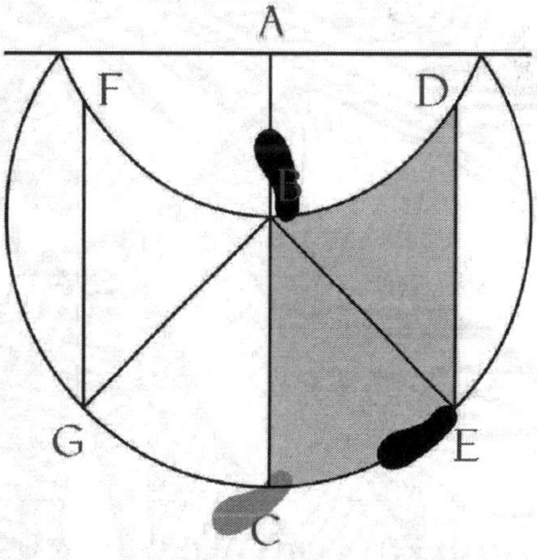

The left foot can step anywhere within the shaded triangles to the right to bring the body and sword further to the right while also preparing the right foot to extend for the Hit

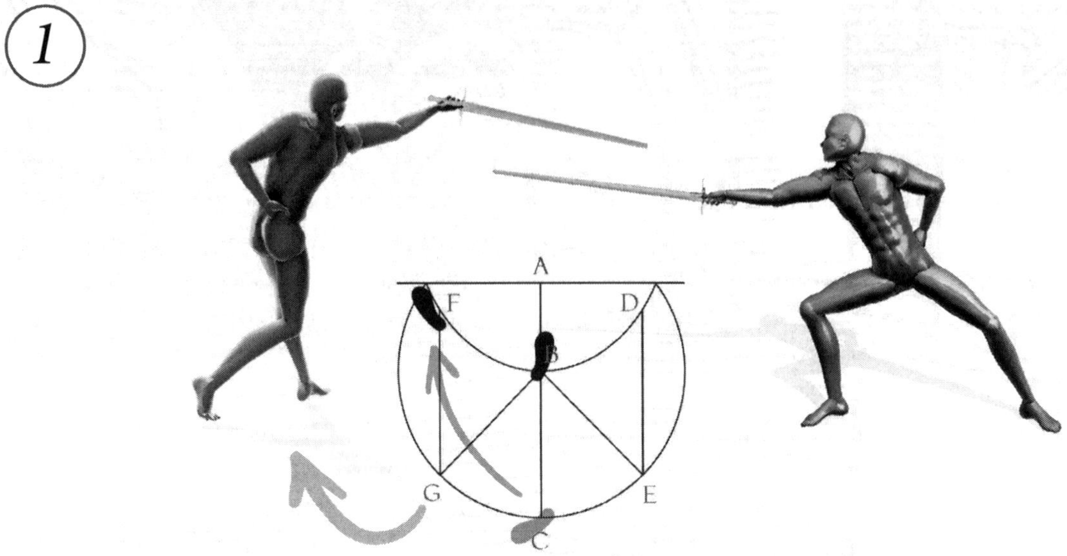

From an initial guard of Straight-Parrying, Iron Gate or Right-Ox for the Thrust, the fencer on the left Provokes with a High Thrust from the left while the left foot steps to F.

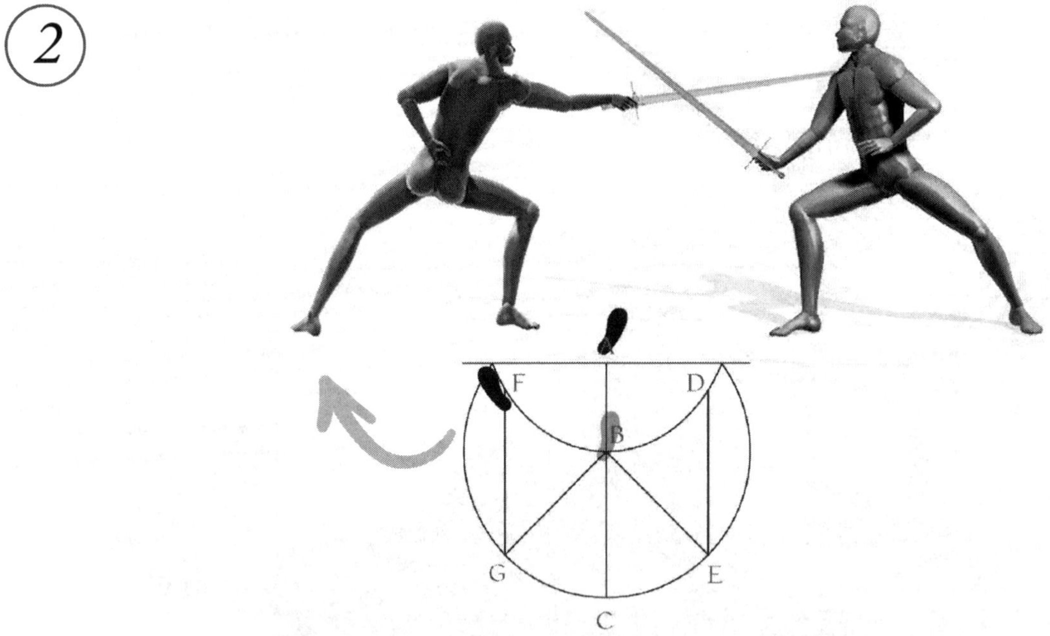

From Left Ox for the Thrust, with the short-edge directed towards the Center, the fencer on the left makes a Crooked Cut into the opponent's weapon, then winds the long-edge against it, delivering a thrust. As the Hit happens, the right foot can step at any point along the horizontal line of A (or beyond) to facilitate the body in bringing the weapon to whichever side the target will be struck.

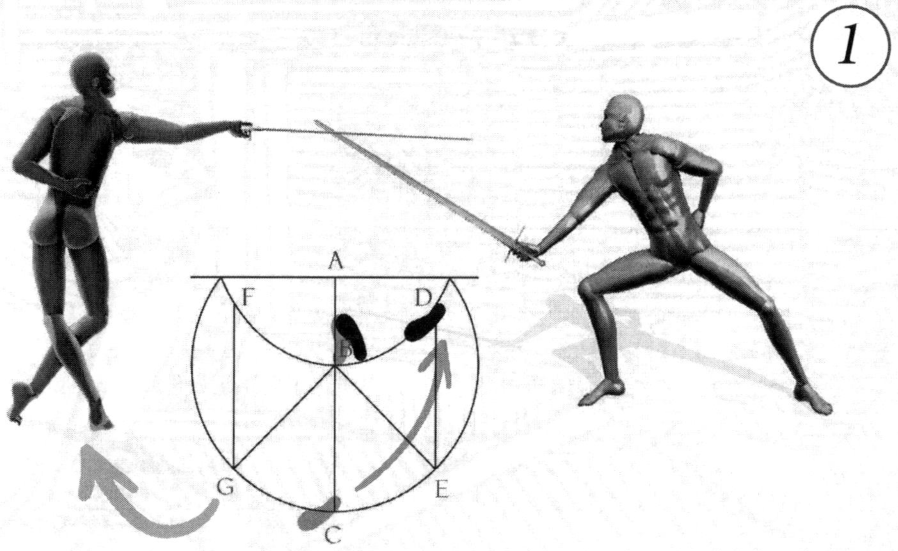

From an initial guard of Straight-Parrying, or Side-Guard (Low Right), the left foot steps to D, brining the body to the right while the weapon extends, Provoking a thrust to the inside. Note, Provoking while stepping in this fashion is seemingly always accompanied with a Taker within the same action.

As the fencer on the right responds the Provocation made by the fencer on the left, the fencer on the left transforms the initial thrust into another while the right foot carries the Hitter into the target.

Provoking on the Front Foot

Provoking with the Hitter

After the step on the rear foot has been made, whether the intent was to Provoke an attack or to simply prepare one, the front foot is next to move. Again, a Provocation can be made during this step – the step where the Hitter will occur. As we raise the front foot for the accompanying action of the sword, we are indicating to our opponent that we are closing the remaining distance.

This raising of the front foot gives the illusion to the opponent that we are intent on Hitting them. However, with this step the foot can linger in the air as the Provocation is turned into the Hitter, or set back down short, meaning that it only extends far enough to threaten sufficiently to draw a motion from the opponent.

From the Onset, standing against the opponent in Straight-Parrying, as the left foot gathers forward, the sword is also 'gathered' or prepared to deliver a cut.

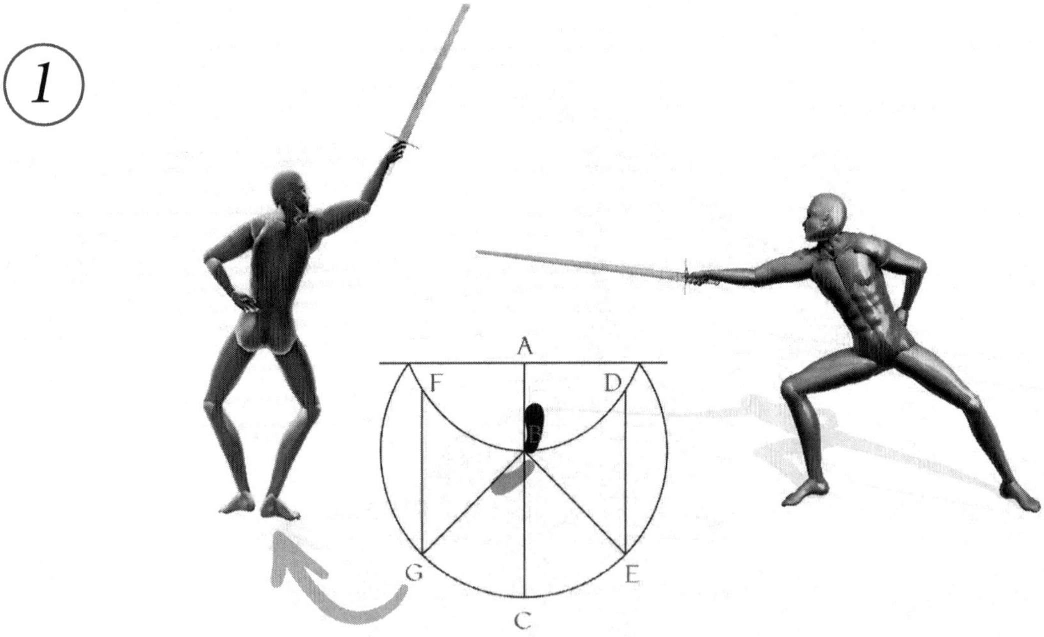

The left foot and sword are gathered and prepared for the cut.

Provoking

2

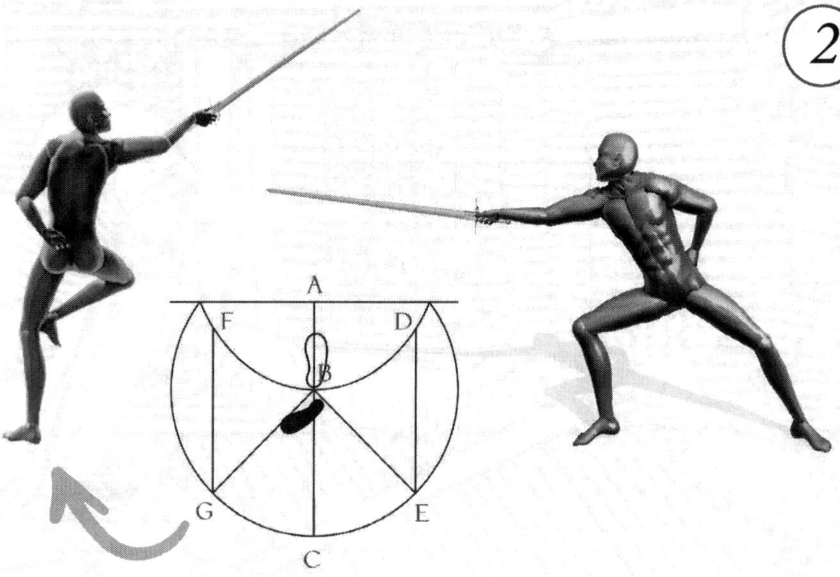

The weapon continues its arc as the right foot raises and remains lifted.

As the cut comes in, the step is held in the air and the foot has three options based on how we decide to follow with the next action:

- The right foot can remain raised as the sword transforms its initial action into another
- The right foot can step laterally along the horizontal line of 'A.' If deceiving with a cut to the right it can step between A&D; or to the left between A&F. Or a short step directly to 'A'
- The right foot can extend past 'A' to allow the action to end as a Hit

With Provocations of the first type, the weight of the body should stay over the left foot so as not to bring the body forward before the second action (the Hitter, or even a second Provocation) so the body is not exposed before the sword is able to defend with a Taker or sufficiently threaten with a Hitter. Remember, the purpose of the Provoker is not to fully commit to an action that could possibly Hit, but rather draw an action from the opponent that will make our Hitter more successful. If the opponent does not see this as a threat, then we can apply the second form of stepping.

When Provoking with the second type of stepping, we are committing the foot and thus the body somewhat more forward than the first type, so again it is important that the sword begins to occupy the space between the fencers before the foot lands. Another way to consider this action is that we are now coming through the Middle;

the single most important aspect of this stage of the fight is having the sword in front of us so that it can Take if need be or Immediately Hit if the opportunity has presented itself. With that being said, if we continue the cut as a Provoker while stepping to the side, it is important that we attempt to avoid contact with the opponent's weapon in order to better transform one action into another. Here, the right foot is landing as the Provocation is made, but it has stepped somewhat short. This means the rear foot can step again as the next action is prepared, moving the sword and body to the opposite side. Then the right foot is free to step again for the final action, the Hitter.

3

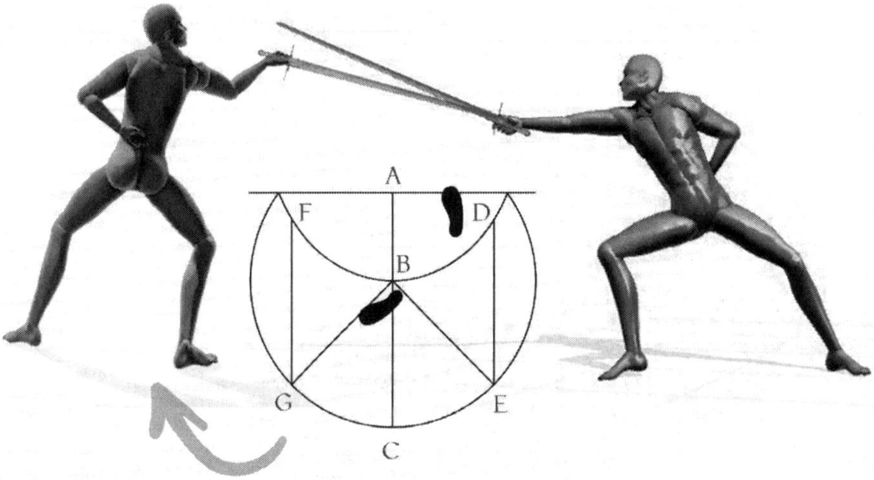

An example of the second form of stepping on the front foot: here, a Squinting Cut on the left is made as the cut descends, turning the short-edge down, stepping to the right with the right foot.

4

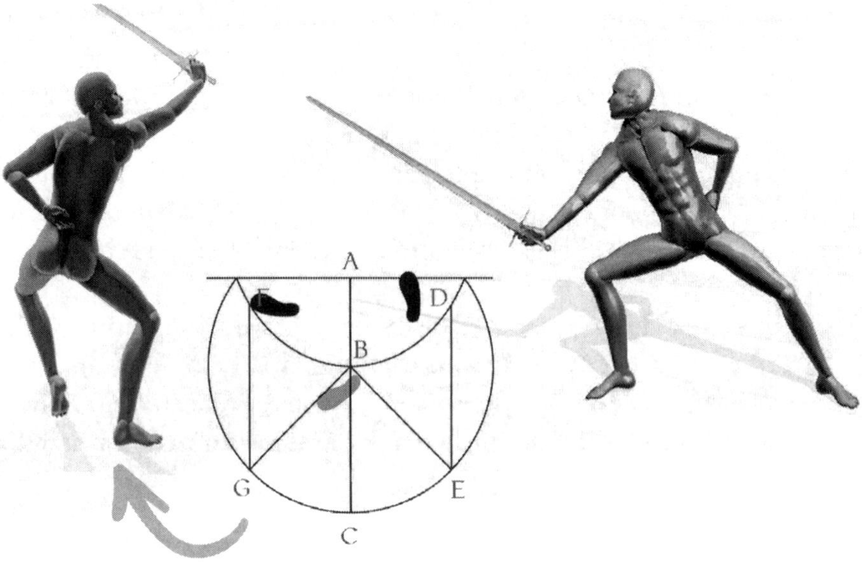

The blade runs-off, circling around the right side, above the head to the left while the left foot steps to the left, preparing a Hitter to that side.

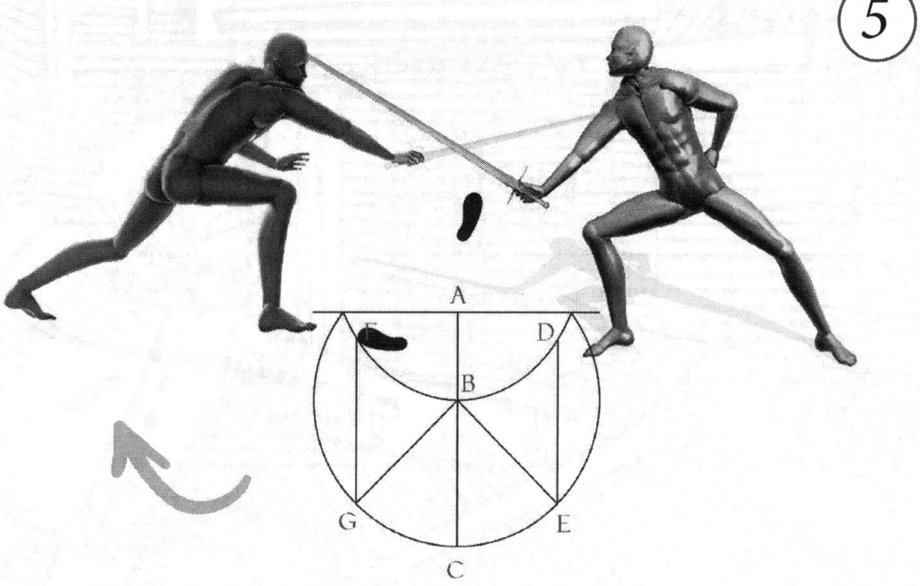

A Wrath Cut from left to right is made to the opponent.*

This raising of the right foot can seem somewhat bizarre, but it serves several purposes. First, it is a means to withhold the step so that the sword has time to transform as necessary, extending out in front of the body before the foot brings the body through the Middle. Second, it gives us time to determine our next course of action.[71] Third, the time of our Hitter is reduced because now the foot only needs to fall, (instead of raising and then falling in the case if it were left on the ground during the Provoker).[72] Lastly, it signals to the opponent that the right foot is stepping and whatever the action of the sword, it is now a potential threat. A smart fencer will realize that the sword cannot be made a threat until the right foot carries it forward, so they will be well aware of where and when that foot moves, not beginning their response until the right foot is raised for the step. This sort of action Meyer refers to as a Provocation with Body Language.

Provoking with Body Language

In sum, if you wish to hit the opponent above, then first glance or threaten below, or if you will hit him on the left, then threaten him first against his right, so that he must slip after with his weapon, and thus give you space on the other side[73] *-Meyer*

Raising the foot, acting as if you will step but then withhold it, is a form of Provoking with Body Language. So are other more subtle actions, but not so subtle that the opponent will not recognize them. These sorts of Provocations are any motion of

** In these instances where the feet leave the diagram, in actuality the diagram follows the fencer, where B is always somewhere near the fencer's center of mass. For clarity, I have chosen to leave the diagram stationary.*

the body that indicates to the opponent that a certain action will be made, while in fact we make another.

Glancing or looking at a certain part of the opponent can indicate that you are ready to strike there. By raising the chin and with a "sneering nose"[74] this can indicate to the opponent that the strike will be through the upper cross or some other high target, while the opposite is true if the head is lowered, staring at their legs. Once it has become obvious that the opponent is expecting a strike high or low, paired with a Provocation of the sword to the same height, the strike can fall or raise to the opposite target. The same can be said with right and left targets by tilting the head in either direction. Though this not something directly talked about by Meyer, it is discussed in other 16th century sources.[75]

While there may be as many Provocations with Body Language as there are body parts, they should always be paired with a Provocation of the sword. Otherwise, an experienced fencer will always use this as an opportunity to distract you with a more credible Provocation, or just Hit you.

On Being Attacked while Provoking

using the Broken/Stolen Step

During our Provocation in the Onset, we first move the left foot and then the right, a literal two step process. During this action the opponent might see an opportunity to strike and we need to be prepared to turn our Provoker into a Taker/Parry. We have looked at many ways to Take and Parry the opponent's blade and the concepts on how to step while doing so. The idea here is we simply need to transition the step that was paired with the Provoker and now pair it with the Taker. This action Meyer refers to as the Broken or Stolen step:

> *act as if you intend to step forward with the one foot, and before you set it down, step backwards with it behind the other foot. Since these properly belong in the rappier section, I will save it for there.*[76] *-Meyer*

Unfortunately, Meyer never uses this term after defining it here, so we are left to infer it from the actions.

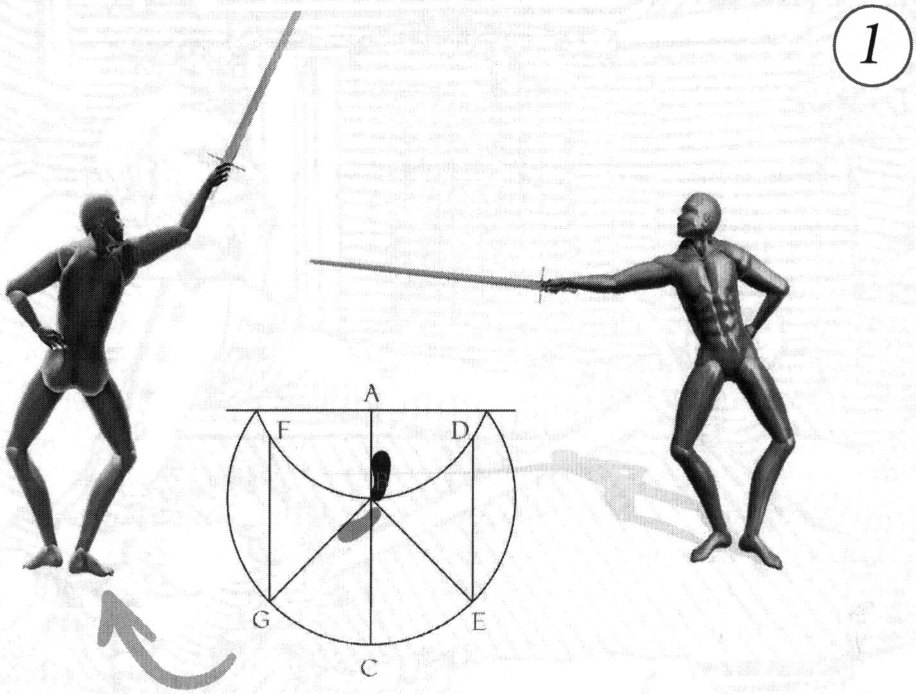

The fencer on the left prepares a cut while gathering the left foot, while Simultaneously, the fencer on the right prepares a thrust by extending the arm and gathering their left foot.

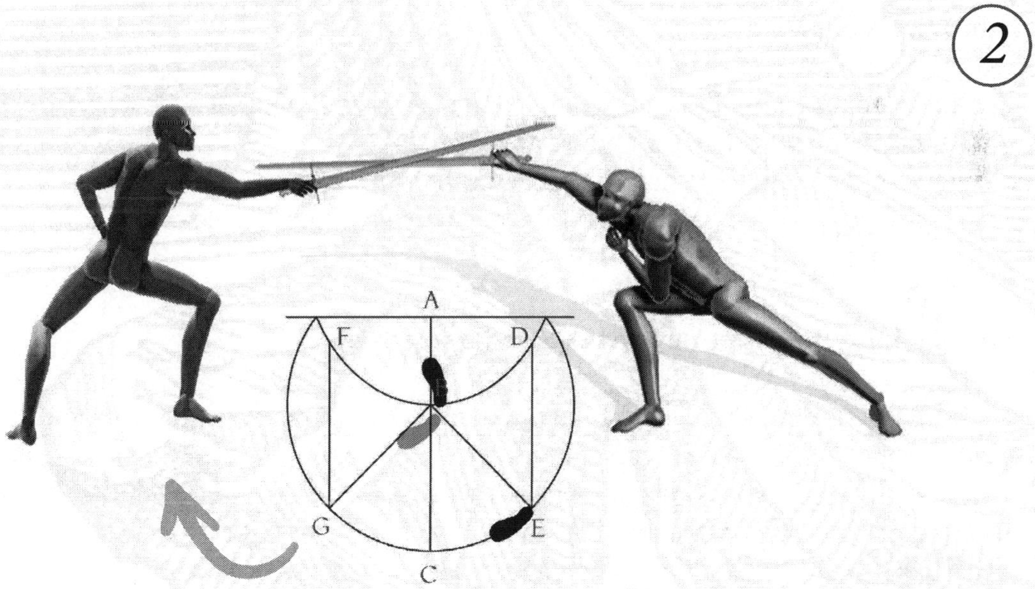

As the fencer on the right delivers a High Thrust on the right, turning the long-edge upward, the fencer on the left steps back and to the right, Setting-Off the thrust to the inside.

To Provoke, to Take, or Both

revisiting space and time

During the course of the fight, it is always important to determine how close or narrow the opponent's sword is to both our sword and to us. The wider, or farther their sword is to us, the more opportunity we have to Provoke a threatening action that looks more like a Hitter. The closer their sword is to the Center, the more we need to pay heed to the threat of their sword, opting to Take it away from the Center instead. To make this determination is simply a matter of space and thus the time their sword can move through space versus ours. If the distance between our point to the target is shorter than the distance between both swords, the more likely our sword is to make a successful Hitter, forcing the opponent to make a Taker/Parry. If, however, the distance between our point and the target is further than the distance between the weapons, then our motion to Hit will be longer than their Parry, meaning we should first move to Provoke instead. Lastly, if the distance between our point and the target is both further than the distance between the swords and the distance between their sword and us, we should Immediately move to Take. These three distinctions should be considered at all times from the Onset, through the Middle and during the Withdrawal, not just at discrete moments but constantly throughout.

In practical terms:

1. If the opponent is wide and we are narrow: Provoke then Hit
2. If the opponent is narrow and we are wide: Take
3. If the opponent is wide and we are wide: become narrow and Provoke
4. If the opponent is narrow and we are narrow: Take and Provoke with the same action

Approaching the Opponent who has Changed-Off

In this first instance, where we are narrow, either in Straight-Parrying or Iron Gate and the opponent has their sword in one of the four openings (Ox for the Thrust, right or left; or Low Guard, right or left), we should threaten the target the opponent has exposed. We should be very wary of attempting to Hit the opening immediately for they have most likely formed one of these guards with the intent to invite an attack there. Or, with their sword unbound, they might seek to Hit in the same instant we attempt to Hit them.

Our goal in dealing with any of these four guards is to make a Provocation by Deception to a target that is somewhat far from where their sword currently lies. In so doing, their attempt to parry the perceived threat will have further to travel. For instance, if they have Changed-Off into Right Ox for the Thrust, then we should threaten a low target, like the belly. If they Changed-Off into the Low Guard on the Left, then we should threaten a high target, like their face or head. As the opponent seeks to parry our feint, or Take our Provocation, we will change our initial action, avoid coming to a bind, and Immediately strike them in another. Alternatively, we can think about this concept as forcing the opponent to move to a location of our choosing so that we can Chase to the opening we know they must necessarily create through forming their defense.

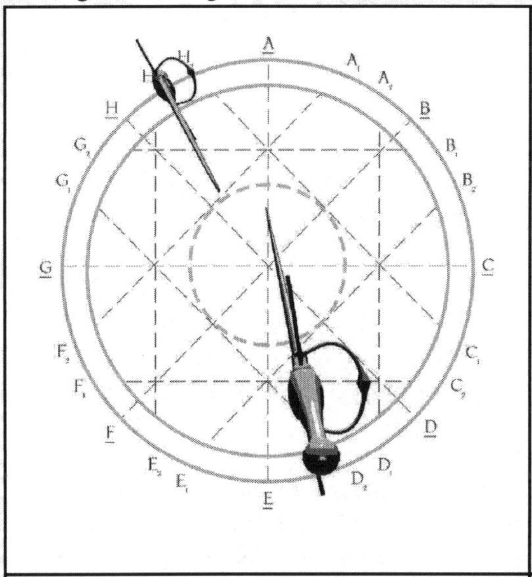

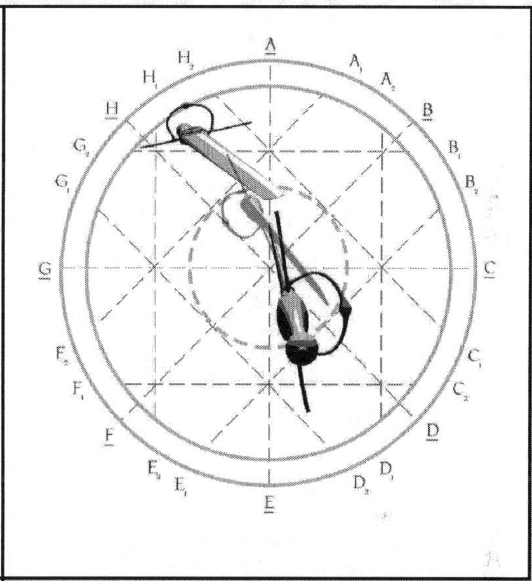

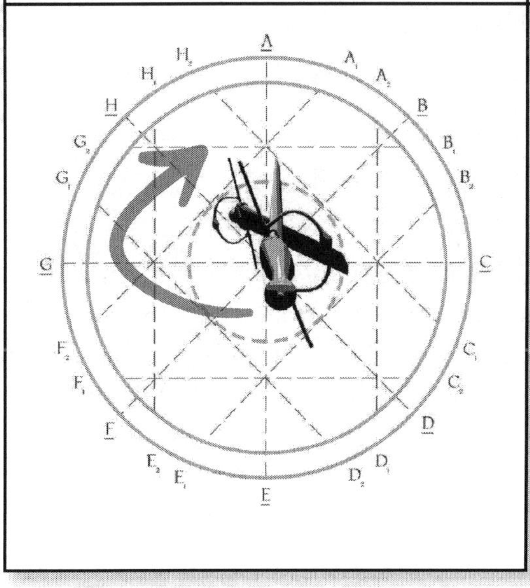

Top Left: opponent lies in Right Ox while we are in Straight-Parrying.

Top Right: a thrust is made to the belly. As the opponent moves to parry the thrust, but before the parry is made, we avoid the parry

Left: as the opponent's blade moves towards the parry, we Change-Through and Chase towards the high-line, thrusting to the upper chest or face

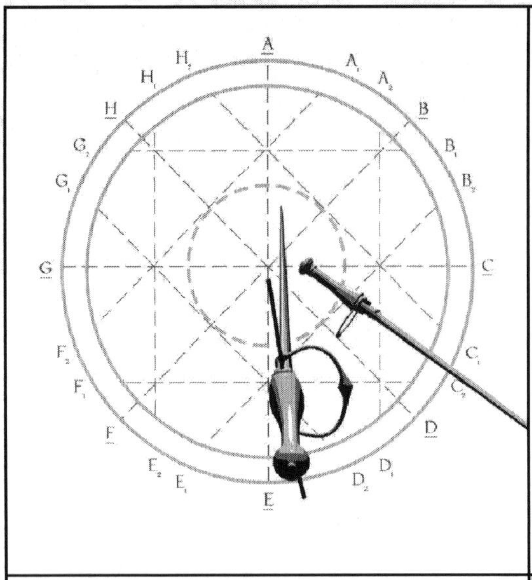

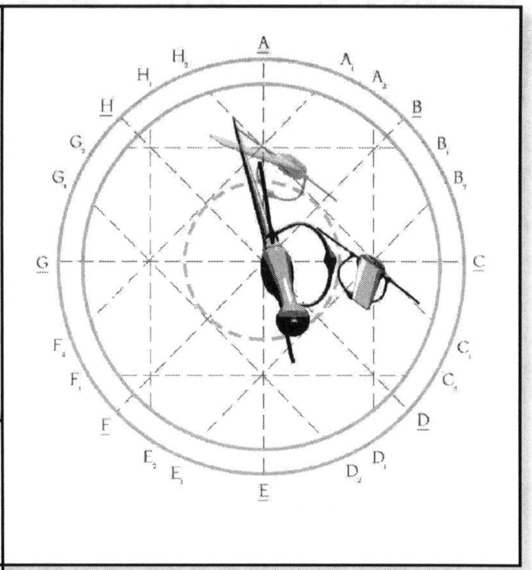

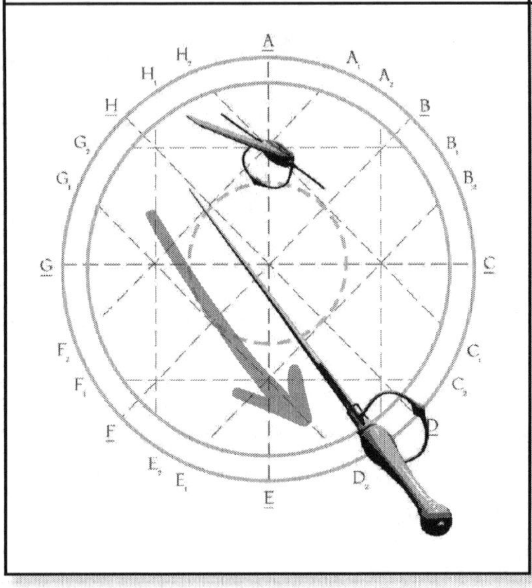

Top Left: opponent lies in The Change while we are in Straight-Parrying

Top Right: a thrust is made to the face. As the opponent moves to parry the thrust, but before the parry is made, we avoid the parry

Left: as the opponent's blade moves towards the parry, we Change-Through and Chase towards the low-line, cutting to the legs or belly

From these two examples we can see that if the opponent rests with their sword wide, then we have an opportunity to make a threat towards their exposed side that they must necessarily move to parry if they do not wish to be struck. As they move to parry the imminent attack, we Chase towards a new exposed opening and strike there. This concept can be applied to an opponent who rests in any guard wide to the Center.

Approaching the Opponent who Threatens with the Point

In the second instance, where they are narrow (in Straight-Parrying or Iron Gate) and we are wide (Ox for the Cut or a low guard), and we wish to act in the *Vor*, then it is more prudent for us to make an action on their blade (a Taker) to force their narrow guard into a slightly wider one. If they threaten us with the point while our point is either not directed towards them or is further from our target than their point to us, then the first step is to remove the threat.

From our wide guard we have each of the seven parries/Takers to remove their sword from the Center at our disposal. However, some of these actions are more suited to some guards rather than others (as indicated in the dashed boxes in the chapter on Parries).

However, depending on the type of fencer they are (which I will talk about next), they might avoid our Taker (either by Changing-Through or Changing-Around), and let our blade fall away, keeping their point remaining as a threat. If Taking or beating their blade aside becomes too laborious then the other method of removing their point is to make a Provocation by Deception, an action meant to draw their sword into a defensive position, while we Chase and Hit.

If they remain with the point as a threat (either not perceiving the Provocation as a threat, by skill or utter ineptness) then we must Provoke and Take simultaneously. These actions are the bread and butter of Meyer's rapier system and mostly involve winding on the blade as we move from the Onset through the Middle.

part vii: the art & practice

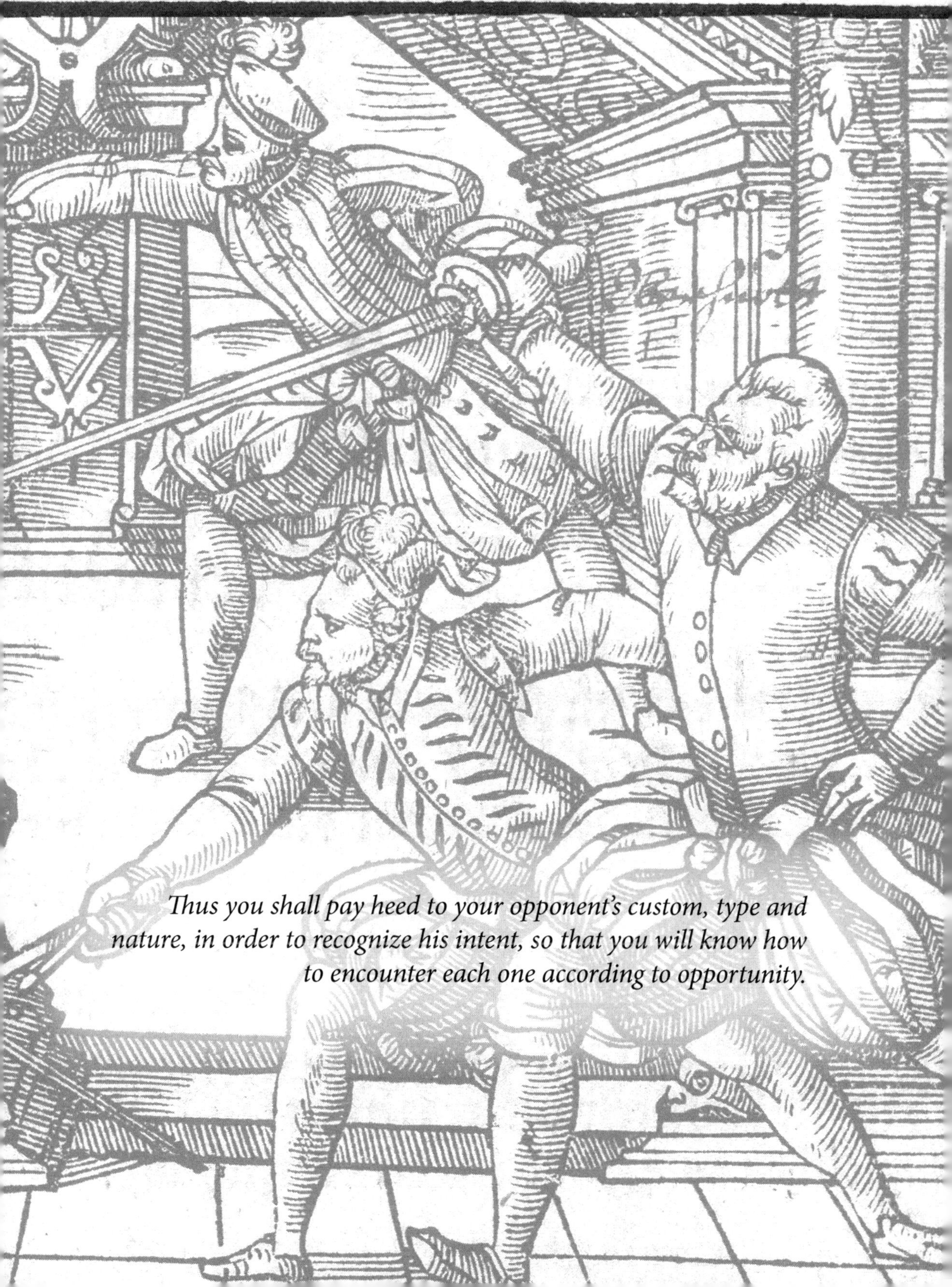

Thus you shall pay heed to your opponent's custom, type and nature, in order to recognize his intent, so that you will know how to encounter each one according to opportunity.

The entire art of Meyer's rapier and fencing as a whole can be distilled into a simple set of rules with the *Vor*, *Nach* and *Indes* along with the Space of the Fencers and the distance of their swords to the Center that make up the core components of the fight. This is the art, but the practice must take into account the temperaments of the fencers and how each approaches the fight (by which I mean both conceptually and tactically). Below I have provided a template flow diagram that can be used to chart any fight.

With the ultimate goal of Hitting the opponent without being Hit ourselves the following rules should be observed:

We have the Vor:

If we are the first to move, threaten the opponent with a cut or thrust to a place where they have not defended themselves. If they move to Take (parry), avoid touching their weapon and strike them somewhere else. Always do this while keeping our own sword in a place where a bind will be in our advantage.

-or-

Remove their sword as a threat by Taking it away from the Center

We are in the Nach:

If they have the Vor, they will either seek to Take our blade or Hit us:

If they want to bind or Take our blade, before they do, Change-Through and do not let them touch it.

If they do bind our blade, Feel the bind and act Instantly from it, obeying the principles laid out in the chapter on Taking.

If they want to Hit us, Take their blade (parry) and seek to Immediately strike them.

If you sense them Provoking us through deception, do not move your sword more than a hands breadth from the Center, and keep the point as a threat.

If they will not move first and do not present an opening to threaten, then we can entice them to attack us by presenting an opening by 'Changing-Off' from guard to guard. When they see an opportunity to Hit us, Take their blade and Hit them.

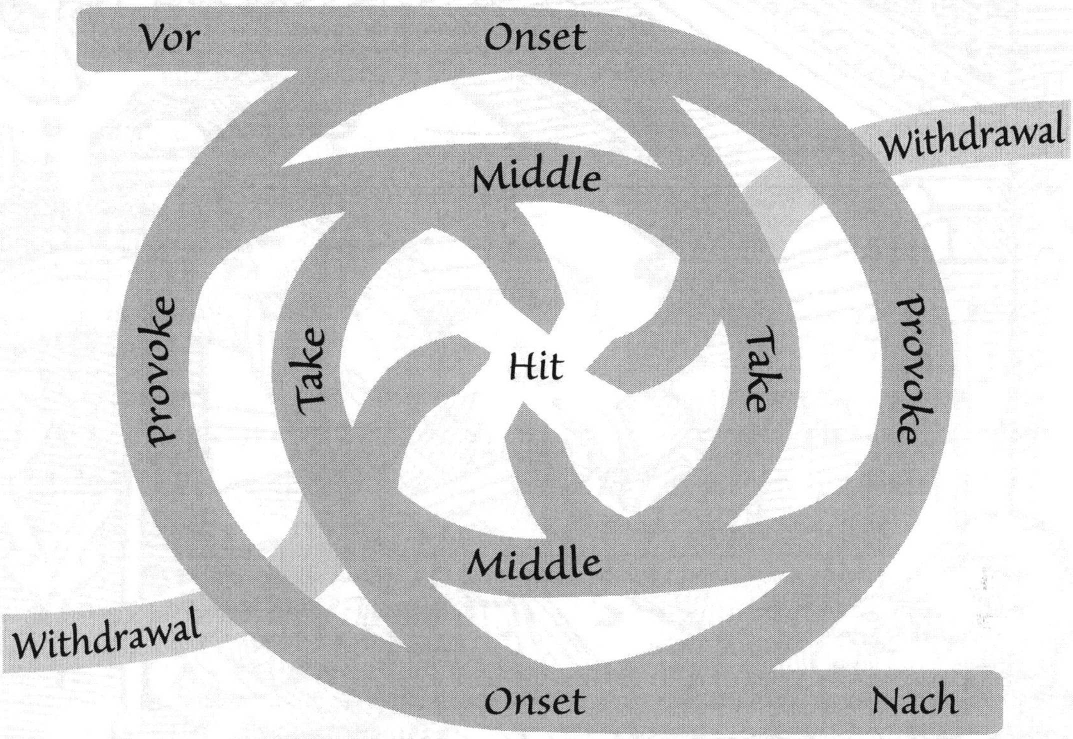

The Above Diagram: The flow chart above is a visual representation of the stages of the fight and their corresponding actions. Each fencer begins in either the upper-left or lower-right depending on who is the first to act. The outer circle is the Onset where both fencers are positioning themselves with various actions to gain the initiative. As each perform their actions and move closer, decreasing the space between them, they move to the inner circle, the Middle. From here both make actions on the others' weapons seeking the ultimate goal in the middle of the diagram, the Hitter. From there, the flow continues out to the opposite side through the Taker and Withdrawal.

The dashed line on the following pages indicates the path each fencer takes through the chart; the longer the line, the more complex the sequence.

To illustrate how this diagram can be used, let us start with a simple action and build a tactical progression...

The Fight

1. From the Onset, the fencer in the Vor prepares their action...

2. and Hits the fencer in the Nach

3. Then withdraws from the engagement

Hitting

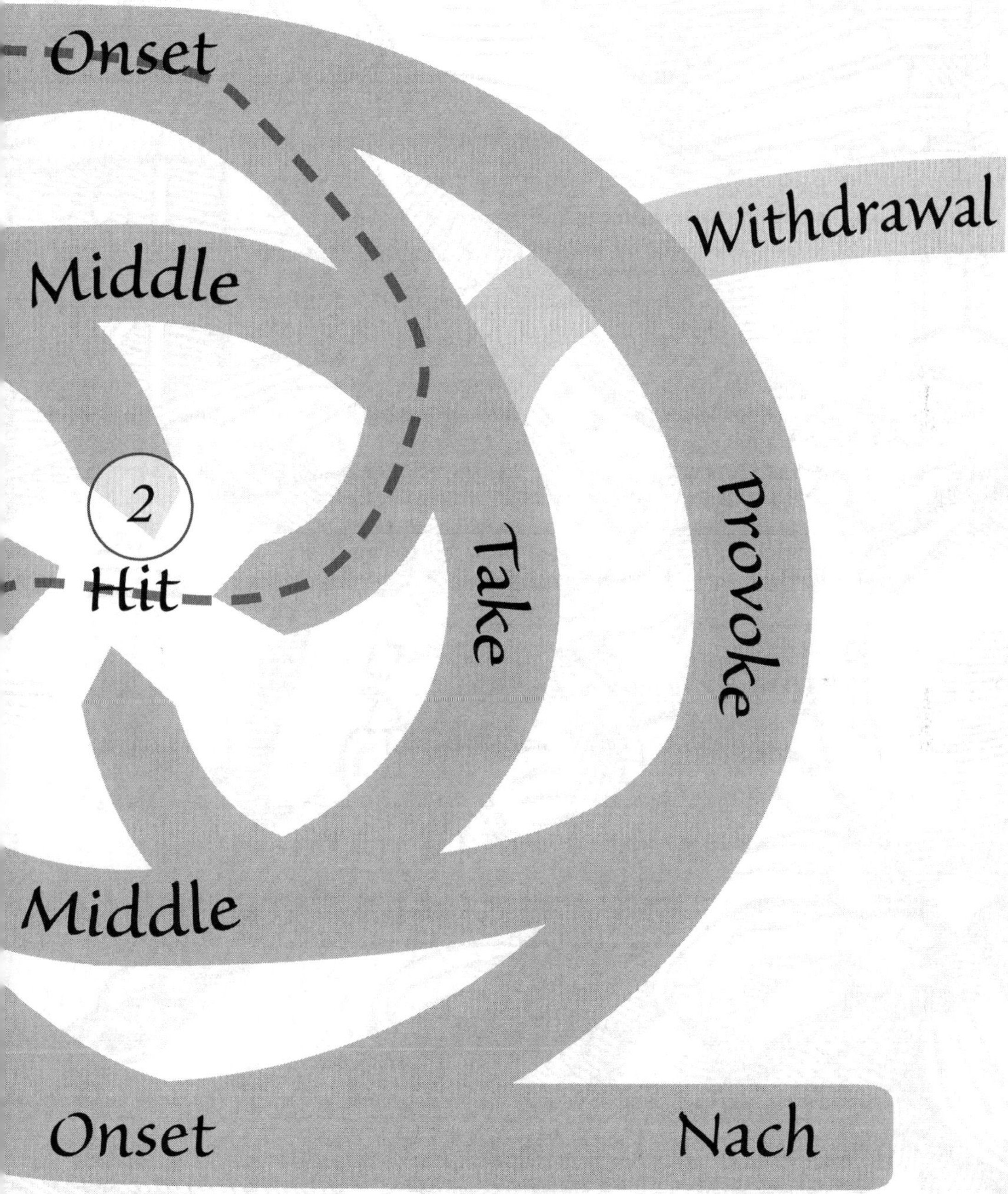

Onset
Withdrawal
Middle
2
Hit
Take
Provoke
Middle
Onset
Nach

...to defeat the fencer who simply seeks to Hit.

The Fight

1. From the Onset, the fencer in the Vor prepares their action and attacks the fencer in the Nach

2. The fencer in the Nach parries/Takes the attack

3. Immediately after parrying the attack, they answer with their own attack and Hits the opponent

4. Remaining safe by making another action (Taking) on the opponent's blade, Withdraws from the engagement

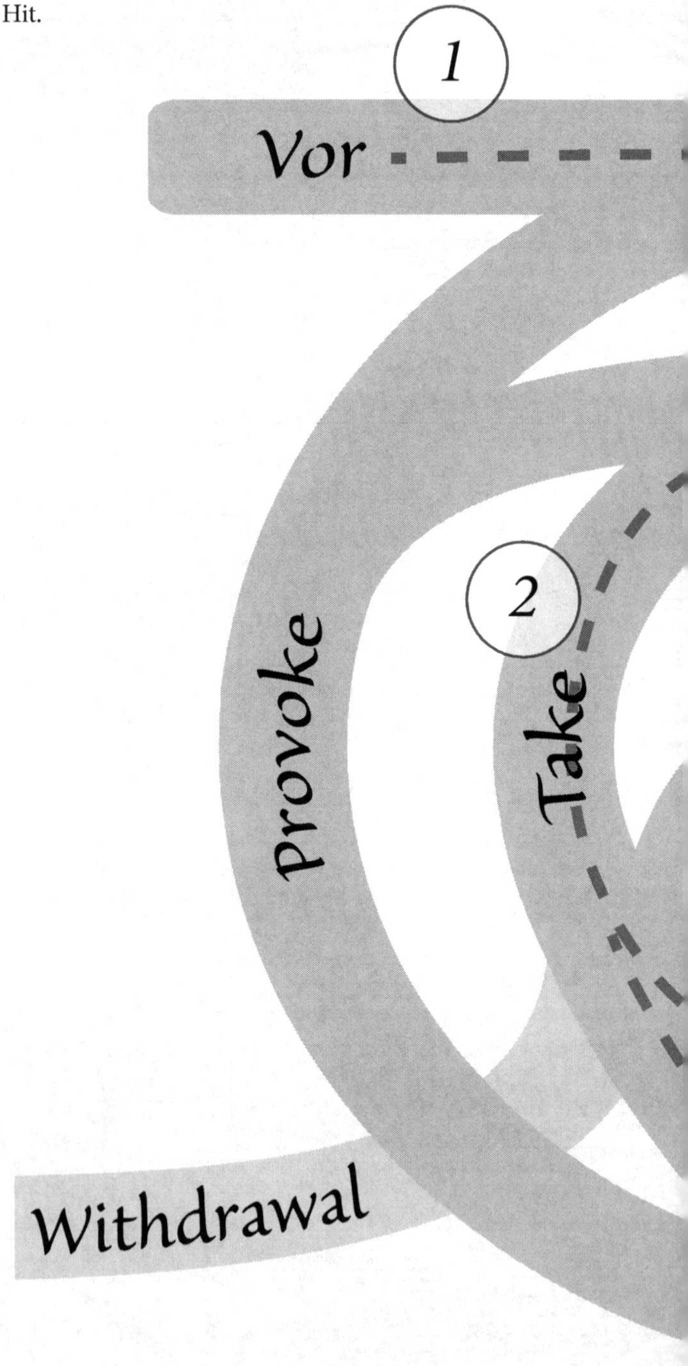

Taking in the Nach

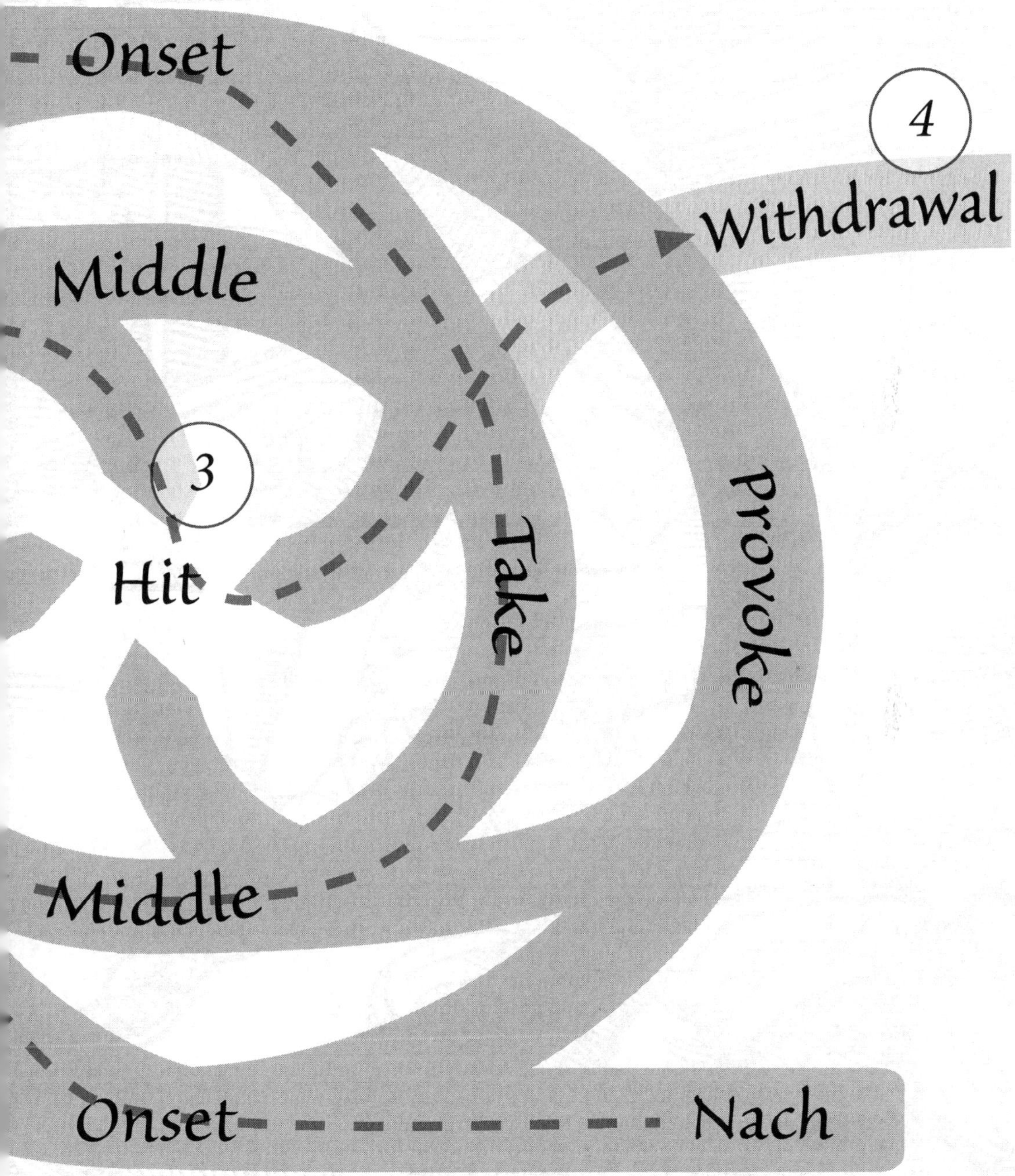

...to safely proceed against an opponent to make their defense (parry) more difficult

The Fight

1. From the Onset, the fencer in the Vor prepares their action...

2. and Takes the fencer in the Nach's weapon (by beating or otherwise displacing it)

3. After Taking their blade, moves to Hit the opponent

4. Remaining safe by making another action (Taking) on the opponent's blade, Withdraws from the engagement

Taking in the Vor

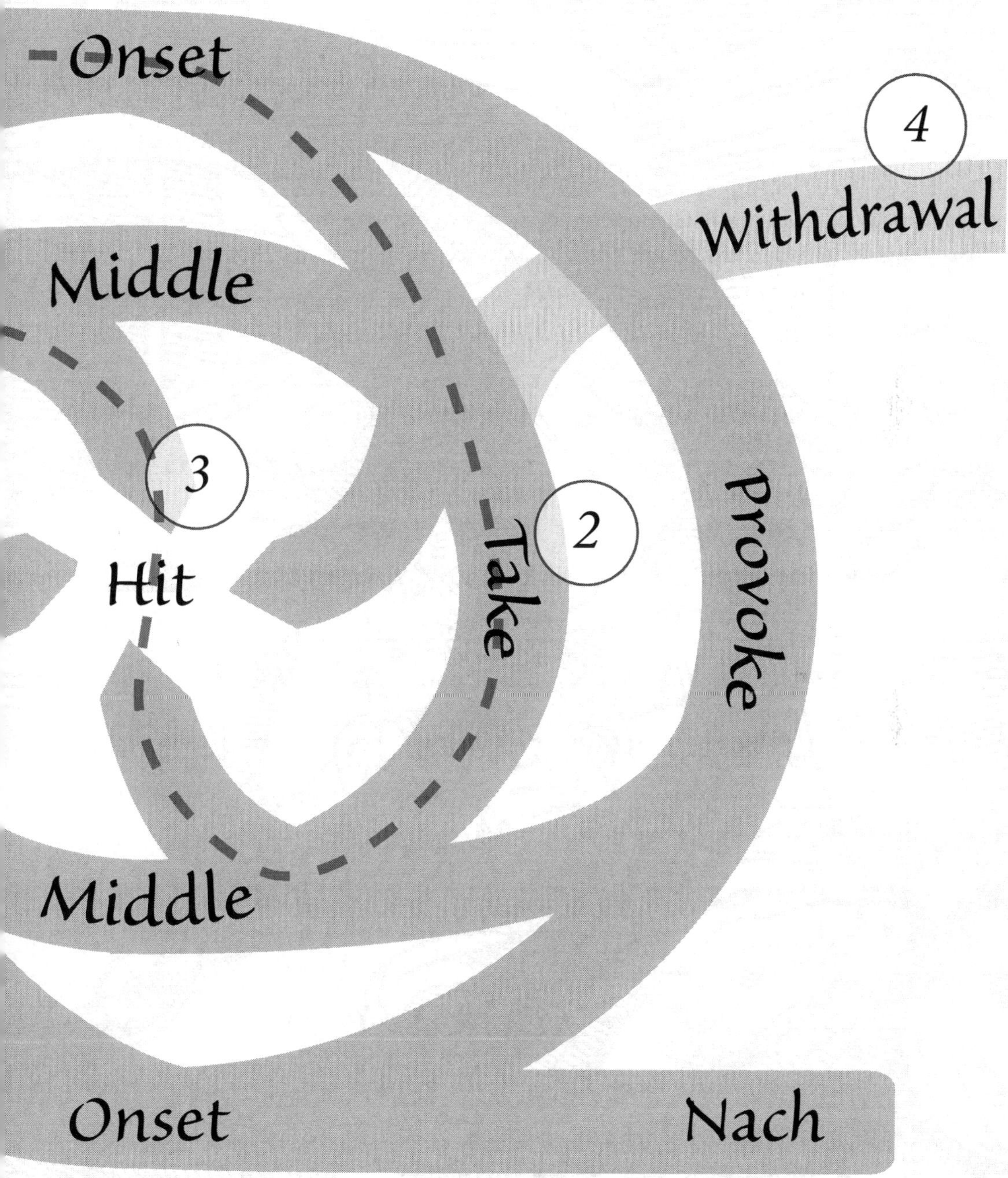

...to operate against an opponent who is hesitant to attack, waiting for an opportunity to do so

The Fight

1. From the Onset, the fencer in the Nach Provokes an attack from the opponent by Changing-Off

2. The opponent sees the opening and opportunity to strike and does so

3. The fencer in the Nach parries the attack and Immediately moves to Hit the opponent

4. Remaining safe by making another action (Taking) on the opponent's blade, Withdraws from the engagement

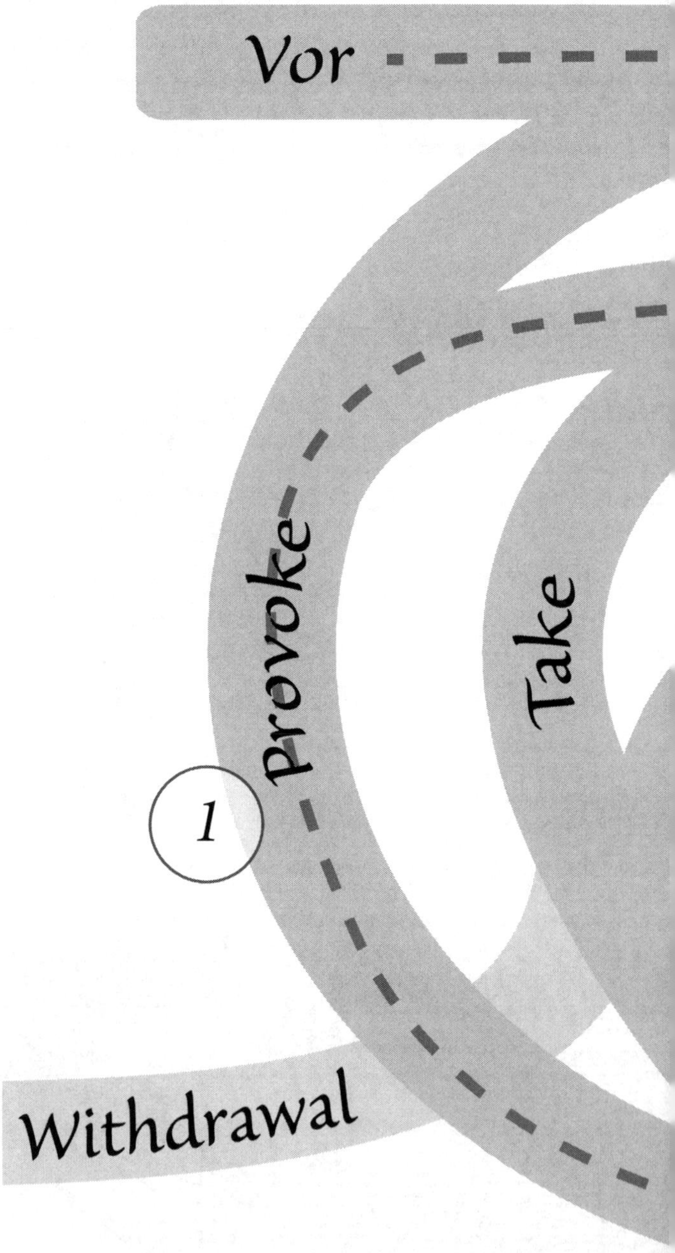

Provoking in the Nach

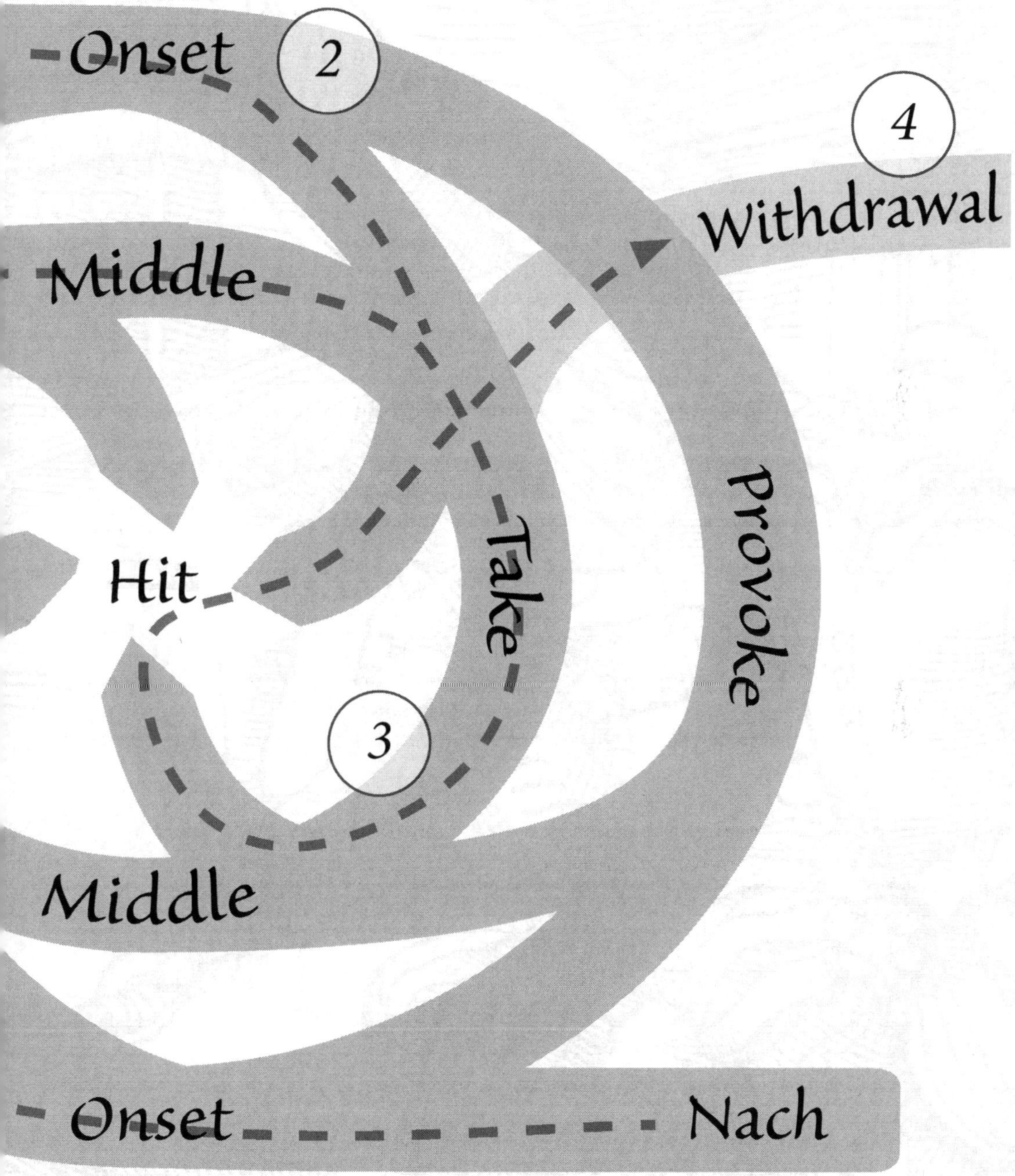

Art & Practice

...to operate against an opponent who will not be the first to initiate an attack

The Fight

1. From the Onset, the fencer in the Vor makes a Provocation by Deception by enticing the opponent to parry an attack that was designed to fail

2. The opponent seeing what they think is an action designed to Hit, moves to parry

3. The fencer in the Vor, seeing the parry, avoids it and strikes to another opening created by the parry

4. Remaining safe by making another action (Taking) on the opponent's blade, Withdraws from the engagement

Provoking in the Vor

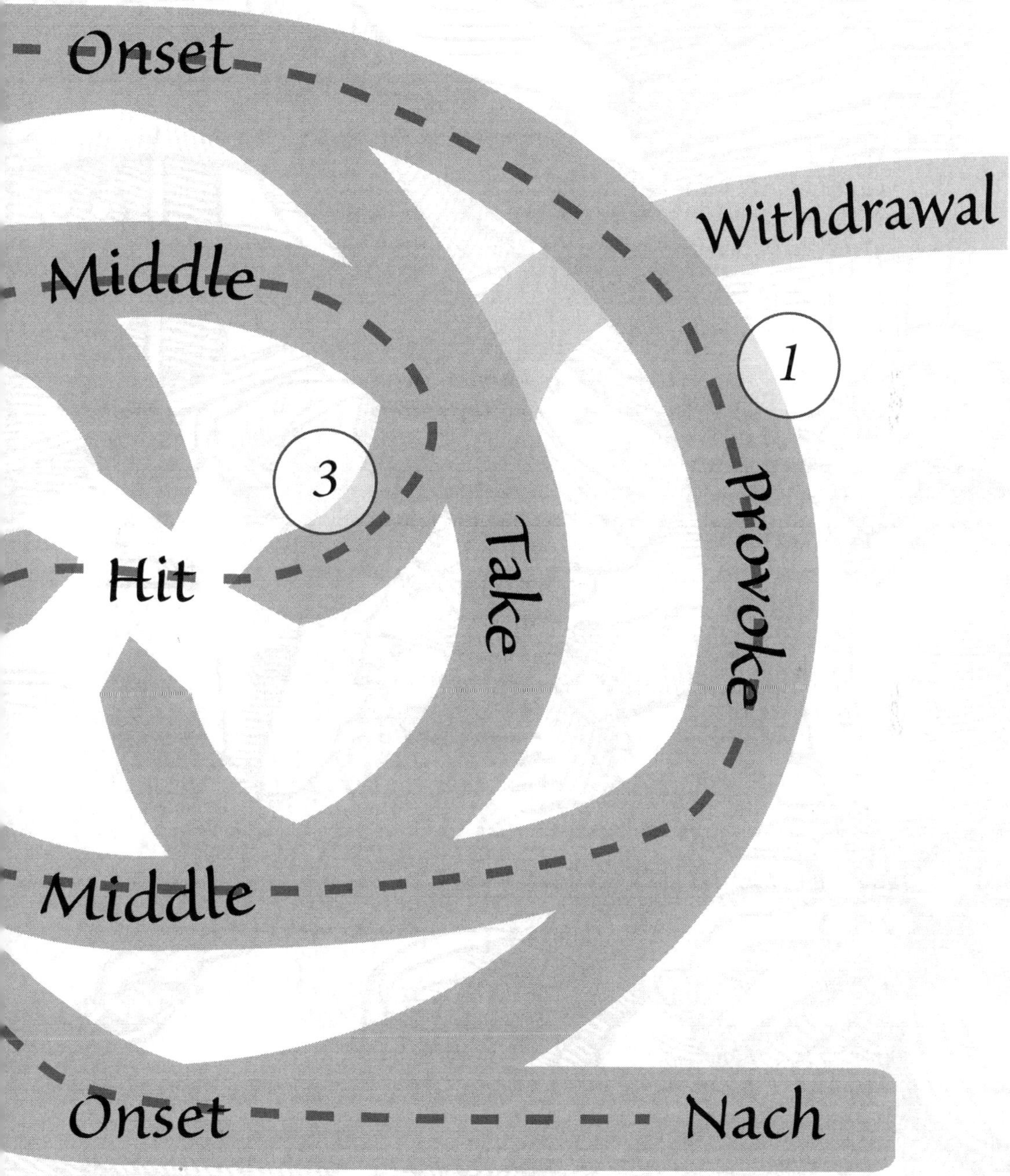

Art & Practice

...to safely attack an opponent who has laid a trap

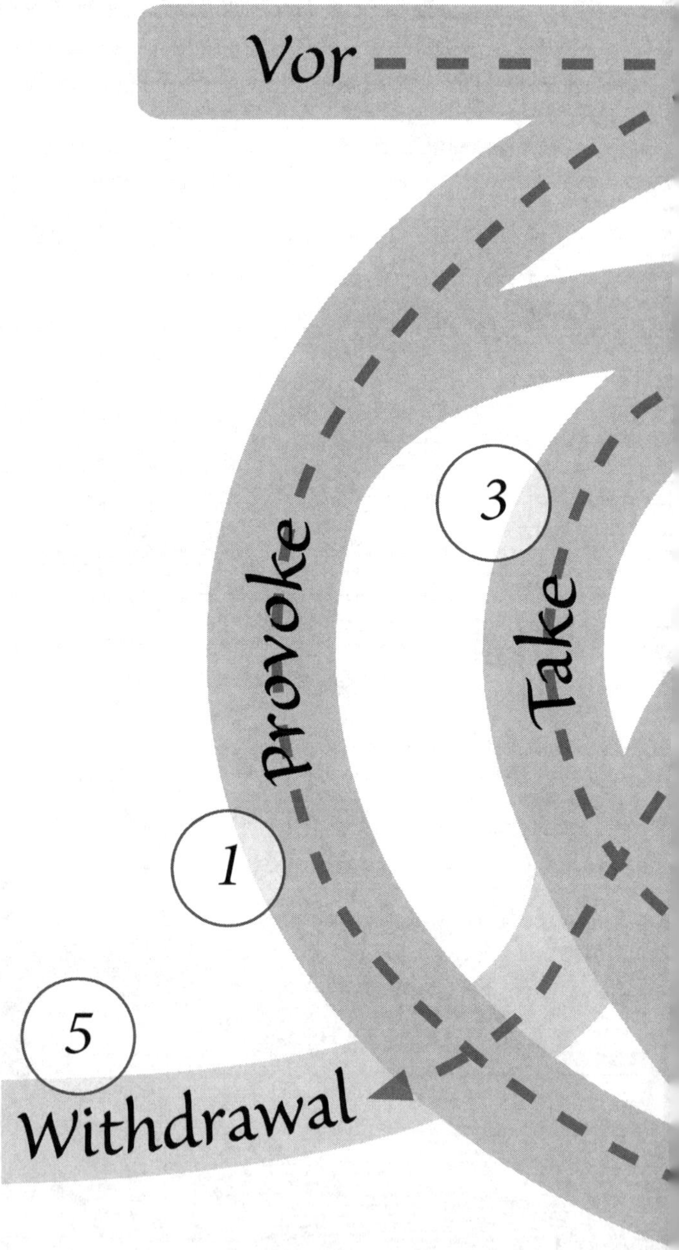

The Fight

1. From the Onset, the fencer in the Nach Provokes an attack from the opponent by Changing-Off or delivering a False Attack

2. The opponent realizing the intentions of their opponent, then makes a Provocation by Deception to draw the parry

3. The fencer in the Nach, not knowing the opponent's action is a feint, moves to parry it

4. The fencer in the Vor, seeing the parry, avoids it and strikes to another opening created by the parry

5. Remaining safe by making another action (Taking) on the opponent's blade, Withdraws from the engagement

Provoking into a Provocation

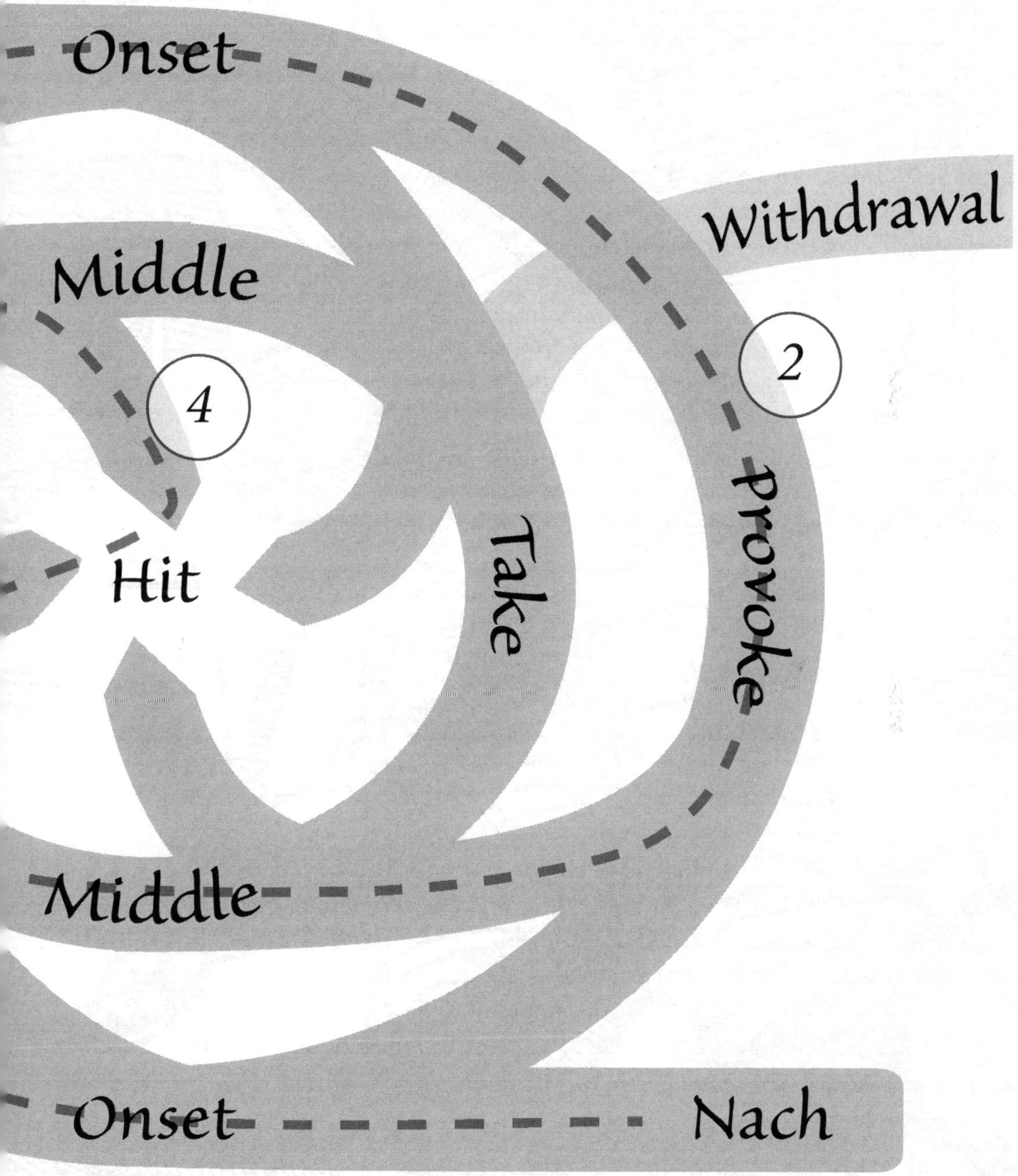

Art & Practice

The Four Types of Fencers

How to fight against them & How to fight like them

Having seen how to diagram the basic tactical actions of rapier combat, we must also remember that fencing is more than just a flow chart: it also encompasses all of the attitudes, qualities and flaws of the people wielding the swords. Meyer divides fencers into four different categories, four different ways fencers can express the singular art. These four categories are as follows:

Type 1: "Violent and Stupid"

These are the fencers that Immediately attempt to Hit their opponent with very little consideration of their own well being once they are close enough. They are violent because they often strike with not one but many blows one after another. Meyer refers to them as Stupid because they lack strategy and do not follow Meyer's 2nd rule of fencing: "You should not cut to the body until you have made yourself secure with [the *Takings*], not only to cut or thrust to his body, but so that after delivering the cut you can recover your weapon and body without harm."[77]

How to Defeat Type 1 Fencers:

Meyer tells us to use Straight-Parrying against these fencers. This will make it difficult for the attacker to Hit to an opening without first dealing with our point. From Straight-Parrying, we are to parry the first few attacks, and while they continue their assault, without warning we remove our blade from the parry and Immediately Hit them as their sword goes by.

How to Act like Type 1 Fencers:

It is beneficial in a fight to make your opponent fear you through violence. The most effective way to accomplish this is to give a few very strong cuts that threaten to Hit. However, we should deliver these cuts in a way that obey Meyer's first rule of fencing: "You should conduct all your cuts such that you do not lose control of your weapon or overcommit with it."[78] We can act or give the impression to our opponent that we have, and once they believe we have overcommitted to our cut and seek to Hit, we Immediately counter in whatever way is most judicious.

Type 2: "Artful and Sharp"

The artful and sharp fencer is one who seeks opportunities to strike their opponent. They may be reluctant to commit to strikes or to even Provoke actions and opt to play in the *Nach* in order to wait for the right moment to strike. They might Change-Off from guard to guard to invite an attack and keep their distance, throwing attacks from the Onset but never closing through the Middle themselves. They wish to goad the opponent to attack so that they may Immediately deal with the threat and counter Simultaneously or just afterwards.

How to Defeat Type 2 Fencers:

Defeating fencers who wish to keep their distance and only strike when they feel they have the opportunity to do so is a game of patience. It is important not to over-commit to an attack or rush in for they will back up and strike when you lose your temperament. To defeat these fencers Meyer tells us to Change-Off, while always keeping the point as a threat. If Type 2 fencers are always seeking just the right opportunity to strike, then to defeat them we should offer them an opportunity of our choosing of which we can Immediately take advantage.

How to Act like Type 2 Fencers:

Artful and Sharp is a sound strategy, especially if the opponent is over eager to close distance and seems to have a distinct action planned for your fight. If the opponent seems intent on making a certain action work, allow them to begin it, creating the illusion it will unfold as they see it, but then Immediately interrupt it, countering it in the Middle. It may take several passes to fully understand what they intend to do, but the Type 2 fencer is patient and not eager to end the engagement within the first action.

Type 3: "Judicious and Deceitful"

Like the Type 2 fencer, these fencers are patient, only seeking to strike when the opportunity presents itself. However, these fencers do not just wait for opportunities, they create them through deception. Meyer notes that these fencers will also Withdraw safely, controlling the entire fight from the Onset, through the Middle and during the Withdrawal.

How to Defeat Type 3 Fencers:

Each action these fencers make should be considered a Provocation. It is difficult to act Within their actions or Immediately respond for fear that we might be responding at the wrong time to an action that was meant to draw us into a specific place. To defeat these fencers it is prudent to see their actions develop and only respond when they have fully committed themselves to a particular action. Waiting might also be disastrous, though, because we will never work our way out of the *Nach*. Meyer would like us keep the initiative by Changing-Off, waiting in the low guards for a moment, then using the action to assume a high guard as a preparation for an attack. This attack should be a False Attack, meant to miss so that they see their opportunity to strike, which we will parry and or otherwise Take and Immediately Hit. This approach denies the opponent opportunities to begin deceits in their own time. By constantly moving, we make them unsure where they should deliver their Provocation, and by the time they see their opportunity, they will have failed to recognize our Invitation (a trap).

How to Act like Type 3 Fencers:

Meyer tells us that he assumes the role of these types of fencers (unless some other method will be more appropriate for the fight). There is no reason with this fencing approach to only 'act' the part. All fencers should be 'Judicious and Deceitful,' and part of this deceit is the ability to adopt the other three methods and change between them at will in order to confuse the opponent as to whom they are fencing. Every fencer should also be judicious, making no extraneous actions; each action should have intent, either to draw an opportunity (Provoke), to Hit, or to Take. Conversely, each action the opponent makes should be exploited, and not after they have made it, but while they are making it (*indes*).

Type 4 : "Foolish or Sharp"

The fencer who is foolish is one who waits in a guard for their opponent to act first. Meyer calls this tactic foolish as they will always be at the mercy of their opponent's design.

How to Defeat Type 4 Fencers:

Defeat the Type 4 fencer by assuming the roll of the Type 1 fencer. If the foolish fencer intentionally fights from the *nach*, the goal should be to keep them in the *nach*, never giving them the opportunity to threaten us with a cut or thrust of their own. If they are able to deliver a cut or thrust, the Type 1 fencer, always having their sword in motion, should use this to their advantage and Immediately parry and counter. The benefit of facing the Type 4 fencer is that they usually give us plenty of time to consider our actions and plan out a strategy. We can see the guard they have formed, carefully plot our steps and blade actions, then begin and most likely complete them all before they choose to make their move.

How to Act like Type 4 Fencers:

A foolish fencer is a dead fencer, but to merely *act* foolishly can lull your opponent into a false sense of security. To pull off this tactic one must be 'especially sharp.' Meaning each action the opponent makes must be perfectly analyzed as to its intent. Is their action meant to Take, to Provoke or to Hit? Misreading intent can spell the Type 4 fencer's demise. The goal of acting foolish is to entice the opponent to be violent and stupid—to be over confident in their actions. This can be done by forming a guard, knowing exactly what actions can be made from it, and then letting the opponent take the Before. When the opponent makes a mistake, that is our opportunity to strike. If the opponent does not assume the roll of the Type 1 fencer, then this tactic can become very dangerous and foolish.

Concluding the Types of Fencers

A way to parse the psychology of assuming the four types of fencers is to understand that two act in the Before, seizing the initiative from Onset of the fight, while the other two act in the After, looking to create or take opportunities as the opponent moves to Hit. Two act wisely, one in the Before, the other in the After; the others act stupidly and foolishly, again, one in the Before, the other in the After.

The Type 1 fencer acts in the Before without regard to their own safety, and is thus stupid. The Type 3 fencer also acts in the Before, but creates smart opportunities to strike.

The Type 2 fencer acts in the After, forcing or enticing the opponent in the Before to commit to a strike so they can take that opportunity to safely counter. The Type 4 fencer, also acting in the After, allows the opponent to develop their approach and execute their actions, subsequently making a counter very difficult for themselves.

The common thread that joins Type 1 fencing with Type 4 fencing, and Type 2 with Type 3, is that Type 1 and 4 lack an awareness for the Middle or Handwork, while Type 2 and 3 use the Middle and its Handworks (Takings) to control the outcome of the fight.

At times it can be appropriate to avoid the Middle, especially if the opponent is not sharp enough to perceive the actions that flow through them. For instance, the time to be Violent and Stupid (Type 1), is when the opponent is Foolish (Type 4). In other words, if the opponent is a "deer in the headlights," the best tactic can be to simply Hit them as quickly as possible. We can say in these cases that Type 1 beats Type 4. Conversely, if we wish for an otherwise calm, smart, fencer to act rashly, we can act like a Type 4 fencer, thus drawing an attack that we can then deal with more easily knowing its intention; and so Type 4 can defeat Type 1.

Type 2 and Type 3 fencers rely on the Middle to act safety. Because all actions with the intent of causing harm (Hitters) happen in the Middle and subsequently during the Withdrawal phase as well, a keen understanding of the Handworks/Takings is paramount to remain safe while striking the opponent and recognizing the opportunity to do so. Type 2 and 3 are in essence the same fencer but assuming different rolls, Type 2 in the After and Type 3 in the Before.

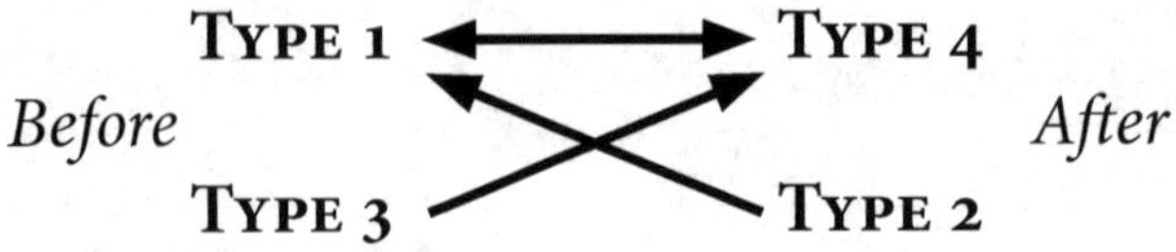

Type 1 & 4 beat each other depending on their use. Type 3 in the Before, beats Type 4 in the After. Type 2 in the After, beats Type 1 in the Before.

Part VIII: Conclusion

Meyer's fight with the rapier was a captivating footnote in the Renaissance fencing of the late 16th century. Many in the modern HEMA community saw, or maybe still do see, him as the "8th Bolognese master;" a nod to the overwhelming and rich amount of extant treatises from Bologna of the 16th century and Meyer's equally impressive tome. Though there are many similarities between Meyer's use of the weapon he calls a 'rappier,' and the sword described by his Italian contemporaries, there exists one key difference that keeps pulling my attention away from the Italians and back to the master who I decided to write this book on – the use of Straight-Parrying. This way of fighting, as I mentioned in the introduction, was not new to German fencing, nor was it something alien to the earlier Italian systems, and definitely not the case in the Italian systems of the 17th century where the fight almost exclusively lives. But, for Meyer's contemporaries, he seems to be a lone wolf, even amongst those who claim the thrust is superior to the cut (a claim Meyer never explicitly makes, but a notion by which he teases his reader).

This stand-out feature of a 16th-century author, wielding a proto-rapier (sidesword), is at minimum noteworthy, and at most, ground-breaking. Meyer seemingly broke with German tradition by abandoning the Master-Cuts as the foundation of the art (entirely in the use of the rapier) and embraced a single guard (Straight-Parrying) with a single, all purpose means of controlling the Center with an extended point—an approach not adopted by the Italians for at least another 25 years.

There is much in Meyer's *Kunst des Fechtens* that I decided to leave out of this publication so I could focus on what I feel are the underlying, fundamental fencing principles required to understand how Meyer is using his single-handed sword, including the use of sword and dagger together, sword and cape, wrestling while armed and unarmed—all contingencies of the realities of fencing in the 16th century. It is my hope to be able to write on these subjects in a future edition, God willing...

~Robert Rutherfoord

Afterward

Meyer's rapier is more than just a set of techniques, no it is in fact a clear look into the system of fighting that Meyer sought to share with his readers. Sadly, the rapier section of Meyer's 1570 treatise is largely overlooked by many modern readers, simply because they are interested in one of Meyer's other weapons. However, it is in the rapier that Meyer clearly describes his approach to a fight and the priorities that one should have. He explains concepts on the types of fighters you will face, the way you protect yourself from an opponent's deceit, and elaborates on his tactical model of Provoker, Taker and Hitter (*Reitzer*, *Nehmer*, *Treffer*) first presented with the dusack.

As you work through and practice the techniques and concepts that Robert has explained throughout his book, keep this in mind: you are not learning to fight with Meyer's rapier, rather you are learning to fight with Meyer's system using a rapier. This more than anything else is what makes this book valuable. Take the teachings outlined here and apply them to the rapier, certainly, but also consider what they teach you about the use of the longsword, the dusack and even the staff.
Take for instance what Robert describes as the Overbind. This piece of rather simple theory will help you to understand the relationship of weak and strong, why you should sometimes maintain contact with the long edge of your blade and other times wind the short. This works equally well with the longsword as it does with the rapier.

Meyer's footwork and hip rotation help to generate power when using one-handed weapons such as the rapier or dusack, but also allows for greater control of the staff or halberd as well as speed and force with the longsword.

Remember at the end of the day that what Meyer, and other masters, seek to teach is not just a collection of techniques that must be followed to the letter only with the weapon shown. Rather they seek to teach a system that solves problems. Yes, the techniques shown will work but the goal is to understand why they work, not just how. Additionally, by studying the material in this book and in Meyer's original, you will hopefully begin to understand when to use a technique and when not to, who your opponent is and who you need to be to defeat them, what your opponent is trying to do and what you should do to counter it.

~Ted Elsner
Sacramento Freifechter Guild, USA

Appendix A - The 'Other' Cutting Diagram

On folio 1v of the 'Rostock' manuscript appears a cutting diagram similar to the one shown on the cover of this book and used throughout, but distorted horizontally. This is the diagram that labels each of the cuts, ie: face, shoulder, arm, etc, and it took some pondering to come up with a purpose to its existence.

The diagram I used to show the fight from a first person perspective is very much symmetrical, and useful to show the engagement of the blades, but makes very little tactical sense if the opponent was not standing like DaVinci's Vitruvian Man.

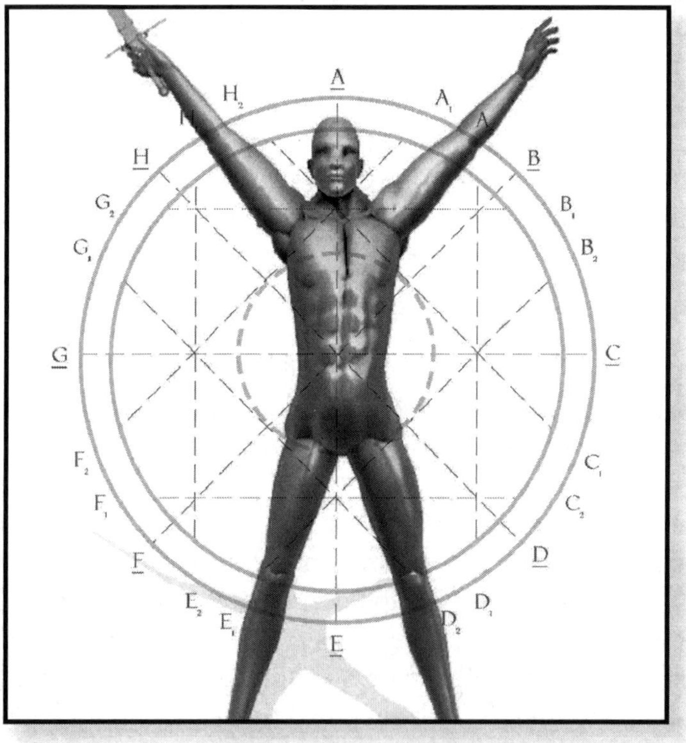

cutting diagram on folio 2v

Because the opponent is not likely to stand this way, but rather in a fencing posture, the diagram I used is not as accurate as it could be. Because the opponent's body is turned, the figure on folio 1v more realistically shows the paths and locations of the cuts in real space.

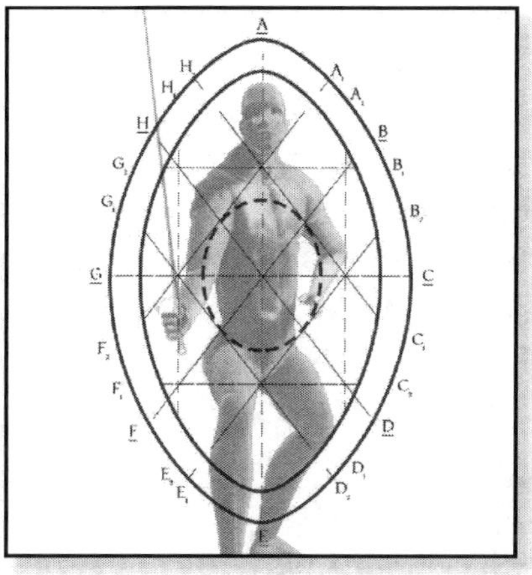

cutting diagram on folio 1v

In fact, if you consider an opponent standing in the Straight-Parrying, with their right side extended towards you and left side refused, the diagram might even become more distorted on its right side.

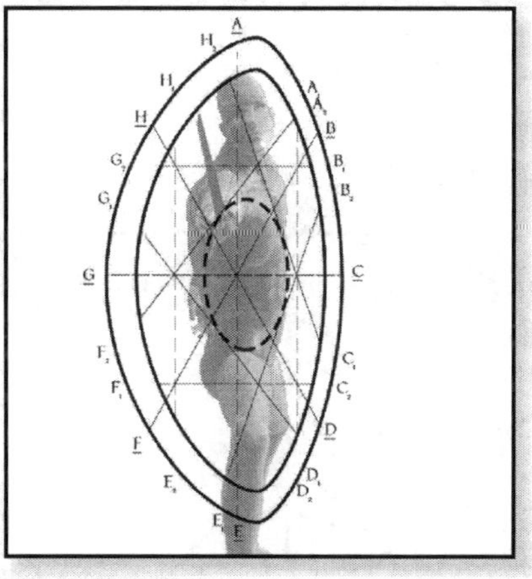

possibly more correct

This condensed cutting diagram is something I have been aware of throughout the writing and production of this book, but I still opted to use the diagram on folio 2v because it is clearer in showing the swords as they exist in this space. But, with the consideration of the opponent standing in a guard where their body is not symmetrical from the left to right, it should be noted that the Center circle is more condensed. This means that the engagements of the weapons becomes 'tighter' and less apparent, but their importance is that much more necessary.

Appendix B - A Note on the Spanish Influence

In the 'Rostock' manuscript, when Meyer explains he has learned this art from various regions across Europe, it is difficult to discern what parts of his art are specifically from one place or another, or if it is a homogenous mix of all of them. But, when it comes to footwork, Meyer's rapier seems decidedly Spanish. With my brief conversations with Ton Puey (an accomplished fencer from Spain practicing the Spanish arts of Destreza), and with Puck Curtis (a maestro here in the USA), both of which I have had the honor to fence, I believe it is clear Meyer has opted to borrow many elements of his footwork from Destreza; specifically from Jerónimo Sánchez de Carranza, a Spanish fencing master, who wrote, "On the Philosophy of Arms and its Skill, and Christian Offense and Defense" in 1569, just one year before Meyer's publication in 1570.

Below is an article published by Puck Curtis in 2009 detailing the use of Carranza's circle (a footwork diagram). The portion of the diagram that exists at both ends of Carranza's circle (where each fencer stands) is remarkably close to the figure Meyer depicts under Plate F (see Appendix E). Though Meyer never makes reference to his diagram, a close study of Carranza's circle should shed some light on how Meyer thought of using it.

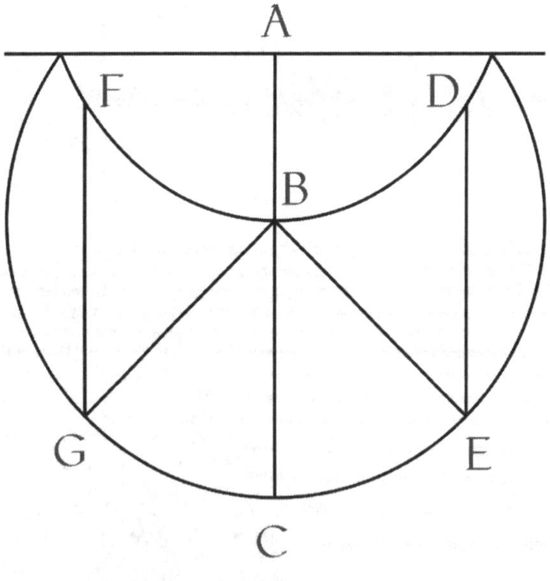

For comparison, here again is my drawing of Meyer's diagram based on what is shown in Plate F (note: the lettering is my own)

"Spanish Fencing Notation Part 2 – Footwork and the Circle"

(Aug. 24, 2009) by Puck Curtis

In the Italian tradition there is an imaginary Line of Direction that describes the shortest path to the adversary.

The Spanish tradition uses this line and expands on the concept to create a 2D planar map of possible footwork laid out in a circle. The Spanish Circle is one of the defining elements of the science and various authors have presented it differently while preserving the core concept.

Carranza's Circle

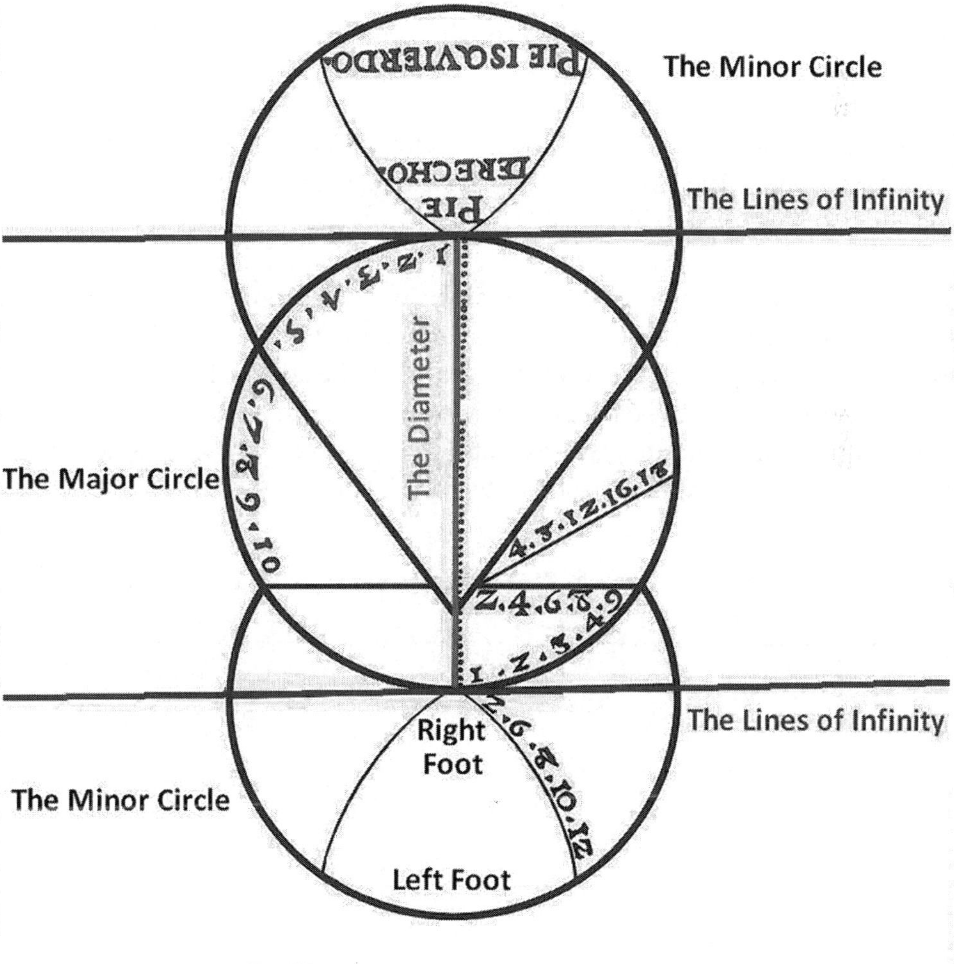

Carranza's Circle from his text in 1569
(with labels)

The Diameter – The imaginary line separating the two fencers is called the Diameter. It represents the shortest path to the target. The Diameter starts at the lead toe of the fencer (bottom of the red line) to the the lead toe of the adversary (top of the red line). The correct length of the Diameter should be the distance at which the fencer can observe the adversary's offensive actions and still respond in time.

The Major Circle (Greater Circle) – The central circle shown between the two fencers is called the Major Circle or sometimes just the Circle. By rotating the Diameter about its center, we can create an imaginary circle which functions as a one piece of a footwork map.

The Lines of Infinity– The two parallel lines shown in green are called the Lines of Infinity or Infinite Lines. In the same manner as the Diameter, the distance between these lines is defined by your ability to observe and react to the adversary's offense. Crossing the Line of Infinity means closing distance into the adversary's offensive measure.

The Minor Circle – The smaller circles on either side of the Major circle are called the Minor Circles. The fencer and the adversary each stand in the center of a Minor Circle which is defined by the positions of the feet.

The Circle represents a moment of fencing time – The circle is not fixed in location, but instead describes the distance and possible steps within a specific fencing action. Just as the Italian Line of Direction changes when the adversaries move, so to does a new circle occur when the fencers change position. If an adversary has broken your defense and closed measure, the text may advise you to step onto a new circle and this represents the need to reestablish correct distance.

-Puck Curtis, 2009

The apparent favor of fencing from the extended Straight-Parrying might also be heavily influenced by the Spanish as well. Carranza refers to the "right angle" (the angle made between the arm and body) as the furthest possible extension of the sword with the arm in a "natural position" (long-edge down).

The following is a passage from Carranza's *Libro de Hieronimo de Caranca, natvral de Sevilla, que trata de la philosophia de las armas y de su destreza y de la aggression y defension christiana,* translated by Dr. Mary Curtis, which illustrates these ideas:

> *And for it is advisable that you all know, that of all the Angles, that are the postures, it is advisable to know the Right, the Obtuse, the Acute, that which reaches furthest is the Right, and that which is in part more entailed for all the movements whether Circular or Straight, [...] because the posture that comes out of the Obtuse Angle, and Acute, is either higher than what is advisable, or lower than is necessary to make up for the lack of place with the favor of the steps and extremes of the body...*

This idea of the right angle continues in later German fencing manuals, such as Joachim Koppe's "New Discourse on the Art of Fencing" published in 1619 (which happens to be heavily influenced in other respects by the Italian master, Salvator Fabris, 1606).

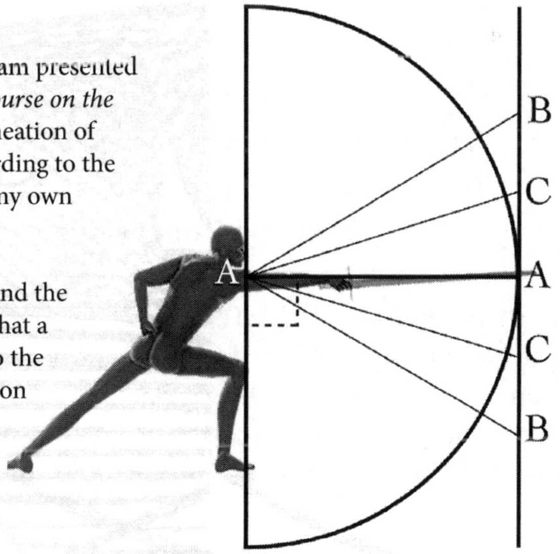

A reconstruction of the diagram presented in Joachim Koppe's *New discourse on the Art of Fencing*, entitled "Delineation of the posture of the body, according to the said Spanish manner" (with my own figure added).

'A' is the dominant shoulder and the point of the sword, showing that a straight line, perpendicular to the vertical is the furthest extension of the thrust. Any deviation departing from 'A' is thus shortened.[79]

Appendix C -
Viggiani's Three Advantages & Italian Initiative

In 2015 I wrote a blog describing how Angelo Viggiani, an Italian contemporary of Joachim Meyer, viewed initiative in a sword fight. I think it would be useful to include it in this book. Meyer describes 'opportunities' and says they must be taken in their correct 'time,' but is quite vague on what exactly those opportunities are and when to take them. Viggiani on the other hand, along with other Italians writing around the same time spills a little more ink on the subject.

As an introduction to this post, I want to quote Marco Docciolini, publishing 31 years after Meyer, in 1601; it is a useful quote that directly ties the Italian term of 'Tempo' to a concept more apt to the Meyer and broader German practitioner.

Since taking the tempo to move our weapons, whether to defend ourselves or to attack our opponent, is of great consequence in this practice, we will consider this subject somewhat, not as a philosophical principle as some do, but only insomuch as is pertinent to our profession.

It should be understood that when we say tempo, we do not mean the space of time between the beginning and the end of the attack, because without any doubt, this should be the shortest possible. By tempo, we mean the opportunity which presents itself, or which we earn, to move our weapon securely to attack our opponent.[80]

"Using Angelo Viggiani's Three Advantages to understand initiative in 16th century, Italian Swordplay" (Mar. 17, 2015) by Robert Rutherfoord

In Lo Schermo (c. 1550, published 1575) Angelo Viggiani dal Montone defines three "advantages", the Guard, Step and Strike, as the most basic means to gain a more favorable position over your opponent. Viggiani, and his contemporaries, though their reasons differ, prefer the thrust to the cut. As a result, guards that naturally delivered a thrust were also preferred. Thus, the importance of placing oneself in a guard with the point in presence – a guardia perfetta – while denying the same to the opponent is defined as the Advantage of the Guard.

Viggiani gives us three methods to gain and maintain the Advantage of the Guard. The first is to make half cuts in order to displace your opponent's blade while keeping your own in presence. The second is to make feints, or *sfalsata* (a disengage), in order to thwart your opponent's attempts at gaining the center-line in the same way. The third is to step offline to reposition the center more favorably to your advantage.

The last method of gaining the Advantage of the Guard should also be understood alongside the second advantage, the Advantage of the Step, which is to place the non-dominant foot (the left foot for us righties) in a position that enables a long and powerful extension of the dominant foot during the attack. Viggiani states this happens when the rear foot is gathered forward to the front foot. With the understanding that stepping offline is a method of gaining Advantage of the Guard, however, one could satisfy both actions in a single step. By taking a step with one's rear foot both offline and somewhat forward, one can reposition the center in his favor while also gaining Advantage of the Step.

If you step into measure while you have Advantage of the Step, you also have Advantage of the Strike. This final advantage is the ability to launch an attack in a single tempo. If you have already established the first two advantages, while also stepping into measure with the rear foot, then a single step on the dominant foot can be made to bring the body and sword forward safely.

The three advantages are Viggiani's general guidelines on how to proceed safely against an opponent. But any proactive motion takes time, and while one attempts to make a motion — a tempo — to gain one of the advantages, that tempo can be exploited by his opponent. Viggani tells us that each of these advantages can actually become disadvantages if the opponent decides to act within the tempo of each action. Here's how it works.

Gaining any Advantage requires one to make a tempo. Delivering a half cut requires one to move from one guard to another, falsing requires the point to leave presence, and stepping offline requires the entire body to move. Each one of these movements (and especially any combination of them) is a perfect opportunity for the opponent to strike. Because the one attempting to gain the advantage is required to leave the safety of his guard and move into another, he is momentarily susceptible to an attack, which is what an opponent should look for when making a strike.

With the Advantage of the Step, especially into a narrow pace of the feet, the same issue exists with the side step. The Agent — the one gaining the advantage — must move a foot to do so, a long tempo that creates substantial opportunity to be struck. Conversely, if he remains with his feet together, he is less apt to receive a blow. The same is also true with the advantage of the strike. To strike one must commit sword and body (with a step) and "be the first to leave the safety of his guard."

The contemporary master Giovanni dall'Agocchie breaks these "disadvantages" down into five categories detailing when it is best to attack:

1. You parry the attack of your opponent.
2. An attack at you traverses outside of your presence.
3. Your opponent raises his sword to attack you.
4. Your opponent injudiciously changes guard, before he settles in the new guard.
5. Your opponent, standing still in guard, raises or moves his foot to change his pace or to move towards you.

Of these, the best time to attack your opponent is when he moves (gives you a tempo). Conversely, a fencer should expect to be attacked if he makes one of these five actions. However, to gain the advantages, one must first move. The advantages come with their liabilities, and may not seem like advantages at all if they are also perfect opportunities for the opponent to strike. The key, however, is that one should expect to be struck at while moving to take advantage. Thus, they are invitations for an opponent to strike. By making a half cut to gain the Advantage of Guard, and a half step to gain the Advantage of the Step, one can entice his opponent to make a full blow, and this large tempo can be exploited in turn with a parry and counter in a single, shorter tempo.

In *Lo Schermo*, which is written as a dialogue, Viggiani is asked by the hypothetical student why it is not prudent to be the first to attack, knowing that the defender will be forced to deal with the oncoming blow. His response is that this would be true if it were not for the fact that a parry can be made in a single tempo; by using a counterattack a fencer can parry and strike in the very moment the first mover meant to land his blow. However, to make a parry succeed in both diverting the blow and striking in a single tempo, one needs to note when and where that blow is meant to be delivered. Rather than simply striking to force a response, seeking to gain the Advantages puts the fencer in a stronger mechanical and tactical position with both sword and body by closing and opening the lines of his choosing, thereby limiting where he can be struck. For example, if the fencer closes the inside line when gaining the Advantage of the Guard, in that instant he is only vulnerable to outside. Having this foresight enables him to reduce his opponent's decision tree: there is one place he can strike, which means that the fencer only has to worry about closing one open line during the parry, thus dramatically increasing his chance to respond with a single-time parry-counter.

With this, we can say that Viggiani's Three Advantages are also a form of provocation, forcing an attack by our opponent to a specific line in a specific tempo that we will be ready to close and respond to in that instant. The ability to force the actions of the opponent when and where a fencer wants is how you control the initiative in fencing, and control of initiative is at the center of how you excel as a swordsman.

Appendix D -
Responding with a Thrust after Parrying with Hanging

Meyer would seem to give a preference to point attacks, though never stating it directly, and even in situations where a thrust will be difficult to perform. After making a parry by Hanging, the natural response is a cut, though to the inside, it is possible to return a thrust to the opponent. This is how Meyer would like it do be done:

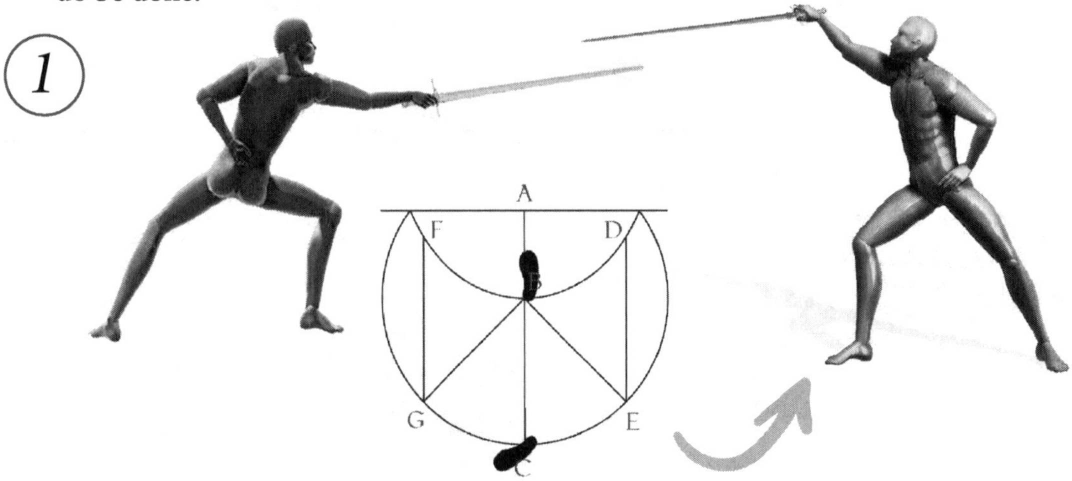

The fencer on the right waits in Right Ox for the Thrust, inviting the opponent on the left to deliver a thrust.

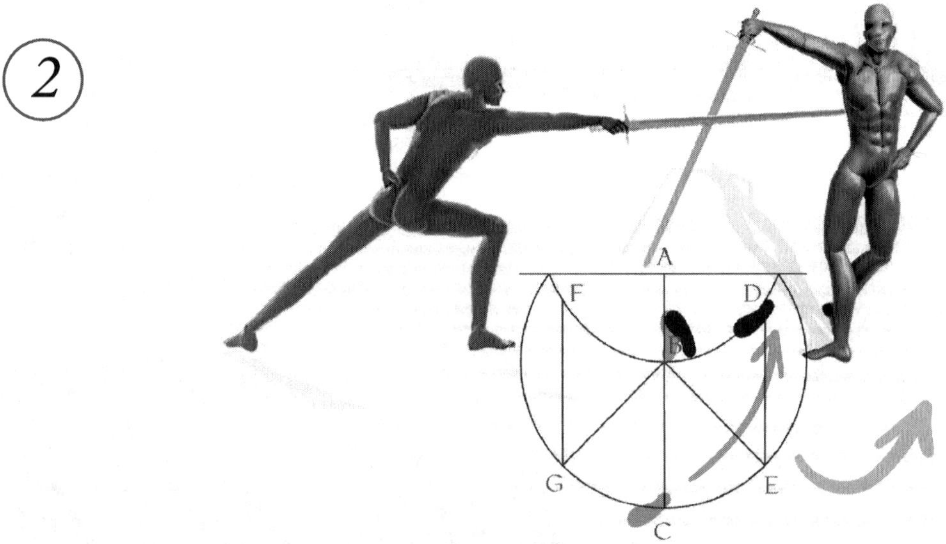

As the fencer on the left gathers the left foot and then extends the right for the attack, the fencer on the right parries with a Hanging while their left foot steps to D, almost turning their back to the opponent.

3

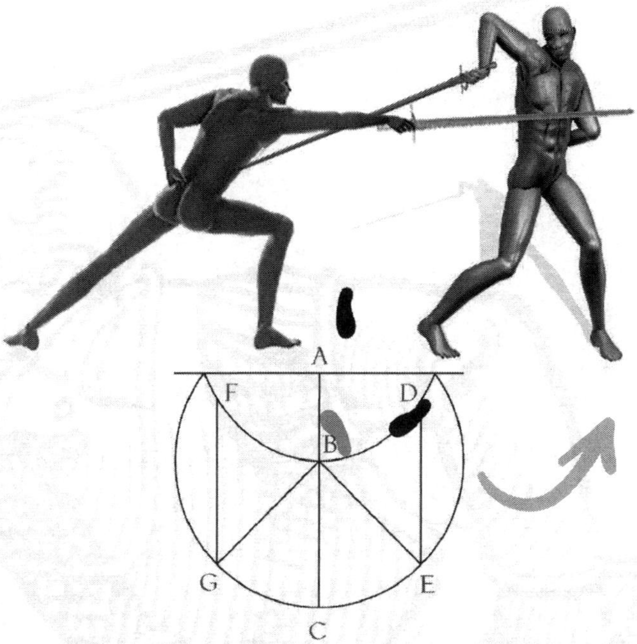

Immediately after the parry is made, the hand is rotated from the palm facing to the right, to facing upward. The elbow is bent to support this rotation. As the thrust is made, the right foot steps forward and also turns to the rear, facilitating the rotation of the entire body, and also moving the body past the opponent's point. After the thrust is made, the right foot passes back, behind the left while making a Scalp Cut during the withdrawal.

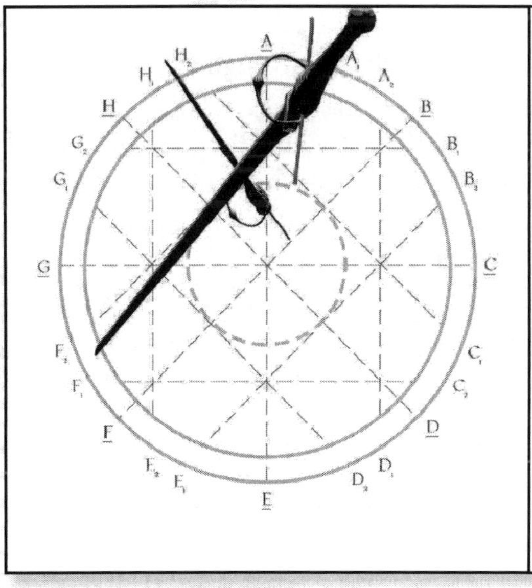

2. From figure 2, a Hanging is made to displace the thrust from the Center

3. From figure 3, the hand is rotated, palm up, delivering the thrust to their belly (the opponent's blade is hidden behind ours)

Appendix E - The Engravings
with explanations

Top Left: Three statues showing the cut lines. Left: the vertical cuts. Middle: the diagonal cuts. Right: the horizontal cuts.

Left: A simplified version of the cutting diagram labeled A through H.

Front Figure: A fencer demonstrating the 'Flying Thrust,' where the feet are situated close together. Then the sword makes a High Thrust, through the Right Ox. 'Flying Thrust' might also be a broad term Meyer uses for a lunge, though he never uses the term again after the initial definition.

Rear Figures: The Face Thrust (see page 160)

Right, Front Figure: Meyer uses this figure to depict Right Ox for the Thrust, though he appears to be mid-thrust.

Middle Figures: Both have made a low bind. One fencer attempts to strike low, while the other makes a low 'Defense Stroke.'

Rear Figures: The fencer on the right performing a 'Hand Cut.' An example of Simultaneous Hitting. The fencer on the left thrusts into a Middle Longpoint, while the fencer on the right steps to the side, making a cut to the other's hand.

Right, Front Figure: A Fencer resting in Iron Gate.

Middle Figures: The fencer on the left is parrying with 'Barring.' The fencer on the right demonstrating the response from Barring, a 'Reversed Thrust' (see page 132).

Rear Figures: The fencers have come to the 'Middle' of the fight, binding each other's blades in their Middles.

Left, Front Figure: A Fencer resting in Low Right or Side Guard.

Middle Figures: Both fencers start to the inside. The fencer on the left makes a High Thrust. The fencer on the right parries by 'Going-Through' (page 129), in this instance slicing into Right-Ox instead of Low Right, in order to deliver his own High Thrust.

Rear Figures: Meyer does not refer to these fencers, but a possible engagement is that the fencer on the right thrusts to the face in High Longpoint while the fencer on the left makes a 'Defense Stroke' against it from right to left.

Front Figures: Another set of fencers Meyer does not reference, but the fencer on the right appears to be making an outside winding through Right Ox.

Rear Figures: The fencer on the left makes a thrust through Middle Longpoint. The fencer on the right parries using 'Hanging' (see page 130).

Front Figures: The fencer on the right thrusts into Middle Longpoint. The fencer on the left, originally in Right Ox for the Thrust, parries by Setting-Off (see page 122) to the inside while stepping away with the rear foot.

Middle Figure*:* A fencer demonstrating Straight-Parrying standing on the foot work diagram Meyer fails to mention once in his text.

Rear Figures: The fencer on the right attempts a Leg Cut. The fencer on the left pulls his leg back, thrusting to the other's face.

Rear Most Figures: The fencer on the left begins in Right Ox for the Thrust and will not attack. The fencer on the right feints a thrust to the inside at his belly. As the fencer on the left moves to parry, while the fencer on the right avoids the parry by 'Changing-Through' and finishes the thrust to the outside.

Top Right Figures: Not referred to by Meyer, but the fencer on the left appears to be making a hip throw: a grappling technique where one steps behind the other.,then using the hip as a fulcrum, pushes the upper chest (or head) over their leg, causing them to fall.

Front Figures: The fencer on the right is performing a 'Heart Thrust.' The name Meyer gives to an action that begins as a Wrath Cut, then mid-way through changes into a High Thrust to the inside (see page 147).

Middle Figure: Not referenced by Meyer, but the two fencers appear to have come to a high bind. Possibly an example of a high 'Defense Stroke.'

Rear Figures: Also not referenced by Meyer, but the fencer on the left stands in a high Longpoint while the fencer on the right rests in The Change or Low Left with the hand inverted. It could be an error but it is reminiscent of the 'Priest's Special Longpoint'[81] from M.S. I.33 (Tower Manuscript). A position favored by the teacher.

Front Figures: The fencer on the left demonstrates a parry by Suppressing (see page 127).

Middle Figure: As the fencer on the left momentarily binds the other's weapon from below, he lets go of the bind, stepping in and thrusting.

Rear Figures (middle and right): Demonstrations of various grapples, a reality of 16th-century fencing.

Front Figure: A fencer resting in Low Left or The Change, while a student mimics the position.

Sources

Gevaert, Bert. *Heinrich von Gunterrodt.* Wheaton, IL: Freelance Academy Press, 2014.

Forgeng, Jeffrey. *The Art of Combat.* London: Greenhill Books, 2006.

Forgeng, Jeffrey. *The Art of Sword Combat.* London: Frontline Books, 2016.

Forgeng, Jeffrey. *The Medieval Art of Swordsmanship.* Texas: Chivalry Bookshelf, 2003.

Fratus, Stephen. *Anonimo Bolognese.* Unpublished, 2018.

Ivonov, Pavel. Jakob Sutor von Baden. Wiktenauer. *https://wiktenauer.com/wiki/Jakob_Sutor_von_Baden*

Leoni, Tommaso. *Art of Dueling.* Texas: Chivalry Bookshelf, 2005.

Leoni, Tommaso. *The Complete Renaissance Swordsman.* Wheaton, IL: Freelance Academy Press, 2010.

Leoni, Tommaso. *Francesco Alfieri, La Scherma.* self published, 2018.

Meyer, Joachim. *Fechtbuch zu Ross und zu Fuss.* Translated by Fortner, Florian & Schrattenecker, Julian. Unpublished, 2018.

Meyers, Keith. *Paulus Hector Mair.* Wiktenauer. *https://wiktenauer.com/wiki/Page:MS_Dresd.C.93_051r.png*

Noort, Reinier van. *New Discourse on the Art of Fencing.* self published. 2018.

Noort, Reinier van. *Proper Description of Thrust-Fencing with the Single Rapier.* Glasgow, UK. Fallen Rook Publishing, 2018.

Reich, Steven & Terminiello, Piermarco. *Marco Docciolini's 1601 Fencing Treatise.* Lexington, KY: self-published, 2017.

Swanger, Jherek. *The Fencing Method of Angelo Viggiani, Lo Schermo, Part III.* self published, 2017.

Tolber, Christian. *In Saint George's Name.* Wheaton, IL: Freelance Academy Press, 2010.

Tolber, Christian. *Secrets of German Medieval Swordsmanship.* Texas: Chivalry Bookshelf, 2007.

Notes

1 Forgeng, *The Art of Combat,* p.173
2 Forgeng, *The Art of Sword Combat,* p. 167
3 Forgeng, *The Art of Combat,* p.173
4 Gavert, *Heinrich von Gunterrodt,* p. 20
5 Forgeng, *The Art of Combat,* p.173
6 Forgeng, *The Medieval Art of Swordsmanship,* p. 23
7 Forgeng, *The Art of Combat,* p.177
8 Forgeng, *The Art of Combat,* p.203
9 Forgeng, *The Art of Combat,* p.215
10 Tobler, *Secrets of German Medieval Swordsmanship, p.*141
11 Other clues, like the blade being rebated, and that there are no depictions of fencers taking wounds, would seem to indicate these are swords for practice
12 Forgeng, *The Art of Combat,* p.186
13 Forgeng, *The Art of Combat,* p.69
14 Leoni, *The Complete Renaissance Swordsman,* p.174
15 Forgeng, *The Art of Combat,* p.177
16 Ivonov, Pavel. Jakob Sutor
17 MS Dresd.C.93, folio 59
18 Swanger, *Lo Schermo,* p.30
19 Leoni, *The Complete Renaissance Swordsman,* p.75
20 Fratus. *Anonimo Bolognese,* p.1
21 Forgeng, *The Art of Combat,* p.206
22 Forgeng, *The Art of Combat,* p.175
23 Forgeng, *The Art of Combat,* p.103
24 Forgeng, *The Art of Combat,* p.175
25 Fortner & Schrattenecker
26 Forgeng, *The Art of Combat,* p.69
27 Forgeng, *The Art of Combat,* p.69
28 Forgeng, *The Art of Combat,* p.69
29 Forgeng, *The Art of Combat,* p.69
30 This is the Italian concept of 'di tempo' or 'in time.' Otherwise 'mezzo-tempo' or 'half-time' when performed as a strike into the preparation of the opponent's strike
31 Forgeng, *The Art of Combat,* p.70
32 Forgeng, *The Art of Combat,* p.61
33 Forgeng, *The Art of Combat,* p.45
34 Forgeng, *The Art of Combat,* p.51
35 Forgeng, *The Art of Combat,* p.45
36 Forgeng, *The Art of Combat,* p.189
37 Forgeng, *The Art of Sword Combat,* p.169
38 Fortner & Schrattenecker
39 Forgeng, *The Medieval Art of Swordsmanship,* p.43
40 Tobler, *In Saint George's Name,* p.131
41 Tobler, *In Saint George's Name,* p.124
42 Leoni, *Art of Dueling,* p167
43 Forgeng, *The Art of Sword Combat,* p.170
44 Forgeng, *The Art of Combat,* p.175
45 Noort, *New Discourse on the Art of Fencing,* p.78
46 Forgeng, *The Art of Combat,* p.180
47 Forgeng, *The Art of Combat,* p.182
48 Forgeng, *The Art of Combat,* p.180 & p.203
49 Forgeng, *The Art of Combat,* p.182 & p.202
50 Forgeng, *The Art of Combat,* p.185 & p.197
51 *"From whichever side he sends his cut, catch and parry his cut, and cut or thrust in at him to the* **same side** *from which he has sent in his cut"* Forgeng, *The Art of Combat,* p.215
52 Forgeng, *The Art of Combat,* p.195
53 Angelo Viggiani also withdraws the arm during a parry to the outside and explains the action in great detail- Swanger, *Lo Schermo, Part III,* p.57
54 Forgeng, *The Art of Combat,* p.60
55 Forgeng, *The Art of Combat,* p.169
56 Forgeng, *The Art of Combat,* p.60
57 Borrowing language from Salvator Fabris, an Italian who published his work in 1606, Leoni, *Art of Dueling*
58 Forgeng, *The Art of Combat,* p.61
59 Forgeng, *The Art of Combat,* p.63
60 Forgeng, *The Art of Combat,* p.215
61 Forgeng, *The Art of Combat,* p.187
62 Forgeng, *The Art of Combat,* p.178
63 Forgeng, *The Art of Combat,* p.204
64 Forgeng, *The Art of Combat,* p.212
65 Forgeng, *The Art of Combat,* p.204
66 Forgeng, *The Art of Combat,* p.45
67 Alfieri's distinction between *Contratempo* & *Incontro*- Leoni, *La Scherma,* p.12
68 Forgeng, *The Art of Sword Combat,* p.170
69 Forgeng, *The Art of Combat,* p.103
70 Forgeng, *The Art of Combat,* p.92
71 Forgeng, *The Art of Combat,* p.75
72 Noort, *Proper Description of Thrust-Fencing,* p.175
73 Forgeng, *The Art of Combat,* p.188
74 Forgeng, *The Art of Combat,* p.188
75 Leoni, *The Complete Renaissance Swordsman,* 113
76 Forgeng, *The Art of Combat,* p.69
77 Forgeng, *The Art of Sword Combat,* p.169
78 Forgeng, *The Art of Sword Combat,* p.169
79 Noort, *New Discourse on the Art of Fencing,* p.48
80 Reich & Terminiello, *Marco Docciolini's 1601,* p.44
81 Forgeng, *The Medieval Art of Swordsmanship,* p. 111